CAMBRIDGE STUDIES IN
ANGLO-SAXON ENGLAND

21

# TRINITY AND INCARNATION IN ANGLO-SAXON ART AND THOUGHT

# CAMBRIDGE STUDIES IN ANGLO-SAXON ENGLAND

GENERAL EDITORS

## SIMON KEYNES
## MICHAEL LAPIDGE

ASSISTANT EDITOR: ANDY ORCHARD

*Volumes published*

# TRINITY AND INCARNATION IN ANGLO-SAXON ART AND THOUGHT

BARBARA C. RAW

*Emeritus Professor of Anglo-Saxon*
*University of Keele*

CAMBRIDGE
UNIVERSITY PRESS

Published by the Press Syndicate of the University of Cambridge
The Pitt Building, Trumpington Street, Cambridge CB2 1RP
40 West 20th Street, New York, NY 10011–4211, USA
10 Stamford Road, Oakleigh, Melbourne 3166, Australia

First published 1997

Printed in Great Britain at the University Press, Cambridge

*A catalogue record for this book is available from the British Library*

*Library of Congress cataloguing in publication data applied for*

ISBN 0 521 55371 7 hardback

# Contents

# Plates

# Acknowledgements

My thanks are due to Malcolm Godden, who has read parts of the book in typescript, and to Janet Bately, Paul Bennett, Kevin Blockley, Mary Clayton, James Cross, David Howlett, Michael Lapidge, Henry Mayr-Harting, Aidan Nichols, Robert Ombres, Paul Parvis and Jean Preston for help and information of various kinds. Specific debts are acknowledged in the footnotes. My thanks are also due to the following institutions for permission to publish photographs: the British Library, London (pls. Ib, II, III, V, VIIa–b, X, XIa, XII, XIII, XVa–b and XVIa–b); the Syndics of Cambridge University Library, Cambridge (pl. VIb); the Master and Fellows of Trinity College, Cambridge (pl. VIII); the Conway Library, Courtauld Institute of Art (pl. IX); the Pierpont Morgan Library, New York (pls. VIa and XIVa–b); the Bodleian Library, Oxford (pls. Ia and IV); the Biblioteca Apostolica Vaticana, Vatican City (pl. XIb).

# Abbreviations and note on the text

| | |
|---|---|
| *AB* | *Analecta Bollandiana* |
| *AntJ* | *Antiquaries Journal* |
| *ArchJ* | *Archaeological Journal* |
| *ASE* | *Anglo-Saxon England* |
| ASPR | *The Anglo-Saxon Poetic Records*, ed. G. P. Krapp and E. van K. Dobbie, 6 vols. (New York, 1931–42) |
| CSASE | Cambridge Studies in Anglo-Saxon England |
| BL | British Library |
| BN | Bibliothèque Nationale, Paris |
| CCCC | Corpus Christi College, Cambridge |
| CCM | Corpus Consuetudinum Monasticarum |
| CCCMed | Corpus Christianorum, Continuatio Mediaevalis (Turnhout) |
| CCSL | Corpus Christianorum, Series Latina (Turnhout) |
| *CH* | Ælfric, *Catholic Homilies* |
| CSEL | Corpus Scriptorum Ecclesiasticorum Latinorum (Vienna) |
| CUL | Cambridge University Library |
| EEMF | Early English Manuscripts in Facsimile (Copenhagen) |
| EETS | Early English Text Society (London) |
| os | original series |
| ss | supplementary series |
| *EL* | *Ephemerides liturgicae* |
| *ES* | *English Studies* |
| HBS | Henry Bradshaw Society Publications (London) |
| *HE* | Bede's *Historia ecclesiastica gentis Anglorum* |
| *JWCI* | *Journal of the Warburg and Courtauld Institutes* |
| L-B | O. Lehmann-Brockhaus, *Lateinische Schriftquellen zur Kunst in* |

England, Wales und Schottland vom Jahre 901 bis zum Jahre 1307, 5 vols. (Munich, 1955-60)

| | |
|---|---|
| LC | *Libri Carolini sive Caroli Magni Capitulare de Imaginibus*, ed. H. Bastgen, MGH, Concilia II, Suppl. |
| LS | Ælfric, *Lives of Saints* |
| MÆ | *Medium Ævum* |
| MGH | Monumenta Germaniae Historica |
| Concilia | Legum Sectio III: Concilia |
| Epist. | Epistolae in quarto |
| N&Q | *Notes and Queries* |
| NY | New York |
| PG | Patrologia Graeca, ed. J. P. Migne |
| PL | Patrologia Latina, ed. J. P. Migne |
| PLS | Patrologia Latina, Supplementum |
| RB | *Revue bénédictine* |
| RS | Rolls Series |

## NOTE ON THE TEXT

Biblical quotations are taken from the Jerusalem Bible unless otherwise stated, but psalm numbers are taken from the Vulgate. The punctuation of quotations in Latin and Old English has been modernized.

# Introduction

In 1963 Francis Wormald published an article entitled, 'Late Anglo-Saxon Art: some Questions and Suggestions'.[1] In it, he drew attention to the large number of representations of the Trinity from late Anglo-Saxon England, and asked, 'Why is there then this remarkable variety of representations of the Trinity current in England at this time?'[2] Wormald linked these pictures to the private prayers in honour of the Trinity in two late Anglo-Saxon manuscripts, suggesting that they mark the beginning of 'an important movement of the later Middle Ages'.[3] A devotional role for the manuscript pictures of the Trinity would certainly be appropriate, given their monastic context and the distinction usually made between monastic theology, which was essentially contemplative, and scholastic theology, which was concerned with question and argument.[4] Both Benedict of Aniane and John of Fécamp, for example, placed belief in the Trinity at the centre of their teaching on prayer and devotion.[5] Concern with Trinitarian doctrine in late Anglo-Saxon England was not a purely monastic matter, however. The repeated references to the Trinity in Ælfric's homilies, which were directed at the laity, and the intensity with which he explains the smallest details of Trinitarian belief, suggest a concern with theology for its own sake.

---

[1] Wormald, *Collected Writings* I, 105–10; the article was originally published in *Studies in Western Art*, ed. M. Meiss (Princeton, 1963), pp. 19–26.

[2] *Ibid.* I, 107.

[3] *Ibid.* I, 108; the manuscripts are BL, Cotton Titus D. xxvii and Oxford, Bodleian Library, Douce 296.

[4] See Chenu, 'The Masters of the Theological Science', in his *Nature, Man and Society*, pp. 270–309.

[5] See below, pp. 15–17.

Some of the pictures to which Wormald referred have been discussed several times: the drawing of the Trinity in the Ælfwine Prayerbook by Kantorowicz and Kidd,[6] and the figures in the frame to the opening of St John's Gospel in the Grimbald Gospels by Jennifer O'Reilly and Richard Gameson.[7] Jane Rosenthal has written extensively on the drawings above the canon tables in the Arenberg Gospels, one of which is related to the drawing in the Ælfwine Prayerbook, and has argued that the scene is a representation of Christ, not of the Trinity; she takes the same view of the drawings of three standing figures in the Sherborne Pontifical, arguing that they show three manifestations of Christ, not the three persons of the Trinity.[8] George Henderson, on the other hand – the only scholar since Wormald to consider the pictures of the Trinity as a group – accepts the figures in the Sherborne Pontifical as representations of the Trinity.[9] More recently, Robert Deshman has written on the painting of the crowned Christ which fills the initial to the Trinitarian blessings for the Sunday after Pentecost in the Benedictional of Æthelwold.[10] So far, however, no one has attempted to relate these pictures to the literature of the late Anglo-Saxon period.

It has been claimed in the past that the tenth century, particularly in England, was a dead period as far as theology was concerned. Knowles is particularly dismissive. He says of the writers of the English monastic revival:

They were men of their period, and it was a period before the reawakening of constructive, independent thought and scientific reasoning. We look in vain to Ælfric, and more vainly still to Byrhtferth, for an original, genial idea or for any of that intellectual self-possession and clarity of criticism that comes in with Anselm and Abelard. Both Ælfric and Anselm draw deeply upon St Augustine, but while Anselm penetrates and transmutes the inmost thought of his model, Ælfric is content with translating or paraphrasing.[11]

---

[6] BL, Cotton Titus D. xxvii, 75v; Kantorowicz, 'Quinity', and Kidd, 'Quinity'.

[7] BL, Additional 34890, 114v; O'Reilly, 'St John', pp. 179–80, and Gameson, 'Manuscript Art at Christ Church', pp. 216–17.

[8] NY, Pierpont Morgan Library, 869, 11v, and Paris, BN, fonds latin 943, 5v–6v; Rosenthal, 'Canon Tables', pp. 219–46, 'Three Drawings', pp. 547–62, and 'Pontifical', pp. 154–9.

[9] Henderson, 'Idiosyncrasy', pp. 242–5.

[10] BL, Additional 49598, 70r; Deshman, *Benedictional*, pp. 92–108.

[11] Knowles, *Monastic Order*, pp. 47–8.

Elsewhere he says of Ælfric, 'As a theologian he has little constructive or speculative power; like Bede, he did little more than translate relevant passages from the Latin fathers and Church historians' and again, 'The more learned monks of the revival aimed at handing on in a simplified form to their countrymen as much as they were capable of receiving of the doctrinal legacy of the ancient civilization; they made no attempt to develop or to discuss dogmas, and no controversies forced them into being apologists.'[12] C. L. Wrenn talks of Ælfric as translating and adapting from the works of the doctors of the church 'without thought of any originality or new intellectual departure',[13] and even Gatch, who speaks of the 'remarkable critical powers' which Ælfric and Wulfstan brought to bear on their sources and who concludes that they can 'be compared favourably with the best theologians of the Early Middle Ages, the group associated with the court of Charlemagne', describes Ælfric as pedantic and unoriginal.[14]

It has become increasingly clear, however, that Ælfric was a highly selective and original writer. Peter Clemoes notes that he 'did not merely assemble patristic homilies as Paul [the Deacon] had done, or compose homilies in Latin by refashioning material from various patristic sources as Haymo had done',[15] and John Pope's detailed study of the sources of Ælfric's later homilies shows the freedom with which he treats his sources, how he 'omits, condenses, expands, rearranges, synthesizes two or more interpretations, rejects one in favour of another, imports examples or parallel texts, reminds us of something he has dealt with more extensively elsewhere'.[16] Eric John has drawn attention to the radical nature of Ælfric's thought, describing his writings as 'a primer of the new theology that, if properly used, can throw light on the more sophisticated continental authors'.[17] He must now be seen as a theologian in his own right, whose writings form an important link between those of the Carolingian period and the theological works of the late eleventh and early twelfth centuries.[18]

The pictures of the Trinity to which Wormald referred, together with the numerous late Anglo-Saxon representations of Christ in glory,

[12] *Ibid.*, pp. 493 and 509.    [13] Wrenn, *Study of Old English*, p. 225.
[14] Gatch, *Preaching and Theology*, pp. 6 and 17.    [15] Clemoes, 'Ælfric', p. 183.
[16] Pope, *Homilies* I, 150.    [17] John, 'The World of Abbot Ælfric', p. 315.
[18] For a discussion of this point in relation to redemption theology, see Raw, *Crucifixion Iconography*, pp. 168–83.

illustrate the same themes as Ælfric's many explanations of the doctrine of the Trinity: the unity of the Godhead; the equality of Christ and his Father; the reality of the Incarnation and the glorification of Christ's human nature; the role of the Incarnation as a making visible of the divine nature. They should not be considered merely as illustrations of theological ideas, however; nor should the religious literature of the period be seen simply as background material for the study of the works of art. Art and literature express religious truths in different, but complementary ways. Whereas the written text is linear, presenting points in sequence, the picture involves spatial relationships; the first is better suited to the definition of theological truths, the second to an intuitive and direct grasp of some truth. Both have a meaning and both have to be read, but in a different way. As Barasch points out, 'Letters, in proper combination, convey a meaning, but they do not resemble the meaning they convey ... Letters are signs, but they are not icons, of ideas.'[19] The method of reception of texts and images is different and so are their functions; in particular, a picture can evoke the presence of a person in a direct and immediate way which is impossible to a text. Moreover, the non-linear nature of the picture allows several ideas to be present simultaneously, and therefore integrates them.[20] Knowledge, however, has to lead to the wisdom which consists in contemplation of God. The distinction is brought out by Bede in the prayer with which he ended his *Historia ecclesiastica*: 'Teque deprecor, bone Iesu, ut cui propitius donasti verba tuae scientiae dulciter haurire, dones etiam benignus aliquando ad te, fontem omnis sapientiae, pervenire, et parere semper ante faciem tuam.'[21] Whereas knowledge could encompass the events of Christ's life on earth, wisdom was concerned with his eternal existence, with the contemplation of one who, after his ascension, was present without limitation. This paradox of physical absence and spiritual nearness is expressed by Leo I in a sermon for the Feast of the Ascension:

Tunc igitur, dilectissimi, filius hominis Dei Filius excellentius sacratiusque innotuit, cum in paternae maiestatis gloriam se recepit et ineffabili modo coepit

[19] Barasch, *Icon*, p. 81.    [20] *Ibid.*, p. 75.

[21] *Historia ecclesiastica* V.xxiv (ed. Colgrave and Mynors, p. 570): 'And I beg you, good Jesus, that as you have graciously allowed me joyfully to drink in the words of knowledge of you, you will also, in your goodness, allow me to come at last to you, the fountain of all wisdom, and to stand before your face for ever.' For the contrast between *scientia* and *sapientia*, see below, p. 84.

esse Divinitate praesentior, qui factus est humanitate longinquior. Tunc ad aequalem Patri Filium eruditior fides gressu coepit mentis accedere, et contrectatione corporeae in Christo substantiae, qua Patre minor est, non egere, quoniam glorificati corporis manente natura, eo fides credentium vocabatur, ubi non carnali manu, sed spiritali intellectu, par Genitori Unigenitus tangeretur.[22]

Ælfric says something similar in a homily for the eve of Ascension:

He [Christ] ferde to heofenum mid þam lichaman þe he on eorðan gefette, ac he is ðurh his godcundan mihte ægðer ge her, ge ðær, swa swa he behet ær ðan ðe he upastige: Efne ic beo mid eow eallum dagum, oð gefyllednysse ðyssere worulde.[23]

This belief in the presence of Christ, everywhere and to all, is reflected in the preference shown in Anglo-Saxon gospelbooks for pictures of the risen and ascended Christ rather than representations of gospel events in which his presence was limited by time and space. These pictures, which portray him in a timeless existence, free of the material items which might tie the figure to this world, invite those studying them to pass beyond the image and to establish a relationship with the reality beyond.

There is, however, a further dimension to this relationship. The contemplation which would be enjoyed in heaven, and which could be anticipated through prayer, was contemplation of the Trinity. The rightness of this expectation was founded on the teaching that God had created man in his own image. As Augustine said, 'Hoc est enim *plenum gaudium* nostrum quo *amplius non est*, frui trinitate deo *ad* cuius *imaginem facti*

---

[22] Leo, 'Tractatus lxxiv, De ascensione Domini', 4 (ed. Chavasse, p. 458, and trans. Modern Roman Breviary for the Friday after Ascension): 'For the Son of man, dearly beloved, was revealed more perfectly and more solemnly as the Son of God once he had returned to the glory of his Father's majesty, and in a mysterious way he began to be more present to them in his godhead once he had become more distant in his humanity. Then faith gained deeper understanding and by a leap of the mind began to reach out to the Son as the equal of the Father. It no longer needed contact with Christ's bodily substance, by which he is less than the Father. For though the glorified body remained a body, the faith of believers was being drawn to touch, not with the hand of the flesh but with the understanding of the spirit, the only-begotten Son, the equal of his Father.' The sermon is included in Paul the Deacon's Homiliary, II, 27; Grégoire, *Homéliaires*, p. 97.

[23] *CH* II.xxii (ed. Godden, p. 211): 'He [Christ] journeyed to heaven with the body that he received on earth, but through his divine power he is both here and there, as he promised before he ascended: Lo I am with you all the days till the end of this world.'

sumus.'[24] This theme of the divine image links art to theology: through material images of Christ, who is himself the true image of God, man, created in God's image, learns to know God, rather than merely knowing about him. The interplay of art and literature in the pursuit of these ends is the theme of this book.

[24] *De Trinitate* I.viii.18 (ed. Mountain, p. 52, and trans. Hill, p. 77): 'The fullness of our happiness, beyond which there is none else, is this: to enjoy God the three in whose image we were made.'

# 1

## 'At this time, which is the ending of the world'

The Church's teaching on the Trinity was clarified during the first five centuries after the death of Christ in response to a series of Christological heresies. The church councils at which the doctrine of the Trinity was progressively defined are listed by Bede in his account of the Synod of Hatfield (AD 679) at which the Anglo-Saxon Church, under Theodore, affirmed its orthodoxy.[1] The Synod accepted the decrees of five general councils,[2] together with those of the first Lateran Council, held in Rome in 649, and proclaimed its faith specifically in 'Patrem et Filium et Spiritum Sanctum trinitatem in unitate consubstantialem et unitatem in trinitate, hoc est unum Deum in tribus subsistentiis vel personis consubstantialibus aequalis gloriae et honoris ... Deum Patrem sine initio, et Filium eius unigenitum ex Patre generatum ante saecula, et Spiritum Sanctum procedentem ex Patre et Filio inenarrabiliter'.[3]

A rather similar list of councils occurs in Ælfric's First Latin Letter to Archbishop Wulfstan, though it is limited to four out of the eight general councils which had taken place up to the end of the tenth century; the other four, Ælfric claims, are of less importance.[4] Ælfric identifies the

---

[1] Bede, *HE* IV.xvii (ed. Colgrave and Mynors, pp. 384–7).

[2] Nicaea I (AD 325), Constantinople I (AD 381), Ephesus (AD 431), Chalcedon (AD 451) and Constantinople II (AD 553).

[3] Bede, *HE* IV.xvii (ed. and trans. Colgrave and Mynors, pp. 386–7): 'The Father and the Son and the Holy Spirit ... a Trinity consubstantial in Unity and the Unity in Trinity, that is, one God in three substances or consubstantial persons equal in glory and honour ... God the Father, who is without beginning, and His only begotten Son, begotten of the Father before all worlds, and the Holy Spirit, ineffably proceeding from the Father and the Son.'

[4] 'First Latin Letter to Archbishop Wulfstan' (ed. Fehr, *Die Hirtenbriefe Ælfrics*, pp. 41–2); the passage is based on Isidore, *Etymologiae* VI.xvi (ed. Lindsay). See also Ælfric, 'First

councils according to the heresies against which they were directed. The Council of Nicaea, he says, condemned the blasphemy of Arius, who would not believe that Christ was truly Son of God, co-eternal and consubstantial with his Father; the Council of Constantinople demonstrated that the Holy Spirit was similarly consubstantial with both Father and Son; the Council of Ephesus condemned the heresy of Nestorius who claimed that there were two persons in Christ, while the Council of Chalcedon condemned the views of Eutyches who claimed that Christ possessed only one nature. Unlike Bede, Ælfric does not stress the procession of the Holy Spirit from both Father and Son, presumably because this teaching did not form part of the definitions of the early councils.[5] More surprisingly, perhaps, in view of the growth of devotion to the Virgin Mary in the late Anglo-Saxon period, Ælfric defines the heresy of Nestorius in purely Christological terms, and says nothing of his claims that Mary should rightly be called 'Mother of Christ' rather than 'Mother of God', or of the approval of the title *Theotokos* for Mary by the Council of Ephesus.[6]

In theory, the disputes over the nature of the Trinity were settled by the fourth General Council, that of Chalcedon (AD 451), but there were further conflicts in the Carolingian period and during the late eleventh and early twelfth centuries. The teaching of Felix, bishop of Urgel, that Christ was the son of God by adoption not by nature, was condemned by the Synod of Frankfurt in 794 and by the Synod of Aachen in 800.[7] Alcuin wrote two works against the Adoptionist heresy,[8] and other contributions to the defence of orthodoxy came from Agobard of Lyons

Old English Letter to Bishop Wulfsige' (ed. Fehr, pp. 21–2). The other councils, which Ælfric considered of lesser importance, are those of Constantinople II (AD 553) and Constantinople III (AD 680–1) on the hypostatic union, Nicaea II (AD 787) on images, and Constantinople IV (AD 869–70).

[5] Kelly, *Creeds*, pp. 296–8. Ælfric certainly accepted the procession from both Father and Son; see *CH* I.xx (ed. Thorpe, p. 278).

[6] The title *Theotokos* is used by Bede, *In Lucam* I.i.35 (ed. Hurst, p. 34); see also below, p. 177. On Nestorius, see Kelly, *Christian Doctrines*, pp. 310–17; the debate over the title *Theotokos* came to the fore again during the Adoptionist controversy of the eighth century, see Pelikan, *Christian Tradition* III, 68–9.

[7] Laistner, *Thought and Letters*, pp. 287–8. For a detailed account of the theological points involved; see Pelikan, *Christian Tradition* III, 52–9.

[8] Alcuin, *Adversus Felicis haeresin* and *Contra Felicem Urgellitanum Episcopum* (PL 101, 85–230).

and Paulinus of Aquileia.[9] More trouble was stirred up by Godescalc of Orbais, better known for his views on predestination, who was condemned in 853 for his use of the term 'trina deitas' in his work on the Trinity.[10] In the course of these controversies both Alcuin and Hincmar composed lengthy works setting out the orthodox doctrine of the Trinity.[11] Another point which came to the fore during the Carolingian period was the teaching that the Holy Spirit proceeded from both the Father and the Son. The text of the Niceno-Constantinopolitan Creed, which was read out at the Council of Chalcedon and accepted as an accurate statement of orthodox belief, referred to the Holy Spirit as proceeding solely from the Father.[12] The phrase *Filioque* was added to the text of the Creed by the Carolingian Church, possibly as a reaction to the Adoptionist crisis, and several Carolingian theologians composed works justifying the change, in particular, Alcuin, Theodulf of Orleans, Smaragdus and, finally, Ratramnus of Corbie in his *Contra Graecorum opposita*.[13] The addition was not accepted by the Roman Church until 1014, and was never accepted by the Greeks.[14] Conflict broke out again in the late eleventh century, first, in connection with disputes with Jewish scholars over the validity of Christian belief and, secondly, as a result of the application of dialectic to the study of theology by scholars such as Roscellin of Compiègne, Peter Abelard and Gilbert de la Porrée.[15]

The period between the debates of the eighth and ninth centuries and the development of dialectic in the late eleventh century produced

---

[9] Agobard, *Liber adversus Felicem Urgellensem* (PL 104, 29–70) and Paulinus, *Libellus contra Elipandum* (PL 99, 151–66).

[10] Pelikan, *Christian Tradition* III, 59–66. For the text of the *De trina Deitate*, see *Œuvres* (ed. Lambot, pp. 81–99).

[11] Alcuin, *De fide sanctae et individuae Trinitatis* (PL 101, 9–58); Hincmar, *De una et non trina Deitate* (PL 125, 473–618).

[12] Kelly, *Creeds*, pp. 297–8.

[13] Laistner, *Thought and Letters*, pp. 291–2. Alcuin, *Libellus de processione Spiritus Sancti* (PL 101, 63–82); Theodulf, *De Spiritu Sancto* (PL 105, 239–76); Smaragdus, *Epistola de processione Spiritus Sancti* (PL 98, 923–9); Ratramnus, *Contra Graecorum opposita* (PL 121, 225–346).

[14] Smith, *Teaching of the Catholic Church*, pp. 155–6; Dix, *Shape of the Liturgy*, pp. 487–8. For the history of the *Filioque*, see Pelikan, *Christian Tradition* II, 183–98 and III, 21–2, and Kelly, *Creeds*, pp. 358–67.

[15] Gilbert Crispin, *Disputatio Judaei cum Christiano* (PL 159, 1011–18). For the problems raised by Roscellin, Peter Abelard and Gilbert de la Porrée, see Pelikan, *Christian Tradition* III, 264–7 and Chenu, *Nature, Man and Society*, p. 276.

relatively little in the way of biblical commentaries or compilations, something Beryl Smalley attributes to a shift of interest in monastic houses, associated particularly with the Cluniac reform, from meditative reading to liturgy; the emphasis is on what she calls 'the dramatic, emotional aspect of Scripture' rather than on theological exegesis.[16] Jaroslav Pelikan draws attention to the Christocentric character of the period, something he too attributes to the influence of the monastic orders.[17] There is certainly a great emphasis on the humanity of Christ in the lavishly illustrated Ottonian gospel-books, which treat the gospels largely as human biography,[18] in the Crucifixion pictures from England and from the Continent which show Christ hanging limply from the cross, and in the desire of people like Odilo of Cluny and Anselm to experience the gospel events for themselves and to share the sufferings of Christ and his mother.[19] But, at the same time, the tenth and eleventh centuries saw a striking development in devotion to the Trinity in both public and private prayer, in church dedications and, at least in England, in art and preaching.

A Feast of the Trinity on the first Sunday after Pentecost was introduced at Liège during the episcopate of Stephen of Liège (902–20).[20] The new feast did not become part of the official Roman liturgy until 1334,[21] but it is clear from the writings of Ælfric and from the *Regularis concordia* that the Anglo-Saxon Church honoured the Trinity in some special way on this day.[22] The *Regularis concordia* says that mass on the Octave of Pentecost is to be of the Trinity: 'Rursus in octavis Pentecostes dominica non repetitur *Spiritus Domini*, eo quod septem tantum colimus dona Spiritus Sancti, sed agitur illa hebdomada de Sancta Trinitate.'[23] The words are echoed by Ælfric in a sermon for the Octave of Pentecost, where he outlines the church's feasts.[24] Scholars have argued that these passages do not

[16] Smalley, *Study of the Bible*, pp. 44–5.  [17] Pelikan, *Christian Tradition* III, 106.

[18] Mayr-Harting, *Ottonian Book Illumination* I, 57–117.

[19] See Raw, *Crucifixion Iconography*, pp. 155–61.

[20] *Leofric Collectar* (ed. Dewick and Frere II, xxiv).

[21] Dix, *Shape of the Liturgy*, pp. 358 and 585.

[22] Gatch, *Preaching and Theology*, p. 96.

[23] *Regularis concordia*, viii.59 (ed. and trans. Symons, p. 58): '*Spiritus Domini* is not repeated on Sunday, the Octave of Pentecost, since we honour no more than seven gifts of the Holy Ghost: instead, the Mass that week shall be of the Holy Trinity.'

[24] *Homilies*, no. xi (ed. Pope I, 418). Cf. no. xia (Pope I, 470–2) and *CH* I.xxii (ed. Thorpe, p. 326).

necessarily refer to an actual feast of the Trinity. Many tenth- and eleventh-century liturgical manuscripts – for example, the Benedictionals of Æthelwold and Archbishop Robert, the Sacramentary of Robert of Jumièges and the *Portiforium Wulstani* – refer to the Sunday after Pentecost simply as 'Octava'. The actual texts, however, are all of the Trinity.[25] The reason for this is that the mass for this Sunday, as for all Sundays which had no proper mass, was normally of the Trinity. Alcuin lists a votive mass of the Trinity for Sundays which do not have their own texts[26] and the *Regularis concordia* states that the morrow mass on Sundays is to be of the Trinity unless some other feast intervenes.[27] The Sacramentary of Robert of Jumièges contains a votive mass of the Trinity, apparently for Sundays,[28] and in the Benedictional of Archbishop Robert the blessings for ordinary Sundays are of the Trinity.[29] Yet Ælfric is clearly referring to something more than the normal Sunday mass in honour of the Trinity, for he describes a celebration lasting for a full week, as would be the case for a major feast. Some manuscripts, in fact, mark the octave as a separate feast. Ælfric's Letter to the Monks of Eynsham includes a reference to the Feast of the Holy Trinity[30] and the Leofric Collectar, a mid-eleventh-century manuscript written in England but based on the collectar of Stephen of Liège, includes a full office of the Trinity, headed 'Dominica de Sancta Trinitate', for the Sunday after Pentecost.[31] The New Minster Missal includes a mass for Trinity Sunday in addition to a votive mass of the Trinity[32] and the *Portiforium Wulstani* contains a group of antiphons headed, 'Antiphonae super Nocturnos in festo Sanctae Trinitatis', followed

---

[25] *Benedictional of Æthelwold* (ed. Warner and Wilson, p. 26); *Benedictional of Archbishop Robert* (ed. Wilson, pp. 22–3); *Missal of Robert of Jumièges* (ed. Wilson, pp. 121–2); *Portiforium Wulstani* (ed. Hughes I, 68–9). In the Sacramentary of Robert of Jumièges, the Preface for the Octave of Pentecost is of the Trinity, though the prayers are not.

[26] *Liber sacramentorum*, i (PL 101, 445); when Stephen of Liège wrote his office for the Feast of the Trinity in the early tenth century he took most of the texts from Alcuin, merely adding music of his own. See *Leofric Collectar* (ed. Dewick and Frere II, xlix–li) for a discussion of the offices of the Trinity in the Collectar and the *Portiforium Wulstani*.

[27] *Regularis concordia*, i.23 (ed. Symons, p. 19).

[28] *Missal of Robert of Jumièges* (ed. Wilson, p. 241).

[29] *Benedictional of Archbishop Robert* (ed. Wilson, p. 48).

[30] Ælfric, *Epistula*, x.53 (ed. Nocent, p. 176).

[31] *Leofric Collectar* (ed. Dewick and Frere I, cols. 187–91).

[32] *Missal* (ed. Turner, pp. 22–3 and 207–8); the readings for the two masses are quite different.

by an office of the Trinity with texts for a commemoration lasting a full week.[33] These formal celebrations were supplemented by daily reminders of the Trinity. The *Regularis concordia* states that the monk's first act on waking should be to invoke the Trinity; in addition, the *Trina oratio*, recited three times each day, is said in honour of the Trinity.[34] Several late Anglo-Saxon manuscripts include sets of private prayers in honour of the three persons of the Trinity[35] and two manuscripts (the Ælfwine Prayerbook and the Crowland Psalter) contain offices in honour of the Trinity.[36]

Church dedications provide further evidence of devotion to the Trinity during the tenth and eleventh centuries.[37] Winchester's New Minster was dedicated in 903 to the Trinity, SS Mary and Peter,[38] and the tower of New Minster, built by Æthelgar between 980 and 988, was decorated with carvings of Mary with her virgins, the Trinity, the cross, All Saints, St Michael and all angels and, finally, the four evangelists.[39] The chapel built by Edith at Wilton in about 984 was dedicated to the Trinity, the Archangel Gabriel and St Denis.[40] Æthelric, bishop of Dorchester (1016–34) had a church built at Ramsey in honour of the Trinity,[41] and Odda's Chapel at Deerhurst, dedicated in 1056, contains an inscription

---

[33] *Portiforium Wulstani* (ed. Hughes II, 48–59); the texts are not the same as those for the Octave of Pentecost (*ibid.* I, 68–9). Some of the manuscripts described by Hesbert include both the Octave of Pentecost and the Feast of the Trinity: *Corpus antiphonalium* I, 232–4 (nos. 97a–b) and II, 454–9 (nos. 97a–c).

[34] *Regularis concordia*, i.15, i.17 and i.27 (ed. Symons, pp. 11, 13 and 23).

[35] BL, Cotton Titus D. xxvii, 86r-87v (ptd Günzel, *Ælfwine's Prayerbook*, pp. 136–8); prayers 1–3 also in CUL, Ff. 1. 23, 276v–277v and BL, Harley 863, 114v–115r; prayers 2–3 in CCCC 391, pp. 582–3 (Günzel, p. 206). Prayers to the Trinity are also found in the Bury Psalter, Biblioteca Apostolica Vaticana, Regin. lat. 12, 168v–169r.

[36] Titus D. xxvii, 76r–80r (ptd Günzel, pp. 128–31) and Oxford, Bodleian Library, Douce 296, 127v–130v.

[37] Of the churches listed by Taylor, *Anglo-Saxon Architecture*, as having remains of Anglo-Saxon work, the following are dedicated to the Trinity: Bosham, Clee, Colchester, Deerhurst (Odda's Chapel), Great Paxton, Stonegrave and Swallow; in all cases Taylor assigns a date late in the Anglo-Saxon period (950–1100).

[38] Biddle, *Winchester in the Early Middle Ages*, p. 313; New Minster, *Liber vitae* (ed. Birch, pp. viii and 214–17).

[39] *Liber vitae* (ed. Birch, p. 10); Quirk, 'Winchester New Minster', pp. 21–2, 33–5 and 38–9; Raw, *Crucifixion Iconography*, pp. 18 and 20–1.

[40] Gem, 'Iconography', pp. 13–14; Goscelin, *De Sancta Editha* I.vii.20 and II.1 (ed. Wilmart, pp. 86, 267 and 269).

[41] L–B 3582 (citing *Historia Ramesiensis, sive liber benefactorum ecclesiae Ramesiensis*).

stating that Earl Odda had the chapel built in honour of the Trinity and for the repose of the soul of his brother, Ælfric.[42] Leofric of Mercia (*ob.* 1057) and his wife Godgifu built a church in honour of the Trinity at Evesham.[43] In addition to these new foundations, two major earlier foundations received additional dedications to the Trinity during the tenth century. Winchester's Old Minster, dedicated originally to SS Peter and Paul,[44] had acquired an additional dedication to the Trinity by the time of Athelstan, for it is referred to as the church of the Holy Trinity, SS Peter and Paul in a grant of 938.[45] Christ Church, Canterbury, seems to have followed suit later in the century. Bartholomew Cotton, writing in the thirteenth century, states under the year 990, 'dedicata est ecclesia sancti Trinitatis Cantuariensis'. Nicholas Brooks has argued that this passage cannot refer to the Anglo-Saxon cathedral, which is invariably referred to as *ecclesia sancti Salvatoris* or *ecclesia Christi*.[46] However, Richard Gem has drawn attention to the fact that the Saxon cathedral, unusually, had two high altars. The more westerly of the two was dedicated to the Saviour; the dedication of the second altar is not known, but Gem suggests that it may have been dedicated to the Trinity and that this dedication is recalled in the later Chapel of the Trinity, built by Anselm to the east of Lanfranc's sanctuary. Gem argues from this that there may have been a rebuilding and rededication of Christ Church under Dunstan.[47] Further evidence for devotion to the Trinity during the second half of the tenth century is provided by Æthelwold's foundation at Thorney. According to the foundation charter (973 × 975), the design of the church, with three

---

[42] Taylor, *Anglo-Saxon Architecture* I, 209.

[43] L–B 1613 (citing *Chronicon abbatiae de Evesham*).

[44] Biddle, *Winchester in the Early Middle Ages*, p. 306; Bede, *HE* III.vii (ed. Colgrave and Mynors, p. 232).

[45] Finberg, *Wessex*, p. 40 (no. 55). The dedication is also given as the Trinity, SS Peter and Paul in a letter from Pope John XIII to King Edgar which is known only from a printed copy; doubts have been expressed about the genuineness of the letter, but, if it is a forgery, it must be an early one; see *Memorials of St Dunstan*, ed. Stubbs, pp. 364–5.

[46] Brooks, *Early History*, pp. 54–5 and p. 340, n. 63.

[47] Gem, 'Anglo-Saxon Cathedral Church at Canterbury', pp. 196–201 and 'Reconstructions', pp. 71–2. The recent excavations under the nave of the present cathedral have revealed traces of at least three earlier buildings, the latest of which, with western apse and south tower, is clearly the building described by Eadmer. An earlier, aisled, building may represent a late tenth-century rebuilding. I am indebted to Paul Bennett and Kevin Blockley for this information.

altars dedicated to Mary, Peter and Benedict, was intended to symbolize the three Persons in one God of the Holy Trinity. Æthelwold also built a private chapel at Thorney which, like the main church, had a triple symbolism.[48]

The drawings and paintings of the Trinity to which Wormald drew attention, most of which occur in manuscripts belonging to monastic houses,[49] are clearly related to this growth in devotion to the Trinity and, in particular, to the central position given to meditation on the Trinity in monastic prayer. The life of contemplation to which the monk aspired was seen as an anticipation of the vision of God he hoped one day to enjoy. Bede defines this life, to be entered into only after long preparation, in a homily for the Feast of St John the Evangelist:

Contemplativa autem vita est cum longo quis bonae actionis exercitio edoctus diutinae orationis dulcedine instructus crebra lacrimarum conpunctione adsuefactus a cunstis mundi negotiis vacare et in sola dilectione oculum mentis intendere didicerit gaudiumque perpetuae beatitudinis quod in futura percepturus est vita etiam in praesenti coeperit ardenter desiderando praegustare et aliquando etiam quantum mortalibus fas est in excessu mentis speculando sublimiter. Haec autem vita divinae speculationis illos maxime recipit qui post longa monasticae rudimenta virtutis secreti ab hominibus degere norunt eo liberiorem ad caelestia meditanda animum habentes quo terrenis separatum tumultibus.[50]

Whereas the active life ends at death, though it receives its reward after death, the contemplative life is perfected after death. It is a life whose happiness will be completed in heaven when we see God face to face,

---

[48] Gem, 'Iconography', pp. 14–15; New Minster, *Liber vitae* (ed. Birch, pp. 286–90); Hart, *Early Charters*, p. 167.

[49] Wormald, *Collected Writings* I, 106–8.

[50] *Homeliae* I.9 (ed. Hurst, pp. 64–5, trans. Martin and Hurst I, 91): 'The contemplative life, however, is [lived] when one who has been taught by the long practice of good actions, instructed by the sweetness of prolonged prayer, and habituated by the frequent sting of tears, learns to be free of all affairs of the world and to direct the eye of his mind toward love alone; and he begins, even in the present life, to gain a foretaste of the joy of the perpetual blessedness which he is to attain in the future, by ardently desiring it, and even sometimes, insofar as is permitted to mortals, by contemplating it sublimely in mental ecstasy. This life of divine contemplation especially takes in those who, after long [practice in] the rudiments of monastic virtue, spend their lives cut off from human beings, knowing that they will have a mind which is freer for meditating on heavenly things inasmuch as it has been separated from earthly tumults.'

rather than through a mirror: 'Speculativa autem felicitas quae hic inchoatur illic sine fine perficitur quando et supernorum civium et ipsius domini praesentia non per speculum et in enigmate sicut nunc sed facie ad faciem videbitur.'[51]

The intimate relationship between meditation on the Trinity, the beatific vision and the monastic life, was set out most fully in the *Forma fidei* of Benedict of Aniane, the early ninth-century reformer of the monastic order.[52] The word *forma* in the title implies a model or image and the work itself, which is heavily dependent on Augustine's *De Trinitate*, was intended for those who had already grasped the basics of Christian belief but who wished to go further on the road which leads from belief, to understanding, to love and, finally, to vision.[53] The focus of Benedict's work is the paradox of a God who is essentially unknowable and yet who offers those he has created a life which is defined as knowledge of God and of Christ.[54] Benedict returns again and again to the subject of God's transcendence: unlike the pagan gods, present in living things, the Christian God is the creator of all things and separate from them; he is not contained in any one place; he is invisible, undivided and uncircumscribed.[55] Who can understand the inner relations of the Trinity, Benedict asks:

Quomodo Pater et Filius et Spiritus Sanctus tres personae sint una natura? Quomodo Pater ingenitus, Filius genitus, Spiritus nempe Sanctus nec genitus nec ingenitus? Quomodo Filius de Patre natus est, Spiritus autem Sanctus de Patre procedat et Filio? Quomodo Filius nascendo procedit, Spiritus Sanctus de Patre et Filio procedendo non nascitur? . . . Quis ista comprehendit?[56]

---

[51] *Homeliae* I.9 (ed. Hurst, p. 65, trans. Martin and Hurst I, 92): 'Contemplative happiness, however, which commences here, will there be made perfect without end when the presence of the heavenly citizens and of the Lord himself will be seen, not through a mirror and in a dark manner as now, but face to face.' Cf. Augustine, *In Iohannis evangelium*, cxxiv.5 (ed. Willems, pp. 685–6) and below, p. 85.

[52] Ed. Leclercq, '*Munimenta fidei*', pp. 28–53.

[53] See esp. *Forma fidei*, i, vi and xii (ed. Leclercq, pp. 28, 34, 38 and discussion, pp. 68–70).

[54] John XVII.3: 'And eternal life is this: to know you, the only true God, and Jesus Christ whom you have sent'; quoted in *Forma fidei*, iii (ed. Leclercq, p. 31).

[55] *Ibid.*, i and iii (ed. Leclercq, pp. 28, 30 and 32).

[56] *Ibid.*, iv (ed. Leclercq, pp. 33–4): 'How Father, Son and Holy Spirit are three persons in one nature? How the Father is unbegotten, the Son is begotten and the Holy Spirit is neither begotten nor unbegotten? How the Son is born of the Father, the Holy Spirit,

But, for Benedict, there is an answer: God, who is invisible, has been described to us in the person of his Son.[57] Moreover, the human mind bears traces of the Trinity, imprinted on it at its creation, and we can therefore come to know and love God through knowing and loving his image within us.[58] Through faith and analogy, therefore, we prepare to contemplate the mystery, a process which will be completed in heaven, when we are conformed to the image in which we were created, when we will see God as he is and know as we are known.[59]

Another monastic writer for whom contemplation of the Trinity was central was John of Fécamp (*ob.* 1078). His earliest work, the *Confessio theologica* which dates from before 1018, ends with a section in which he describes how he has written the book in order that he may always have it with him, to rekindle the love of God in himself.[60] John reworked the material in this book twice: the *Confessio fidei*, written about 1050, includes a commentary on the Creed and a treatise on the eucharist in addition to a new version of the *Confessio theologica* and was similarly intended for his personal use; the *Libellus de scripturis et verbis patrum* was intended for use by others and includes psalms and prayers as well as the more meditative and discursive material.[61] The *Confessio theologica* is divided into three sections which treat, first, the Trinity, then the redemption and, finally, the desire for heaven; the *Libellus*, on the other hand, moves from meditation on the Incarnation, to love of Christ and desire for heaven and, in third place, what John calls a higher form of contemplation, that of the Trinity. This is probably the work, 'de contemplatione divina Christique amore et de illa superna Ierusalem', which he sent to an unnamed nun and, later, to the Empress Agnes, to be read frequently, with tears and devotion, when they were filled with the desire for contemplation and for the sweetness of heaven.[62]

on the other hand, proceeds from the Father and the Son? How the Son proceeds by being born, the Holy Spirit, proceeding from the Father and the Son is not born? . . . Who can grasp these things?'

[57] *Ibid.*, xiii (ed. Leclercq, p. 40), quoting John I.18, 'unigenitus Filius, qui est in sinu Patris, ipse narravit'.

[58] *Ibid.*, viii (ed. Leclercq, pp. 36–7).

[59] *Ibid.*, xii, xiii and xv (ed. Leclercq, pp. 38, 42, 46 and 50).

[60] *Confessio theologica* III, Recapitulatio (ed. Leclercq and Bonnes, pp. 182–3).

[61] Leclercq and Bonnes, *Jean de Fécamp*, pp. 31–2 and 37.

[62] *Ad sanctimonialem*, iv and v and *Ad imperatricem viduam*, vii and x (ed. Leclercq and Bonnes, pp. 207, 214 and 215).

Like Benedict of Aniane, John stresses the inability of the human mind to understand the mystery of the Trinity and the importance of faith as a prerequisite for vision.[63] Where Benedict, following Augustine, quoted Isaiah, 'Nisi credideritis, non intelligetis',[64] John says: 'Corde credo, ore confiteor, quia vera sunt omnia quae illa [the Church] credit, confitetur et docet. Certe videbimus in re, quod tenemus in spe.'[65] While emphasizing the inability of mortals to see or understand God's inner being, he argues that those who truly love God are sometimes allowed a faint glimpse of the reality:[66] the contemplative life begins on earth but is perfected in heaven, where God 'sine aspectu cernitur, sine sono auditur, sine motu suscipitur, sine corpore tangitur, sine loco retinetur'.[67]

The primacy of faith in the search for God is a commonplace in the writings of the early medieval period.[68] Augustine began his treatise on the Trinity by attacking those who thought that it was possible to understand the Trinity through reason: 'Lecturus haec quae de trinitate disserimus prius oportet ut noverit stilum nostrum adversus eorum vigilare calumnias qui fidei contemnentes initium immaturo et perverso rationis amore falluntur.'[69] He returns to this point at the end of bk VII where he says: 'Quod si intellectu capi non potest, fide teneatur donec inlucescat in cordibus ille qui ait per prophetam: *Nisi credideritis non intellegetis.*'[70] The theme of faith in search of understanding is best known, however, from

---

[63] *Confessio theologica* I.vi (ed. Leclercq and Bonnes, pp. 112–13).

[64] Isaiah VII.9, Old Latin: 'Unless you believe you will not understand'; *Forma fidei*, i (ed. Leclercq, p. 28); Augustine, *De Trinitate* VII.vi.12 and XV.ii.2 (ed. Mountain, pp. 267 and 461).

[65] *Confessio theologica* I.vii (ed. Leclercq and Bonnes, p. 113): 'I believe in the heart, I confess with the mouth, because all the things that she believes, confesses and teaches are true. Certainly we shall see in reality what we hold in hope.'

[66] *Ad sanctimonialem*, vi and *Ad imperatricem viduam*, xi (ed. Leclercq and Bonnes, pp. 208 and 215).

[67] *Ad sanctimonialem*, vii and *Ad imperatricem viduam*, xiv (ed. Leclercq and Bonnes, pp. 208 and 216): '[God] is perceived even though he has no visible form, is heard without any sound, is received without any movement, touched though he has no body, is grasped though he occupies no space.'

[68] For a discussion of the material, see Pelikan, *Christian Tradition* III, 258–60.

[69] *De Trinitate* I.i.1 (ed. Mountain, p. 27, trans. Hill, p. 65): 'The reader of these reflections of mine on the Trinity should bear in mind that my pen is on the watch against the sophistries of those who scorn the starting-point of faith, and allow themselves to be deceived through an unseasonable and misguided love of reason.'

[70] *Ibid.* VII.vi.12 (ed. Mountain, p. 267, trans. Hill, p. 232): 'If this cannot be grasped by

17

the work of a writer very different from Augustine, namely Anselm of Canterbury.

Anselm's two early works, the *Monologion* and *Proslogion*, were written for his fellow monks as meditations on the nature of God.[71] The themes of the *Monologion*, which was based on Augustine's *De Trinitate* and originally given the title, 'Exemplum meditandi de ratione fidei', are those of Benedict of Aniane's *Forma fidei*: that God cannot be known in his essence, but only through analogy;[72] that the memory of the Trinity is imprinted on the human mind through its capacity to remember, to understand and to love;[73] that the mind (*mens*) is both a mirror (*speculum*) and an image (*imago*) of God.[74] For Anselm, however, reason plays a far larger part than it did for Augustine, Benedict or John of Fécamp. He quotes no authorities. In fact, in the Prologue to the *Monologion* he states quite clearly that his aim was to rely on logic rather than on quotation from scripture. The *Proslogion*, to which Anselm gave the title, 'Fides quaerens intellectum', carries this principle further for it was designed, as Anselm himself says, to see whether it was possible to find a single argument, needing no proof outside itself, for the existence of God.[75] The method and style, therefore, are very different from those of the earlier writers, yet the focus is the same. Anselm wonders how it is possible to see God, who lives in a light which dazzles the human eye.[76] He urges the reader to shut out the world and to seek God, the one necessary being, creator of all that is, possessor of all goodness and beauty, in whom there is no place or time.[77] Finally, he prays to God that he may so love him in this world that he may at last enter into the joy of his Lord, the God who is both Three and One.[78]

Benedict of Aniane, John of Fécamp and Anselm were writing for monks, though the latter sent copies of some of his prayers and

understanding, let it be held by faith, until he shines in our minds who said through the prophet, *Unless you believe, you will not understand* (Isaiah VII.9).'

[71] *Monologion*, Prol. and *Proslogion*, Proemium (ed. Schmitt, I, 7 and 93–4). For an account of these two works, which date from 1077 and 1078, see Southern, *Anselm*, pp. 47–66.

[72] *Monologion*, lxvi (ed. Schmitt I, 77).

[73] *Ibid.*, xlviii and lx (ed. Schmitt I, 63 and 70); see also *Proslogion* i (ed. Schmitt I, 100).

[74] *Monologion*, lxvii (ed. Schmitt I, 77–8).

[75] *Proslogion*, Proemium (ed. Schmitt I, 93–4).

[76] *Ibid.*, i, xiv and xvi (ed. Schmitt I, 98 and 111–13).

[77] *Ibid.*, xxiii, v and xix (ed. Schmitt I, 117, 104 and 115).

[78] *Ibid.*, xxvi (ed. Schmitt I, 120–2).

meditations to at least two pious laywomen, Adelaide, daughter of William the Conqueror, and Matilda, countess of Tuscany.[79] Ælfric, on the other hand, wrote his Catholic Homilies for lay people. The homilies belong, of course, to a monastic tradition of exegesis and it seems likely that Ælfric's patrons at Cerne Abbas, Æthelweard and Æthelmær, used them for private, devotional reading, but they were also intended for preaching in public[80] and their content must therefore be related to the needs of a wider audience.

A major preoccupation for Ælfric, and for his contemporary, Wulfstan, was the approaching judgement. Both writers were well aware that no one knew the date when the world would end, but they were also very conscious of the wars and other disturbances which the New Testament warned them were signs of the approaching end, and there are many passages in their writings which show that they believed that the end was near, even if they did not put an exact date on it.[81] Ælfric, talking of the wise and foolish virgins, says:

Oft cweðað men, efne nu cymð domes dæg, for ðan ðe ða witegunga sind agane, þe be ðam gesette wæron. Ac gefeoht cymð ofer gefeohte, gedrefednys ofer gedrefednysse, eorðstyrung ofer eorðstyrunge, hungor ofer hungre, þeod ofer ðeode, and þonne gyt ne cymð se brydguma. Eac swilce þa six ðusend geara fram Adame beoð geendode, and ðonne gyt elcað se brydguma. Hu mage we þonne witan hwænne he cymð? Swa swa he sylf cwæð, on middre nihte. Hwæt is on middre nihte buton þonne ðu nast, and þu his ne wenst ðonne cymð he. Nis nan gesceaft þe cunne ðone timan þyssere worulde geendunge buton gode anum.[82]

Elsewhere, he quotes Christ's words, that no one except God knows the time or day of the world's end, but adds: 'Þeahhwæðere, be ðam tacnum þe Crist sæde, we geseoð þæt seo geendung is swiðe gehende, þeah ðe heo

---

[79] Southern, *Anselm*, p. 37.      [80] Gatch, *Preaching and Theology*, p. 53.

[81] *Ibid.*, pp. 78–84; Ælfric, *Homilies* (ed. Pope II, 585). The biblical passages are Matt. XXIV.3–36, Mark XIII.5–27 and Luke XXI.8–28.

[82] *CH* II.xxxix (ed. Godden, pp. 330–1): 'Often men say, Even now doomsday is coming, because the signs which were described have passed. But battle comes after battle, affliction after affliction, earthquake after earthquake, famine after famine, nation after nation, and yet the bridegroom still does not come. Also, in the same way, the six thousand years since Adam have ended, and yet the bridegroom still delays. How then may we know when he will come? As he himself said, In the middle of the night. What does, In the middle of the night mean except, When you do not know, and when you do not expect him then he will come. There is no creature who knows the time of this world's end but God alone.'

us uncuð sy.'[83] In the English Preface to the first set of Catholic Homilies he talks of 'this time, which is the ending of this world', and he returns to this theme in his homilies for Advent, a period when the Church traditionally reflected on Christ's second coming.[84] In a homily for the First Sunday in Advent, he recalls St Paul's warning: 'You know the time has come: you must wake up now: our salvation is even nearer than it was when we were converted.'[85] In the homily for the following Sunday he reminds his audience of the signs of the approaching end: 'Sume ðas tacna we gesawon gefremmede, sume we ondrædað us towearde.'[86] The homily ends with a renewed warning: 'Se witega cwæð, þæt se miccla Godes dæg is swiðe gehende, and þearle swyft. Þeah ðe gyt wære oðer þusend geara to ðam dæge, nære hit langsum; forðan swa hwæt swa geendað, þæt bið sceort and hræd ... Uton forði brucan þæs fyrstes ðe us God forgeaf, and geearnian þæt ece lif mid him.'[87] Again, in a homily on the memory of the saints, he says:

Nu on urum dagum on ende þyssere worulde,
swicað se deofol digollice embe us

...

forðan þe he wat geare þæt þysre worulde geendung
is swyðe gehende and he onet forði.[88]

---

[83] *CH* I.xxi (ed. Thorpe, p. 298): 'However, by the signs of which Christ spoke, we see that the end is very near, even though it is unknown to us.'

[84] 'on þisum timan þe is geendung þyssere worulde', *CH* I, Preface (ed. Thorpe, p. 2). The Preface occurs only in CUL, Gg. 3. 28; it was later discarded and the greater part of it (Thorpe, pp. 2–6) transferred to the end of the homily for the First Sunday in Advent, *CH* I.xxxix; see Sisam, 'MSS Bodley 340 and 342', pp. 168 and 178, and Pope, *Homilies* I, 60–2 and II, 611.

[85] Romans XIII.11, from the Epistle for the day; *CH* I.xxxix (ed. Thorpe, pp. 600–2).

[86] *CH* I.xl (ed. Thorpe, p. 608): 'We have seen some of these signs come about, some we fear are at hand'; based on Luke XXI.25–33; Ælfric is drawing on a homily by Gregory the Great, *Homiliae in evangelia* I.i.1 (PL 76, 1078).

[87] *CH* I.xl (ed. Thorpe, p. 618): 'The prophet said that the great day of God is very near and very swift. Even though there were still a further thousand years till that day, it would not be long; because whatever ends, is short and swift ... Therefore let us make use of the time which God has given us and earn that eternal life with him'; quoted by Gatch, *Preaching and Theology*, p. 79.

[88] *LS* I.xvi (ed. Skeat, I, 352): 'Now in our days, at the end of this world, the devil plots secretly against us ... because he knows well that the end of this world is very near, and so he hastens.'

Wulfstan is equally convinced that the world is approaching its end. His exhortation to the English in 1014, the 'Sermo ad Anglos', begins, 'Þeos world is on ofste, and hit nealæð þam ende.'[89] Like Ælfric, he identifies contemporary conflicts with those mentioned in the gospels,[90] and in a sermon on Mark XIII, based on the Preface to Ælfric's first set of Catholic Homilies, he says: 'Æfter þusend gearum bið Satanas unbunden. Þusend geara and eac ma is nu agan syððan Crist wæs mid mannum on menniscum hiwe, and nu syndon Satanases bendas swyðe toslopene, and Antecristes tima is wel gehende.'[91]

It is this figure of Antichrist which provides the link between the doctrine of the Trinity and the last days. Ælfric treats the subject of Antichrist several times: in the English Preface to the first set of Catholic Homilies,[92] in three of the second set of Catholic Homilies,[93] in the Life of Saints Chrysanthus and Daria,[94] and in a late homily, 'De die iudicii'.[95] Wulfstan devoted several complete homilies to the subject of Antichrist, as well as making frequent references to him elsewhere.[96] Both writers describe the disastrous effect Antichrist's lies will have on Christians and both draw attention to the need for good teaching at this time.[97] Wulfstan, typically, calls for repentance, a strict attention to religious duties like the payment of tithes and the giving of alms, and an increase in love for Christ.[98] Ælfric, on the other hand, stresses the need for sound

---

[89] *Homilies*, no. xx (ed. Bethurum, p. 261): 'This world is in haste and is approaching the end.'

[90] *Homilies*, no. iii (ed. Bethurum, p. 124).

[91] *Homilies*, no. v (ed. Bethurum, pp. 136–7): 'After a thousand years Satan will be unbound. A thousand years and more has now passed since Christ was among men in the form of a man, and now Satan's bonds are greatly loosened and the time of Antichrist is very close'; see also *Homilies*, no. vi (ed. Bethurum, p. 155): 'Antecristes tima bið æfter ðysum, and nu swyðe raðe his man mæg wenan.'

[92] *CH* I, Preface (ed. Thorpe, pp. 4 and 6).

[93] *CH* II.vii, xxx and xxxvii (ed. Godden, pp. 60, 263 and 312–13).

[94] *LS* II.xxxv (ed. Skeat II, 398).

[95] *Homilies*, no. xviii (ed. Pope II, 603–4 and 608).

[96] *Homilies*, ed. Bethurum, nos. ia, ib and iv, and references in homilies ii, iii and v (ed. Bethurum, pp. 121, 125 and 136). For discussion of the Antichrist theme in the writings of Ælfric and Wulfstan, see Gatch, *Preaching and Theology*, pp. 80, 224–5 (nn. 22 and 23) and 105–16.

[97] Wulfstan, *Homilies*, no. ia (ed. Bethurum, p. 114); Ælfric, *CH* I, Preface (ed. Thorpe, p. 6).

[98] *Homilies*, nos. iii, iv and vi (ed. Bethurum, pp. 124, 126–7, 133 and 154–6); cf.

learning and right belief in addition to the active virtues of helping the poor. His references to the Last Judgement, based on the account in St Matthew's Gospel,[99] emphasize the importance of good works, and in a sermon for the Ninth Sunday after Pentecost he quotes Christ's warning: 'Ne færð into heofonan rice ælc ðæra ðe cweð to me, Drihten, drihten, ac se ðe wyrcð mines Fæder willan þe on heofonum is, se færð into heofonan rice.'[100] The homily ends, however, with a definition of good works which is very different from what one might expect:

Þæt is Godes weorc, þæt ge on ðone gelyfan þe he asende. Ðis is þæt fyrmeste weorc and se fyrmesta willa, þæt we gelyfon on ðone ancennedan Godes sunu hælend Crist, þone ðe se ælmihtiga Fæder for ure alysednysse asende, and ðone geleafan we sceolon mid hluttrum mode and eawfæstum ðeawum geglengan, þæt we habbon infær to heofenan rice, swa swa Crist sylf eallum geleaffullum behet.[101]

For Ælfric, it is ultimately faith which saves[102] and the faith which is needed is steadfast belief in the Trinity and in the Incarnation.

By the late Anglo-Saxon period preachers were able to draw on a well-established tradition of writing about Antichrist. One of the most popular works was the *De ortu et tempore Antichristi* of Adso of Montier-en-Der, written between 949 and 954 for Gerberga, sister of Otto I.[103] The work was translated into Old English and was known to both Ælfric and Wulfstan, though neither follows it precisely.[104] Adso claimed that

---

*Blickling Homilies*, no. vii (ed. Morris, p. 91), *Vercelli Homilies*, no. viii (ed. Scragg, pp. 143–8) and *Christ III* 1487–8 (ASPR III, 44).

[99] *CH* II.vii (ed. Godden, pp. 65–6).

[100] Matt. VII.21; *CH* II.xxvi (ed. Godden, pp. 235 and 239): 'Not everyone who says to me, Lord, Lord, will go into the kingdom of heaven, but he who does the will of my Father who is in heaven, he will go into the kingdom of heaven.'

[101] *CH* II.xxvi (ed. Godden, pp. 239–40): 'That is God's work, that you should believe in the one whom he sent (John VI.29). This is the foremost work and the foremost desire, that we believe in the only-begotten Son of God, the saviour Christ, whom the almighty Father sent to free us, and we must adorn that faith with a pure mind and pious habits, so that we may have entry to the kingdom of heaven, as Christ himself promised to all believers.'

[102] *CH* I, Preface (ed. Thorpe, p. 4): 'Þa beoð gehealdene þe oð ende on geleafan þurhwuniað' ('Those who continue in faith to the end will be saved'), cf. Matt. XXIV.13. See also *CH* II.xxii (ed. Godden, p. 212).

[103] *Adso Dervensis*, ed. Verhelst, pp. 1–3.

[104] Gatch, *Preaching and Theology*, pp. 223–4, n. 21; Ælfric, *Homilies* (ed. Pope II, 588); Wulfstan, *Homilies* (ed. Bethurum, pp. 281–2 and 288–92).

Antichrist was born of human parents, though he was inspired by the devil.[105] Ælfric and Wulfstan, on the other hand, saw him as a parody of Christ: just as Christ was true God and true man, so Antichrist was true man and true devil.[106] His role is to draw men away from right belief: 'Ælcne mann he wile awendan of rihtan geleafan and of cristendome and bespannan to his unlarum gif he mæg.'[107] He claims to be God's son and therefore draws many into error.[108] He even claims to be God himself.[109] Finally, he raises himself up, not only above the classical gods, but above the Trinity, which alone is to be worshipped and adored. As Haymo says: 'Extollet se Antichristus supra omne quod dicitur deus ... et non solum super illos, sed etiam (quod maius est) supra omne quod colitur, id est supra sanctam Trinitatem, quae solummodo colenda et adoranda est ab omni creatura.'[110] Antichrist, therefore, promotes heresy and, in particular, heretical beliefs about the Trinity.

This view of Antichrist is brought out most clearly in the work of two continental writers, Adémar of Chabannes and Ralph Glaber. Adémar, who was born in about 988 and died in Jerusalem in 1034, is credited with the forgery of two Trinitarian documents: the so-called Creed of Leo, based on Alcuin's *De fide sanctae et individuae Trinitatis*, and the letter from the monks of the Mount of Olives to

---

[105] *De ortu* (ed. Verhelst, p. 23); cf. Haymo, *In Epistolam II ad Thessalonicenses*, ii (PL 117, 779).

[106] Ælfric, *CH* I, Preface (ed. Thorpe, p. 4): 'Se bið mennisc mann and soð deofol, swa swa ure Hælend is soðlice mann and God on anum hade' ('He is true human and true devil, as our Saviour is truly man and God in a single person'); Wulfstan, *Homilies*, no. iv (ed. Bethurum, p. 128): 'Crist is soð God and soð mann, and Antecrist bið soðlice deofol and mann' ('Christ is true God and true man, and Antichrist is truly devil and man').

[107] Wulfstan, *Homilies*, no. iv (ed. Bethurum, pp. 128–9): 'He will turn every man away from right belief and from Christendom and entice him to his evil teaching if he may.' Cf. II Thess. II.9–10: 'There will be all kinds of miracles and a deceptive show of signs and portents, and everything evil that can deceive those who are bound for destruction because they would not grasp the love of the truth which could have saved them.'

[108] Wulfstan, *Homilies*, no. v (ed. Bethurum, pp. 138–9).

[109] Ælfric, *Homilies*, no. xviii (ed. Pope II, 603).

[110] Haymo, *In Epistolam II ad Thessalonicenses*, ii (PL 117, 779–80): cf. Adso, *De ortu* (ed. Verhelst, p. 27). These references represent a modification of the biblical passage on which Haymo is commenting: 'This is the Enemy, the one who claims to be so much *greater than all* that men call "god", so much greater than anything that is worshipped, that *he enthrones himself* in *God's* sanctuary and claims that he is God' (II Thess. II.4).

Charlemagne.[111] Adémar's interest in the Trinity, apparent in his sermons as well as the two documents already mentioned, is clearly connected with his expectation that the world was nearing its end. Heretics are the messengers of Antichrist, he says; Christians who do not openly profess the faith embodied in the Creed are easily led astray by these messengers; without this faith no one will attain the vision of Christ.[112] The heretics of Aquitaine and Orleans were described by Adémar as Manichaeans.[113] Ralph Glaber (*ob. c.* 1046), however, says that the Orleans heresy of 1023 was a new one, previously unknown, and that the heretics denied the unity of the Trinity and the creation of the world by God.[114] Ralph sets the events at Orleans in an account of history which is consistently eschatological. He connects an outbreak of heresy at Ravenna with St John's prophecy that the devil would be freed after 1000 years,[115] and begins the final book of his history with a reference to the prodigies surrounding the millennium and with prophecies of further marvels at the millennium of Christ's passion.[116] He describes the famine which preceded the year 1033 and notes that it was thought to indicate the approaching end of the world.[117] He talks of the crowds who flocked to Jerusalem in 1033, expecting the world to end, and adds that this signified the appearance of Antichrist when even the elect might give way to temptation.[118] He draws the same conclusion from these events as Adémar: that people need a firm belief in the Trinity if they are to resist the attacks of Antichrist, a point brought out most strongly in the lengthy exposition of Trinitarian doctrine which he adds to his account of the Orleans heresy.[119]

Similar attitudes can be detected at Winchester, though they appear rather earlier. Æthelwold introduced three votive offices (in honour of the Virgin Mary, SS Peter and Paul and All Saints) at the Old Minster, Winchester. These offices were to be recited privately as additions to the regular office and were intended to strengthen those reciting them against

---

[111] Callahan, 'The Problem of the "Filioque"', pp. 89–90.
[112] *Ibid.*, pp. 91, 96, 120–1, 124 and 129.
[113] Adémar, *Historiae* III, 49 and 59 (ed. Waitz, pp. 138 and 143).
[114] Ralph Glaber, *Historiae* III.viii.27 (ed. France, pp. 140–2).
[115] *Ibid.* II.xii (ed. France, p. 92).    [116] *Ibid.* IV.i (ed. France, p. 170).
[117] *Ibid.* IV.iv.9–10, 13 and v.14 (ed. France, pp. 184–8 and 190–4).
[118] *Ibid.* IV.vi.18–21 (ed. France, pp. 198–204).
[119] *Ibid.* III.viii.28–30 (ed. France, pp. 142–8).

'the manifold trickery of the shape-shifting Antichrist and his associates', so that their faith would not waver.[120] As far as is known, Æthelwold's office for SS Peter and Paul has not survived but the office in honour of All Saints, which is mentioned in the *Regularis concordia*, may be that found in a manuscript containing a copy of the *Regularis concordia* and other items, written at Christ Church, Canterbury about 1050.[121] An office in honour of Mary, which may be Æthelwold's, was copied into the Ælfwine Prayerbook, written at New Minster, Winchester, between 1023 and 1032.[122] This manuscript also contains offices in honour of the cross and the Trinity, arranged on the same pattern as the office in honour of Mary, and perhaps modelled on it in response to changing devotional needs.[123]

Ælfric, who was Æthelwold's pupil, seems relatively untroubled by the possibility of heresy. He frequently refers to Arius, for example, yet he never links him to contemporary problems; on the contrary, he seems to view him as a figure from the distant past.[124] Wulfstan similarly says nothing of contemporary heresy in the long lists of sins in his address to the English of 1014.[125] What does seem to concern Ælfric is Jewish beliefs. Like Bede, he compares Jewish denials of the divinity of Christ to Arian denials of his equality with the Father.[126] He stresses the continuity of revelation in Old and New Testaments but at the same time he points to a break with Jewish tradition in the law revealed by Christ.[127] In a sermon for the dedication of a church he talks of Christ as the living stone,

---

[120] *Wulfstan of Winchester* (ed. Lapidge and Winterbottom, p. lxviii and n. 115); the offices must date from 963–84, the period of Æthelwold's episcopacy.

[121] BL, Cotton Tiberius A. iii, 57r–v; see *Wulfstan of Winchester* (ed. Lapidge and Winterbottom, pp. lxxv–lxxvii).

[122] BL, Cotton Titus D. xxvii, 81v–85v (ptd Günzel, *Ælfwine's Prayerbook*, pp. 133–6).

[123] Titus D. xxvii, 76r–80r (Office of the Trinity) and 80r–81v (Office of the Cross), *ibid.*, pp. 128–33.

[124] *CH* I.xx (ed. Thorpe, p. 290), *LS* I.xvi (ed. Skeat I, 350), *Homilies*, no. x (ed. Pope I, 403), 'In natale unius confessoris' (ed. Assmann, p. 59), 'First Latin Letter to Wulfstan' and 'First Old English Letter to Wulfstan' (ed. Fehr, pp. 41 and 92). For a note on the sources of the references, see *Homilies*, ed. Pope I, 394–5.

[125] 'Sermo Lupi ad Anglos' (ed. Bethurum, pp. 267–75).

[126] Bede, *Homeliae* I.23 (ed. Hurst, p. 169); Ælfric, *CH* I.xx (ed. Thorpe, p. 290). See also Blumenkranz, 'Altercatio', p. 17, n. 37. Pelikan, *Christian Tradition* I, 71 and II, 201, points out that 'to Judaize' was used by early theologians as a term for teaching false doctrine.

[127] Cf. Ælfric, 'Preface to Genesis' (ed. Crawford, *Heptateuch*, p. 80), a reference I owe to Malcolm Godden, and Raw, 'Verbal Icons', pp. 121–8.

rejected by the unbelieving Jews,[128] and in two places he describes how the whole of creation recognized Christ as God, with the one exception of the Jews.[129] Ælfric's references to the unbelieving and impious Jews belong to literary tradition but his taunt that God works miracles at the tombs of saints 'ðe gelyfdon on ða Halgan Ðrynnysse, and on soð Annysse anre Godcundnysse' but not at Jewish tombs suggests that he had some actual contact with Jews.[130] The earliest reference to Jews living in Winchester seems to be the Winton Domesday[131] but there is some evidence for the presence of Jews in England before that date. The illustrations to the Old English Hexateuch portray Jews wearing distinctive head-dresses and at least one of the literary debates between Synagogue and Ecclesia seems to have been written in England between 938 and 966, suggesting that theological disputes between Christians and Jews were a reality in tenth-century England.[132] A major theme of such disputes was the conflict between Christian belief in the Trinity and Jewish belief in the One God who spoke to Moses.[133] There is, then, a clear link between Ælfric's repeated expositions of the doctrine of the Trinity and his attitude towards the Jews. There is also a link with the Last Days, for Bede claims that the Jews will accept Antichrist in place of Christ:

Christum namque quem fides orthodoxa verum Deum verum confitetur et hominem illi purum tantummodo hominem futurum non autem Deum esse credebant memores videlicet quia de humanitate ipsius iuravit dominus David de fructu ventris eius sedere super sedem suam (Ps. CXXXI.11) sed obliti quod ipse de sua divinitate per eundem David cecinit dicens: *Dominus dixit ad me, filius meus es tu* (Ps. II.7). Credebant ergo Christum de stirpe David nasciturum et regem ceteris omnibus excellentiorem esse venturum qua etiam dementia posteri eorum

---

[128] *CH* II.xl (ed. Godden, p. 338); see I Pet. II.4–10, Matt. XXI.42 and Ephes. II.20–2. Cf. Bede, *De templo* I.i (ed. Hurst, p. 147).

[129] *CH* I.vii and xv (ed. Thorpe, pp. 108 and 228) and *Vercelli Homilies*, no. xvi (ed. Scragg, p. 270), based on Gregory, *Homiliae in evangelia* I.x.2 (PL 76, 1111). See Blumenkranz, 'Altercatio', pp. 14–16 and 46–8 for discussion of anti-Jewish writings.

[130] *CH* I.xx (ed. Thorpe, p. 292): 'who believed in the holy Trinity and in the true Unity of a single Godhead'. See also *LS* II.xxxii (ed. Skeat II, 334).

[131] Biddle, *Winchester in the Early Middle Ages*, p. 101.

[132] BL, Cotton Claudius B. iv, see Mellinkoff, 'Round, Cap-Shaped Hats', pp. 159–60 and Blumenkranz, 'Altercatio', pp. 31–5.

[133] 'Altercatio' (ed. Blumenkranz, pp. 69–77). See also Pelikan, *Christian Tradition* II, 200–15 and III, 34–42.

usque in praesens et donec antichristum pro Christo suscipiant errare non cessant.[134]

What is clear in all this is Ælfric's deep sense of the urgency of the situation, and of his own duty to teach others: 'We ne durran forsuwian, þæt we eow ne secgan þa deopan lare and ures drihtenes beboda, þy-læs-þe we scyldige beon, gif we hit forsuwiað.'[135] The frequency and detail with which he returns to the subjects of the Trinity and the Incarnation demonstrate the importance these beliefs held in his view of salvation.[136] Other homilists had talked of the three persons in one God,[137] and of the two natures in one person of Christ,[138] but none equals the complexity of

---

[134] *Homeliae* II.24 (ed. Hurst, p. 359, trans., Martin and Hurst II, 243): 'They believed that the Christ, whom orthodox faith confesses to be true God and true man, would be only a man, not God. They were mindful that the Lord swore to David concerning [Christ's] humanity that the fruit of [David's] body would sit upon his throne, but they forgot what [the Lord] chanted concerning [Christ's] divinity through the [mouth of] David, saying, *The Lord said to me, You are my Son.* They therefore believed that the Christ would be born of the stock of David and would come as a king surpassing every other. [They believed this] with the same lack of sense that their descendants possess even at the present time, and they will not cease to err until at length they accept the antichrist in place of Christ.' For discussion of the prophecy in Psalm CXXXI.11 in relation to pictures of the Trinity, see below, p. 151.

[135] 'First Old English Letter to Wulfstan' (ed. Fehr, pp. 68–70): 'We dare not keep silent and not tell you the deep teaching and our Lord's commands, lest we are guilty if we keep silent about it'; see also *CH* I, Preface (ed. Thorpe, p. 6) and 'In natale unius confessoris' (ed. Assmann, pp. 56–7):

> Nu sceole we eac secgan ða soðan lare
> eow nu on urum timan, elles we beoð gehatene
> yfele þeowan and unnytwyrðe.

('Now we must also tell you the true teaching in our days, otherwise we will be called evil and unprofitable servants.')

[136] See, for example, *CH* I.i, ii, vii, viii, ix, xv, xviii, xx, xxii (ed. Thorpe, pp. 10, 24, 40, 116, 134, 150, 228, 248, 274 and 326), *CH* II.i, iii, iv, xiv, xv, xxii, xxiv (ed. Godden, pp. 3–4, 22–3, 29–31, 146, 154, 208–9, 211 and 224), *Homilies*, nos. i, vi, vii, viii, x, xia, xxi (ed. Pope I, 196–204, 322–5, 346–7, 365–7, 402–3, 463–4, 469, 471–2; II, 677–8 and 712).

[137] E.g. *Vercelli Homilies*, nos. iii and v (ed. Scragg, pp. 73 and 117); *Blickling Homilies*, nos. vi and x (ed. Morris, pp. 81 and 111).

[138] E.g. *Blickling Homilies*, nos. i, ii, iii, vii, xi and xii (ed. Morris, pp. 11, 19, 29, 31, 33, 91, 115–17, 121, 123, 127 and 131).

Ælfric's exposition. 'Gyt her is oðer cnotta, eal swa earfoðe',[139] he says, in a discussion of how it can be the case that 'No one has gone up to heaven except the one who came down from heaven, the Son of Man who is in heaven' (John III.13), apparently forgetting that he is supposedly writing 'ob aedificationem simplicium ... ad utilitatem idiotarum'.[140] The passage is based on part of a homily by Bede for the Octave of Pentecost; Bede, however, gives a quite different emphasis, saying, 'Cuius tamen nodum quaestionis apertissima ratio solvit.'[141] No one can enter heaven, Ælfric says, unless Peter opens to him, and this means that he must share the faith which Peter professed.[142] And what is that faith? 'Þæt is ece lif, þæt hi ðe oncnawon soðne God, and ðone ðe þu asendest Hælend Crist.'[143] The righteous man lives by faith in God, a faith which requires that he should understand the nature of the Trinity:

Geleafa is ealra mægena fyrmest; buton þam ne mæg nan man Gode lician; and se rihtwisa leofað be his geleafan. Uton gelyfan on þa Halgan Ðrynnysse, and on soðe Annysse, þæt se Ælmihtiga Fæder and his Sunu, þæt is his wisdom, and se Halga Gast, seðe is heora begra lufu and willa, þæt hi sind þry on hadum, and on namum, and an God, on anre godcundnysse æfre wunigende, butan angynne and ende.[144]

---

[139] Ælfric, *CH* II.xxiv (ed. Godden, p. 224): 'Here is another knotty point, equally difficult.'

[140] *CH* I, Preface (ed. Thorpe, p. 1): 'To teach the simple ... for the benefit of the unlearned.'

[141] *Homeliae* II.18 (ed. Hurst, p. 315, trans. Martin and Hurst II, 183): 'Yet a very clear argument unties the knot of this question.'

[142] *CH* I.xxvi (ed. Thorpe, p. 370); cf. Bede, *Homeliae* II.24 (ed. Hurst, p. 363).

[143] *CH* I.ii (ed. Thorpe, p. 42): 'That is eternal life, that they should know you the true God and the one whom you have sent, the Saviour Christ'; cf. *CH* II.xxii (ed. Godden, p. 208): 'Ðeos tocnawennys is ece lif for ðan ðe we habbað þæt ece lif ðurh geleafan and oncnawennysse þære halgan ðrynnysse gif we ða oncnawennysse mid arwurðnysse healdað' ('This knowledge is eternal life, because we have that eternal life through faith and belief in the holy Trinity, if we honourably maintain that belief').

[144] *CH* I.viii (ed. Thorpe, p. 134): 'Faith is the first of all virtues, without which no man may please God; and the righteous man lives by his faith. Let us believe in the holy Trinity and in the true Unity, that the almighty Father and his Son, that is his wisdom, and the Holy Spirit, who is the love and will of both, that they are three in person and in name, and one God, always living in a single Godhead, without beginning and end.'

# 2

## 'If anyone wishes to be saved'

The belief in the Trinity and in Christ as both God and man which lay at the centre of Ælfric's teaching was set out in the Creeds of the Church. The simplest of the three Creeds (the Apostles' or baptismal Creed) provided the basis of Christian teaching, and all Christians were expected to know it by heart, in the vernacular if necessary. Wulfstan, for example, says in his sermon on baptism:

And æfre swa þæt cild raðost ænig ðing specan mæge, tæce man him sona ealra þinga ærest Pater noster and Credan; þonne sceal him ðananforð a þe bet gelimpan. And eac ic on Godes naman bidde and beode, gyf ænig Cristen man þe ylde hæbbe swa sy forgymed þæt he hit ne cunne, leornige hit georne; and ne sceamige ænigum men for his ylde, ac do swa him þearf is, helpe his sylfes, forðam he ne bið wel cristen þe þæt geleornian nele, ne he nah mid rihte æniges mannes æt fulluhte to onfonne, ne æt bisceopes handa se ðe þæt ne cann, ær he hit geleornige, ne he rihtlice ne bið husles wyrðe ne clænes legeres, se ðe on life þæt geleornian nele, huru on Englisc, buton he on Læden mæge.[1]

---

[1] *Homilies*, no. viiic (ed. Bethurum, pp. 182–3): 'And as soon as that child can speak, let him immediately be taught first of all the *Pater noster* and the Creed; he will always be the better for it. And I also ask and command in God's name, if any Christian man who is adult is so ignorant that he does not know it, let him eagerly learn it; and let no man be ashamed on account of age, but let him do as is necessary for him, help himself, because he is not truly Christian who will not learn that, nor can he rightly accept any man for baptism nor at the hands of the bishop who does not know that, until he learns it, nor is he rightly worthy of communion nor of Christian burial, who will not learn that while alive, at least in English, if he is unable to do so in Latin.' See also *Homilies*, no. viia (ed. Bethurum, pp. 166–7) and Paulinus of Aquileia, 'Let every Christian know the Creed and the Lord's Prayer by heart ... because without this blessing no one will be able to receive a portion in the kingdom of heaven', quoted by Pelikan, *Christian Tradition* II, 185–6.

Priests had the duty of explaining the *Pater noster* and the Creed to their congregations as often as they could.[2] Translations by Ælfric of the *Pater noster*, the Apostles' Creed and the Niceno-Constantinopolitan Creed are included at the end of one of the copies of the Catholic Homilies and various Old English paraphrases exist of the *Pater noster*, the *Gloria* and the Apostles' Creed.[3] Ælfric and Wulfstan preached on the subject of the Creed, Wulfstan in his 'De fide catholica',[4] and Ælfric in a series of sermons for Rogation days:[5] the understanding of the Creed which they envisaged, however, was very different.

Wulfstan's approach is simple and practical: Christians pray to God in the *Pater noster* and proclaim their faith in the Creed.[6] Prayer depends on belief: 'Hu mæg þonne æfre ænig man hine inweardlice to Gode gebiddan buton he inwerdlice on God hæbbe rihtne geleafan.'[7] Wulfstan's main expansions to the text of the Creed are therefore devotional ones: Christ is born to save the human race, which has been deceived by the devil; he demonstrates his divine nature through miracles; through his death he frees us from everlasting death and now we can choose either death or life; we must consider how to repay Christ for all that he has done for us, for the world is nearing its end.[8] Faith is required, of course, but it is a blind faith, for we can never understand the nature of God: 'Nis æfre æniges mannes mæð þæt he þa godcundnesse asmeagan cunne; ac us is þeah mycel þearf þæt we aa habban rihtne geleafan on God ælmihtigne þe us ealle gescop and geworhte.'[9] Wulfstan's conclusion is that, if we wish to get to heaven, we should love God: 'Utan we don swa us mycel þearf is,

---

[2] Ælfric, 'Letter to Bishop Wulfsige' (ed. Fehr, p. 15).

[3] CUL, Gg. 3. 28, 261v–262v (ptd Thorpe, *Catholic Homilies* II, 596–8); *The Lord's Prayer I* (ASPR III, 223–4), *The Lord's Prayer II*, *Gloria I*, *The Lord's Prayer III* and Apostles' Creed (ASPR VI, 70–80).

[4] *Homilies*, nos. vii and viia (ed. Bethurum, pp. 157–68 and 299–307).

[5] *CH* I.xviii, xix and xx (ed. Thorpe, pp. 244–94).

[6] Cf. Ælfric, *CH* I.xx (ed. Thorpe, p. 274): 'Ælc cristen man sceal æfter rihte cunnan ægðer ge his Pater noster ge his Credan. Mid þam Pater nostre he sceal hine gebiddan, mid ðam Credan he sceal his geleafan getrymman.'

[7] *Homilies*, no. vii (ed. Bethurum, p. 157): 'How then can any man ever pray inwardly to God unless he has right belief in God within him.'

[8] *Ibid.* (Bethurum, pp. 158–65).

[9] *Homilies*, no. vi (ed. Bethurum, p. 152): 'It is never within any man's power to think about the divine nature; but we have great need, however, always to have right belief in almighty God, who created and made us all.'

lufian Godd eallum mode and eallum mægene and healdan his bebodu
georne; þonne geearnige we us ece blisse æt ðam sylfum Gode þe leofað
and rixað a butan ende.'[10]

In theory, Ælfric would have agreed. In a sermon on the text, 'Unus est
Dominus, una fides, unum baptisma, unus Deus et Pater omnium, qui est
super omnes, et per omnia, et in omnibus nobis. Ex quo omnia, per quem
omnia, in quo omnia; ipsi gloria in secula',[11] he ends his definition of the
Trinity with the remark:

> Selre us is soðlice to gelyfanne
> on þas halgan Þrynnysse, and hi geandettan,
> þonne us sy to smeagenne to swiðe embe þæt.[12]

Elsewhere, however, theology takes over, and faith becomes a means to
understanding, rather than a virtue in itself: 'Seðe understandan ne mæg,
he hit sceal gelyfan, þæt he hit understandan mæge; forðan þæs witegan
word ne mæg beon aidlod, ðe þus cwæð, Buton ge hit gelyfan, ne mage ge
hit understandan.'[13] Whereas Wulfstan sees love as the way to heaven,
Ælfric stresses belief. Moreover, it is a belief which involves detailed
understanding of two things, the nature of the Trinity and the nature of
Christ.[14]

Ælfric's view of this belief which leads to salvation is set out in his 'De
fide catholica', which forms the final item in a group of three homilies for

---

[10] *Ibid.* (Bethurum, p. 156): 'Let us do as is very necessary for us, love God with all our
mind and all our power and eagerly keep his commandments; then we will earn eternal
happiness for ourselves from God himself, who lives and reigns for ever without end.'

[11] 'There is one Lord, one faith, one baptism, and one God who is Father of all, over all,
through all and within all. All that exists comes from him; all is by him and for him.
To him be glory for ever' (Ephes. IV.5–6 + Rom. XI.36). Augustine interprets this
passage as proof that the three persons of the Trinity are one God, *De Trinitate* I.vi.12
and V.viii.9 (ed. Mountain, pp. 41–2 and 215–16). The word *Pater* is used here of the
Godhead, source of creation, not of the first person of the Trinity; cf. Augustine, *De
Trinitate* V.xiii.14 (ed. Mountain, pp. 220–2).

[12] *Homilies*, no. xxi (ed. Pope II, 678): 'Truly it is better for us to believe in the holy
Trinity and to confess it than it is to consider the matter too carefully.'

[13] *CH* I.xx (ed. Thorpe, p. 280): 'The one who cannot understand, must believe it in order
to understand, because the prophet's word cannot be denied who said as follows: Unless
you believe it you cannot understand it.' See above, p. 17.

[14] *CH* I.xxii (ed. Thorpe, p. 326): 'Se ðe wile to ðisre geðincðe becuman, he sceal gelyfan
on ða Halgan Ðrynnysse, and on soðe Annysse.'

31

Rogationtide.[15] The first homily in the group, 'In letania maiore', is concerned partly with repentance and partly with petition; it deals, first, with the story of Jonah and the repentance of the people of Nineveh, and, secondly, with the parable of the man who rouses his friend in the middle of the night to borrow three loaves (Luke XI.5–13). The same two themes are taken up in the second homily, 'De dominica oratione': the prayer which embraces all our needs, both material and spiritual, and which was taught to his disciples by Christ himself.[16] The final item in the group is concerned with the Creed but whereas the commentary on the *Pater noster* follows the text phrase by phrase, the homily on the Creed consists of a wide-ranging discussion on the Trinity, based, so Ælfric says, on the writings of St Augustine. James Cross sees the homily as based on Augustine's sermons rather than the *De Trinitate*: 'a free composition fed by a retentive memory'.[17] There are certainly echoes of passages from several of the sermons, and Ælfric's theology of the Trinity is unashamedly Augustinian, but the overall content and shape of the homily are so close to the Athanasian Creed that it seems likely that this was the immediate model.[18]

The Athanasian Creed (sung at the office of Prime on Sundays other than major feasts) opens with the blunt statement: 'Quicumque vult salvus esse, ante omnia opus habet ut teneat catholicam fidem: quam nisi quisque integram inviolatamque servaverit, absque dubio in aeternum peribit.' It ends: 'Ad cuius adventum omnes homines resurgere habent cum corporibus suis, et reddituri sunt de factis propriis rationem; et qui bona egerunt ibunt in vitam æternam, qui vero mala in ignem æternum. Haec est fides catholica; quam nisi quisque fideliter firmiterque crediderit, salvus esse non poterit.'[19] The Creed admits the need for good works, but the bulk of

---

[15] *CH* I.xviii, xix and xx (ed. Thorpe, pp. 244–94).

[16] *CH* I.xix (ed. Thorpe, p. 272): 'Crist gesette þis gebed, and swa beleac mid feawum wordum, þæt ealle ure neoda, ægðer ge gastlice ge lichamlice ðæron sind belocene.'

[17] Cross, 'Ælfric and the Mediaeval Homiliary', pp. 24–34, at 34. The sermons quoted by Cross are cxvii, cxviii, cxx and ccxlv (PL 38, 661–71, 671–3 and 676–8, and PL 39, 2196–8).

[18] The importance of understanding the Athanasian Creed in eleventh-century England can be inferred from the fact that the copies of it in BL, Harley 863, 107r–v, and Cotton Vespasian A. i, 155r–156r, have been given an Old English gloss; see *Golden Age*, pl. 160, *Vespasian Psalter* (ed. Wright) and *Leofric Collectar* (ed. Dewick and Frere II, 611).

[19] *Quicumque* (ed. Mountain, pp. 566–7): 'Whoever wishes to be saved, it is above all

the text is concerned with faith, not deeds, as a means to salvation. It is a faith of daunting complexity, set out in a series of statements devised to discern any hint of heresy in relation to the Trinity and the nature of Christ. Father, Son and Holy Spirit are all divine, equal in glory and majesty, uncreated, immense, eternal, omnipotent, and yet they are not three gods but one, in whom there is no before or after, no greater or less. All this must be believed if one is to be saved. Moreover, it is also necessary to believe in the incarnation of Christ, perfect God and perfect man and yet one person, born of the Father before all ages and born in time from his mother.

Ælfric's exposition rivals the original in its piling up of one definition on another. After a brief account of creation and of the difference between Creator and created, he embarks on a series of statements about God, who lives 'on Ðrynnysse untodæledlic, and on annysse anre Godcundnysse'.[20] Father, Son and Holy Spirit are distinct, Ælfric says, yet they share one divine nature, and are alike in glory and power. All three persons are almighty, yet there are not three almighty gods but one. They share one mind and will, and none of them acts apart from the other two.[21] All three are eternal; the Father is so named because he has a Son, born from him without any mother; the Holy Spirit proceeds from Father and Son together.[22] The Athanasian Creed is fuller, but the structure is the same: 'Alia est enim persona Patris, alia Filii, alia Spiritus Sancti: sed Patris, et Filii, et Spiritus Sancti una est divinitas, æqualis gloria, coæterna maiestas ... Similiter omnipotens Pater, omnipotens Filius, omnipotens Spiritus Sanctus. Et tamen non tres omnipotentes, sed unus omnipotens.'[23] After

---

necessary that he should hold the Catholic faith: and unless he holds it whole and untouched, without doubt he will perish eternally ... At whose coming all men will rise again in their bodies, and will give an account of their own deeds. And those who have done good will go into eternal life; those indeed who have done evil will go into eternal fire. This is the Catholic faith, and unless a man believes it faithfully and firmly, he will not be able to be saved.'

[20] *CH* I.xx (ed. Thorpe, p. 276): 'in undivided Trinity and in the unity of one divine nature'.

[21] *Ibid.* (Thorpe, pp. 276–8); cf. *Homilies*, no. xxi (ed. Pope II, 677) and 'Letter to Wulfgeat' (ed. Assmann, pp. 1–2) on the Trinity as having one nature, one purpose and one work.

[22] *CH* I.xx (ed. Thorpe, p. 284).

[23] 'There is one person of the Father, another of the Son, another of the Holy Spirit; but there is one divine nature of Father and Son and Holy Spirit, equal in glory, coeternal

his lengthy exposition of the Trinity, Ælfric turns, as the Athanasian Creed does, to the Incarnation. Only Christ was incarnate, he says, though the other two persons of the Trinity were always with him in all that he did.[24] Finally, like the authors of the Athanasian Creed, Ælfric considers the judgement and the need for good works:

We sceolon gelyfan þæt ælc lichama ðe sawle underfeng sceal arisan on domes dæge mid þam ylcum lichaman þe he nu hæfð, and sceal onfon edlean ealra his dæda: þonne habbað ða godan ece lif mid Gode, and he sylð þa mede ælcum be his geearnungum. Þa synfullan beoð on hellewite a ðrowigende, and heora wite bið eac gemetegod ælcum be his geearnungum. Uton forði geearnian þæt ece lif mid Gode þurh ðisne geleafan, and ðurh gode geearnunga, seðe þurhwunað on Ðrynnysse an Ælmihtig God, aa on ecnysse.[25]

Ælfric's determination that his listeners should grasp the difficult ideas he is presenting to them is clear. 'Þas word sind sceortlice gesæde', he says, 'and eow is neod þæt we hi swutelicor eow onwreon.'[26] Much of the sermon therefore consists of further statements clarifying the status of God the Son, who is begotten by his Father and is, nonetheless, his equal in power and age, and the nature of the Holy Spirit who proceeds from them both, but, like them, has no beginning.[27] Typically, Ælfric illustrates his points through comparisons with material objects. The relationship between Father and Son is like that between fire and the brightness it emits; the brightness is produced by the fire but neither can exist without the other.[28] The Trinity consists of three persons and one nature just as

---

in majesty … Similarly, the Father is almighty, the Son is almighty, the Holy Spirit is almighty. And yet they are not three almighties but one almighty.'

[24] *CH* I.xx (ed. Thorpe, pp. 284–6).

[25] *Ibid.* (Thorpe, p. 294): 'We must believe that each body which received a soul shall rise on the Day of Judgement with the same body that he has now, and shall receive payment for all his actions. Then the good will have eternal life with God and he will reward each according to his deserts. The sinful will be in hell torment, for ever suffering, and their torment will also be measured to each according to his deserts. Therefore let us earn that eternal life with God through this faith and through good works, he who remains in Trinity, one almighty God, for ever in eternity.'

[26] *Ibid.* (Thorpe, p. 278): 'These words are said briefly and it is necessary to explain them to you more clearly.'

[27] *Ibid.* (Thorpe, pp. 280–2). Cf. Augustine, *De doctrina Christiana* I.v.5 (ed. Martin, p. 9).

[28] *CH* I.xx (ed. Thorpe, p. 278). Cross ('Ælfric and the Mediaeval Homiliary', pp. 29–30) suggests Augustine, *Sermo cxviii* (PL 38, 673) as a source.

the sun has three properties, and just as God is present everywhere, so the sun shines over the whole world.[29] The comparisons are not original to Ælfric. The author of the Vercelli Epiphany homily compares the persons of the Trinity to the three properties of fire – heat, brilliance and light – all inseparably linked.[30] Augustine talked of the relationship between God's Wisdom and his light in terms of the sun whose brightness cannot be separated from it.[31] Quodvultdeus talks of fire with its flame, light and heat which are yet one thing, just as the Trinity is three Persons but one God.[32] Alcuin uses the same image in his *Quaestiones xxviii de Trinitate*.[33]

Ælfric's favourite Trinitarian image, however, is that of Augustine: the image in the human soul. In his attempts to understand the paradox of the one God who is at the same time three persons, Augustine considered several different triads. His first attempt at definition consisted of mind, its self-knowledge and its self-love (*mens, notitia sui* and *amor sui*).[34] The parallel was not sufficiently exact, however, for the word 'mind' refers to a substance and is used absolutely, whereas 'knowledge' and 'love' refer to actions and are used relative to something else.[35] Augustine therefore replaced the absolute term, *mens*, by the relative term, *memoria sui*.[36] This image, though better, was still unsatisfactory because it placed the image of God in transient actions whereas the true image of God must be eternal.[37] In bk XIV of the *De Trinitate*, therefore, Augustine considered the way in which memory works and concluded that, in addition to memories of things which enter the mind through the senses, there is a memory of God which has always been there and which enables humans to

---

[29] *CH* I.xx (ed. Thorpe, pp. 282 and 284–8); cf. *Homilies*, no. viii (ed. Pope I, 367). Pope (*Homilies* I, 371) and Cross ('Ælfric and the Mediaeval Homiliary', pp. 26–7) suggest Augustine, *Sermo cxx* (PL 38, 676–7) as a source. Ritzke-Rutherford ('Anglo-Saxon Antecedents of the Middle English Mystics', pp. 225–6), says Ælfric is drawing on John Scotus, *Periphyseon*. Malcolm Godden (personal communication) suggests Augustine, *Sermo ccclxxxiv*, ii.2 and ps.-Augustine, *Sermo ccxlvi*, 4 (PL 39, 1689 and 2199).

[30] *Vercelli Homilies*, no. xvi (ed. Scragg, pp. 272–3). Szarmach (*Vercelli Homilies*, p. 43) gives as source, Quodvultdeus, *De symbolo II*, ix (ed. Braun, pp. 345–6).

[31] Augustine, *In Iohannis evangelium*, xx.13 and xxii.10 (ed. Willems, pp. 211 and 229); see Cross, 'Coeternal Beam', pp. 75–8.

[32] *De symbolo II*, ix, see above, n. 30.     [33] PL 101, 62–3.

[34] Augustine, *De Trinitate* IX.v.8 (ed. Mountain, pp. 300–1).

[35] This triad would correspond to God, Son and Holy Spirit rather than Father, Son and Holy Spirit; see Hill, *Trinity*, pp. 52–3.

[36] Augustine, *De Trinitate* X.xi.18 (ed. Mountain, pp. 330–1).

[37] *Ibid*. XIV.ii.4–5 (ed. Mountain, pp. 425–7).

remember, understand and love God rather than self.[38] This is still a very imperfect image of the Trinity, for the human soul is distinct from its ability to remember, to understand and to will, whereas the divine nature actually *is* three persons.[39] Even so, contemplation of this image offers a way to God, provided that one remembers that it *is* an image:

Sed hanc non solum incorporalem verum etiam summe inseparabilem vereque immutabilem trinitatem cum venerit visio quae *facie ad faciem* nobis promittitur, multo clarius certiusque videbimus quam nunc eius imaginem quod nos sumus. *Per* quod tamen *speculum* et *in* quo *aenigmate* qui vident sicut in hac vita videre concessum est non illi sunt qui ea quae digessimus et commendavimus in sua mente conspiciunt, sed illi qui eam tamquam imaginem vident ut possint ad eum cuius imago est quomodocumque referre quod vident et *per imaginem* quam conspiciendo vident etiam illud videre coniciendo quoniam nondum possunt *facie ad faciem.*[40]

Ælfric follows Augustine very closely, distinguishing the soul from its activities of memory, understanding and willing, and pointing out that, although there is a parallel between the Trinity in Unity and the three activities within the human soul, man is not a trinity as God is:

Wite eac gehwa, þæt ælc man hæfð þreo ðing on him sylfum untodæledlice and togædere wyrcende, swa swa God cwæð, þaþa he ærest mann gesceop. He cwæð, Uton gewyrcan mannan to ure gelicnysse. And he worhte ða Adam to his anlicnysse. On hwilcum dæle hæfð se man Godes anlicnysse on him? On þære sawle, na on ðam lichaman. Þæs mannes sawl hæfð on hire gecynde þære Halgan Þrynnysse anlicnysse; forðan þe heo hæfð on hire ðreo ðing, þæt is gemynd, and andgit, and willa. Þurh þæt gemynd se man geðencð þa ðing ðe he gehyrde, oþþe geseah, oþþe geleornode. Þurh þæt andgit he understent ealle ða ðing ðe he

---

[38] *Ibid.* XIV.xii.15 (ed. Mountain, pp. 442–3). For Augustine's thoughts on memory, see *Confessiones* X.viii.12–xxvi.37 (ed. Verheijen, pp. 161–75) and *De civitate Dei* XI.xxvi (ed. Dombart and Kalb, pp. 345–6).

[39] Augustine, *De Trinitate* XV.xxii.42–xxiii.43 (ed. Mountain, pp. 519–21).

[40] *Ibid.* XV.xxiii.44 (ed. Mountain, p. 522 and trans. Hill, p. 429): 'But when the sight comes that is promised us *face to face*, we shall see this trinity that is not only incorporeal but also supremely inseparable and truly unchangeable much more clearly and definitely than we now see its image which we ourselves are. However, those who do see *through this mirror and in this puzzle*, as much as it is granted to see in this life, are not those who merely observe in their own minds what we have discussed and suggested, but those who see it precisely as an image, so that they can in some fashion refer what they see to that of which it is an image, and also see that other by inference *through its image* which they see by observation, since they cannot see it *face to face*.'

gehyrð oððe gesihð. Of ðam willan cumað geðohtas, and word, and weorc, ægðer ge yfele ge gode. An sawul is, and an lif, and an edwist, seoðe hæfð þas ðreo ðing on hire togædere wyrcende untodæledlice; forði þær þæt gemynd bið þær bið þæt andgit and se willa, and æfre hi beoð togædere. Þeahhwæðere nis nan ðæra ðreora seo sawul, ac seo sawul þurh þæt gemynd gemanð, þurh þæt andgit heo understent, þurh ðone willan heo wile swa hwæt swa hire licað; and heo is hwæðere an sawl and an lif. Nu hæfð heo forði Godes anlicnysse on hire, forðan ðe heo hæfð þreo ðing on hire untodæledlice wyrcende. Is hwæðere se man an man, and na ðrynnys: God soðlice, Fæder and Sunu and Halig Gast, þurhwunað on ðrynnysse hada, and on annysse anre godcundnysse. Nis na se man on ðrynnysse wunigende, swa swa God, ac he hæfð hwæðere Godes anlicnysse on his sawle þurh ða ðreo ðing þe we ær cwædon.[41]

Ælfric echoes Augustine again in a passage in a homily for the Feast of the Nativity, where he draws a distinction between the term 'soul', which is used absolutely, and the activities of the soul which are described relative to one another:

Seo sawul hæfð swa swa we ær cwædon on hire gecynde, þære halgan Þrynnysse anlicnysse, on þan þe heo hæfð gemynd, and andgit, and wyllan. An sawul is, and an lif, and an edwist, þe þas ðreo þing hæfð on hire, and þas ðreo þing na synd na ðreo lif ac an, ne þreo ædwiste ac an. Seo sawul, oððe þæt lif, oððe seo edwist, synd gecwædene to hyre sylfra, and þæt gemynd, oððe þæt andgit, oþþe seo

---

[41] Ælfric, *CH* I.xx (ed. Thorpe, pp. 288–90): 'Know also that each man has three things in himself, working together without division, as God said when he first created man. He said, Let us make man in our likeness, and then he created Adam in his likeness. In which part of him does man have God's likeness? In the soul, not in the body. Man's soul has the likeness of the Holy Trinity in its very nature, because it has within it three things, that is, memory, and understanding and will. Through the memory, man thinks of those things that he has heard or seen or learned. Through the understanding, he understands all the things that he hears or sees. From the will come thoughts and words and actions, both evil and good. There is one soul, and one life and one substance which has these three things together in it working indivisibly, because where memory is, there are understanding and will, and they are always together. Yet the soul is none of these three things, but the soul remembers through the memory, understands through the understanding, and through the will it wills whatever pleases it and yet it is one soul and one life. Now therefore it has God's likeness within it, because it possesses three things working within it without division. However, the man is a single man and not a trinity. Truly, God, Father and Son and Holy Spirit, exists as three persons and one divine nature. Man does not exist as a trinity as God does, yet he has God's likeness in his soul through the three things we have spoken about.' For Augustine's teaching, see Kelly, *Christian Doctrines*, pp. 271–9.

wylla, beoð gecwædene to sumum þinga, ed-lesendlice, and þas ðreo þing habbað annysse him betwynan.[42]

Again, like Augustine, Ælfric stressed the unity of the divine nature, while at the same time distinguishing his position from that of the Sabellians, who claimed, 'þæt se Fæder wære, þaþa he wolde, Fæder; and eft, ðaða he wolde, he wære Sunu; and eft, ðaða he wolde, wære Halig Gast; and wære forði an God'.[43] For both writers, the three persons of the Trinity were distinguished on the basis of their relationships to one another rather than their attributes or actions. Augustine says:

Omnes quos legere potui qui ante me scripserunt de Trinitate quae Deus est, divinorum librorum veterum et novorum catholici tractatores, hoc intenderunt secundum scripturas docere, quod Pater et Filius et Spiritus Sanctus *unius substantiae* inseparabili aequalitate divinam insinuent unitatem, ideoque *non* sint *tres dii sed unus deus* – quamvis Pater Filium genuerit, et ideo Filius non sit qui Pater est; Filiusque *a Patre* sit *genitus*, et ideo *Pater non sit qui Filius* est; *Spiritus*que *Sanctus nec Pater sit nec Filius*, sed tantum *Patris et Filii Spiritus*, Patri et Filio etiam ipse coaequalis et ad Trinitatis pertinens unitatem.[44]

---

[42] *LS* I.i (ed. Skeat I, 16–18): 'As we said before, the soul has in its nature a resemblance to the holy Trinity, in that it possesses memory, and understanding and will. It is one soul, and one life and one substance, which possesses these three things in itself, and these three things are not three lives but one, not three substances but one. The soul, or the life, or the substance, are considered absolutely, and the memory, or the under-standing, or the will, are considered relative to something else, and these three things are united.' See also above, p. 35.

[43] *CH* I.xx (ed. Thorpe, p. 290): 'that the Father was, when he wished, Father and again, when he wished, he was Son, and again, when he wished, he was the Holy Spirit, and therefore he was One God'; cf. Augustine, *De Trinitate* VII.iv.9 (ed. Mountain, pp. 259–60), *Sermo lxxi* (PL 38, 448) and Bede, *Homeliae* I.8 and II.24 (ed. Hurst, pp. 53 and 362). On Sabellius, see Kelly, *Christian Doctrines*, pp. 121–3.

[44] Augustine, *De Trinitate* I.iv.7 (ed. Mountain, pp. 34–5, and trans. Hill, *Trinity*, p. 69): 'The purpose of all the Catholic commentators I have been able to read on the divine books of both testaments, who have written before me on the Trinity which God is, has been to teach that according to the scriptures Father and Son and Holy Spirit in the inseparable equality of one substance present a divine unity; and therefore there are not three gods but one God; although indeed the Father has begotten the Son, and therefore he who is the Father is not the Son; and the Son is begotten by the Father, and therefore he who is the Son is not the Father; and the Holy Spirit is neither the Father nor the Son, but only the Spirit of the Father and of the Son, himself co-equal to the Father and the Son, and belonging to the threefold unity.' See also *De Trinitate* V.v.6, V.vii.8 and V.xiv.15 (ed. Mountain, pp. 210–11, 212–15 and 222–3), *De civitate Dei* XI.x (ed. Dombart and Kalb, pp. 330–2) and Kelly, *Christian Doctrines*, pp. 274–6.

Ælfric makes the same point: 'Þonne ðu gehyrst nemnan þone Fæder, þonne understenst ðu þæt he hæfð Sunu. Eft, þonne þu cwyst Sunu, þu wast, butan tweon, þæt he hæfð Fæder.'[45]

Ælfric's 'De fide catholica' contains his fullest and most elaborate discussion of the Trinity, but it is a subject he returns to again and again in his preaching, sometimes with the slimmest of connections to his main theme. The passage on the Trinity in his sermon 'De Sancta Trinitate et de festis diebus per annum' is understandable, since it is attached to a reference to the Sunday after Pentecost, though it is noticeably long and detailed.[46] Other accounts of the Trinity, however, appear in less obvious places. In a sermon for Rogationtide, the three loaves which a man asks his neighbour to lend him (Luke XI.5) turn into a reference to the three persons of the Trinity, belief in whom is the food which brings man to eternal life:

Se Ælmihtiga Fæder is God, and his Sunu is Ælmihtig God, and se Halga Gast is Ælmihtig God: na ðry godas, ac hi ealle an Ælmihtig God untodæledlic. Þonne ðu becymst to ðisum ðrym hlafum, þæt is, to andgite ðære Halgan Ðrynnysse, þonne hæfst ðu on ðam geleafan lif and fodan ðinre sawle, and miht oðerne cuman eac mid ðam fedan, þæt is, ðu miht tæcan ðone geleafan oðrum frynd þe þe ðæs bitt. He cwæð, Cuma, forðan ðe we ealle sind cuman on ðisum life, and ure eard nis na her; ac we sind her swilce wegferende menn; an cymð, oðer færð; se bið acenned, se oðer forðfærð and rymð him setl. Nu sceal gehwa forði gewilnian þæs geleafan þære Halgan Ðrynnysse, forðan ðe se geleafa hine gebrincð to ðam ecan life.[47]

---

[45] *CH* I.xx (ed. Thorpe, p. 284): 'When you hear the Father named, then you understand that he has a Son. Again, when you speak of the Son, you know for certain that he has a Father.' See also *CH* I.xx, 'Se is Fæder gehaten, forðan ðe he hæfð Sunu' (Thorpe, p. 278).

[46] *Homilies*, no. xia (ed. Pope I, 471–2).

[47] *CH* I.xviii (ed. Thorpe, p. 248): 'The almighty Father is God, and his Son is almighty God, and the Holy Spirit is almighty God, not three gods, but they are all one almighty God, undivided. When you come to these three loaves, that is to the understanding of the holy Trinity, then you will have in that belief life and food for your soul, and might also feed another stranger, that is, you might teach that faith to another friend who asks it of you. He says, One who comes, because we are all strangers in this life, and our home is not here, but we are here as travellers. One comes, another goes, One is born, another dies and leaves his place to him. Now therefore everyone must desire faith in the holy Trinity, because that belief will bring him to eternal life.' Cf. Augustine, *Quaestiones evangeliorum* II.xxi (ed. Mutzenbecher, pp. 64–5).

In a sermon on prayer, based on John XVI.23–30, Ælfric suddenly digresses, via a quotation from John X.30, 'Ego et Pater unum sumus', to talk about the Trinity in relation to the vision of God which Christ's followers will enjoy in heaven:

> Ic and min Fæder syndon witodlice an.
> Þæt is, soðlice, an God, on anre godcundnysse,
> and him bam is gemæne æfre an soð Lufu,
> þæt is se Halga Gast, þe gæð of him bam.
> He cwæð, wyt syndon, for ðan þe se Sunu
> is æfre swa wunigende, and ne awent na of ðam,
> ne heora nan ne bið abroden to oþrum,
> þæt he elles beo of ðam þe he ær wæs.
> He cwæð, wyt syndon an, for ðære annysse,
> þæt seo an godcundnyss, and seo an mægenþrymnys,
> and þæt an gecynd þe him is gemæne
> nele geþafian þæt hi þry godas syndon,
> ac an ælmihtig God æfre on ðrym hadum;
> and þis oncnawað þa halgan þonne hi hine geseoð.[48]

The emphasis here, as in 'De fide catholica', is on the unity of the Godhead. Elsewhere, it is the question of relationship which concerns Ælfric. In two homilies he moves from an account of the raising from the dead of Jairus's daughter, the widow of Naim's son and Lazarus to a discussion of the Trinity and, specifically, the distinction between the Son and the Holy Spirit.[49] The relations between the three persons, he says, are not the same. The Father, for example, is the Father of the Son but not of the Holy Spirit. All three persons work together but they have distinct roles. So, forgiveness belongs to the Holy Spirit and being born belongs to Christ alone. The superficial link in Ælfric's argument is the way in which the soul which is dead through sin can be brought back to life by God,

---

[48] *Homilies*, no. viii (ed. Pope I, 365–6); 'I and my Father are truly one. That is, truly one God, in a single divine nature, and one true Love is always common to them both, that is the Holy Spirit, who proceeds from them both. He said, We are, because the Son is always thus living with him, and never departs from him, and none of them is separated from the other so that he is anything other than what he was before. He said, We are one, because of the unity, that the one divine nature, and the one mighty power, and the one nature that is common to them will not allow of their being three gods, but one almighty God always in three persons; and the saints will know this when they see him.'

[49] *CH* I.xxxiii (ed. Thorpe, pp. 498–500) and *Homilies*, no. vi (ed. Pope I, 322–4).

and the one sin which cannot be forgiven, namely, the sin against the
Holy Spirit; the connection is very slight, however, and one is left, as so
often, with the sense that there is some deep, unstated reason for Ælfric's
repeated explanations of Trinitarian doctrine.[50]

A clearer example of what may be a fear of error occurs in the sermon
for Epiphany in the second set of Catholic Homilies, where the descent of
the dove on Christ's head at his baptism, and the voice from heaven, 'Ðes
is min leofa Sunu ðe me wel licað',[51] prompt a definition of the relationship between the three persons of the Trinity:

Þær stod se Sunu on ðære menniscnysse, and se Fæder clypode of heofonum, and
se Halga Gast niðer astah to Criste. Þær wæs ða eal seo halige Ðrynnys, seo ðe is
an God untodæledlic. Se Fæder nis of nanum oðrum gecumen, ac he wæs æfre
God. Se Sunu is of ðam Fæder eall þæt he is na geworht, ne gesceapen, ac acenned
æfre of ðam Fæder, for þan ðe he is ðæs Fæder wisdom, þurh ðone he geworhte
ealle gesceafta. Se Halga Gast is lufu and willa þæs Fæder, and þæs Suna, and hi
sindon ealle gelice mihtige, and æfre hi ðry an God untodæledlic, þry on hadum,
and an on godcundnysse, and on gecynde, and on eallum weorcum. Ne trucað
heora nan ana ðurh unmihte, ac ðurh gecynde anre godcundnysse, hi wyrcað ealle
æfre an weorc. Nis na se Fæder mid þære menniscnysse befangen, ne se Halga
Gast, ac se Sunu ana, ðeahhwæðere hi ealle ðry þæt geræddon, and gefremedon
þæt se Sunu ana þa menniscnysse underfeng.[52]

Christ's baptism, when he was acknowledged publicly as God's Son, was

---

[50] It is perhaps worth noting that Carolingian theologians identified the sin against the
Holy Ghost as a rejection of the *Filioque* clause of the Creed, so placing it in a
Trinitarian context: see Ratramnus, *Contra Graecorum opposita* I.i (PL 121, 227) and
Pelikan, *Christian Tradition* II, 186.

[51] 'This is my beloved Son in whom I am well pleased.'

[52] *CH* II.iii (ed. Godden, pp. 22–3): 'There stood the Son in his humanity, and the Father
called from the heavens, and the Holy Spirit descended on Christ. There was, then, all
the holy Trinity, which is one undivided Godhead. The Father is descended from no
other, but he was always God. The Son derives all that he is from the Father, not made
or created but eternally begotten from the Father, because he is the Father's wisdom,
through whom he created everything. The Holy Spirit is the love and will of the Father
and of the Son, and they are all alike mighty, and all three are one undivided Godhead,
three in persons and one in divinity, and in nature and in all their works. None of
them, when alone, is lacking in power, but through the nature of a single Godhead
they all always do one work. The Father was never enclosed in human nature, nor the
Holy Spirit, but only the Son, though they all three advised that and brought it about
that the Son alone received a human nature.' Cf. Bede, *Homeliae* I.12 (ed. Hurst,
pp. 83–4).

one of the key items in the Adoptionist controversy of the eighth century.[53] By reminding his hearers of Christ's eternal birth from the Father, Ælfric asserts the orthodox view against the heretical one that Christ became the son of God at his baptism. Similar statements occur in both the Blickling and Vercelli homilies:

And þa wæs þæs Heahfæderes stefn geworden of heofonum and seo wæs sprecende and þus cweðende: 'Þis is min se leofa Sunu in þam me wel licade'. Efne swa he cwæde: 'Þis me is gecyndelic Sunu.' In managum stowum we þæt leorniaþ, in conone þære boc and in oðrum Godes bocum, þæt ure Dryhten ealle halige men on þyssum middangearde him to bearnum nemneð for heora rihtum dædum and for heora eadmedum and for heora clænum geþohtum, and for his þære myclan lufan þe he to his þam halgan hafað. Ac seo syb bið hwæðre þurh Dryhtnes gife and þurh his mildheortnesse. And nu ure Dryhten Hælenda Crist, he wæs þam ælmihtigan Godfæder gecyndelic Sunu, for þan þe he wæs of Godfæder acenned ær eallum gesceaftum, soð God of soðum Gode and se ælmihtiga of ðam ælmihtigan, and ealle gesceafta þurh hine gesceapene and geworhte wæron.[54]

Most of Ælfric's references to the Trinity are simple statements of doctrine, elaborations of the paradox of three persons in one God.[55] The Trinity is a mystery, a series of relations, static, timeless and remote. Yet this hidden life, invisible and incomprehensible, is what man is destined to share. This sharing comes about through the Incarnation, when God,

[53] Pelikan, *Christian Tradition* I, 176 and III, 52–5.

[54] *Vercelli Homilies*, no. xvi (ed. Scragg, pp. 271–2): 'And then the almighty Father's voice came from the heavens, speaking and saying, This is my beloved Son in whom I am well pleased, as though he said: This is my Son by nature. We learn in many places, in canonical books and other religious works, that our Lord calls all holy men in this world his sons because of their righteous deeds and humility and pure thoughts and his own great love which he has towards his saints. But that relationship, however, is through God's gift and mercy. And now our Lord and Saviour Christ was the Son of the Almighty Father by nature because he was begotten of God the Father before all creation, true God of true God, and the almighty from the almighty, and all creation was shaped and made through him.' See also *Blickling Homilies*, no. iii (ed. Morris, p. 29): 'Halige men þonne ongeaton þæt he wæs soþ Godes Sunu; forþon þe God Fæder stemn wæs gehyred æt his fulwihte, þus cweþende: Þis is min se leofa Sunu, on þæm me wel gelicode' ('Holy men then recognized that he was the true Son of God, for the voice of God the Father was heard at his baptism, saying, This is my beloved Son, in whom I am well pleased').

[55] E.g. *CH* I.i, viii, ix, xv, xxii (ed. Thorpe, pp. 10, 134, 150, 228 and 326); *Homilies*, nos. i, vi and xxi (ed. Pope I, 204 and 322–5, and II, 677).

who had created man in his image, redeemed that image by joining it to himself.[56]

The Church's teaching on the relationship between Christ, the perfect image of God, and humanity, created in God's image, was developed by Augustine in his *De Trinitate*. Christ is not simply a model to be imitated. He is the means by which man can be restored to his original likeness to God:

Quia enim homo ad beatitudinem sequi non debebat nisi Deum et sentire non poterat Deum, sequendo Deum hominem factum sequeretur simul et quem sentire poterat et quem sequi debebat ... Non igitur mirum si propter exemplum quod nobis ut reformemur ad imaginem Dei praebet *imago aequalis Patri*, cum de sapientia scriptura loquitur, de Filio loquitur quem sequimur vivendo sapienter, quamvis et Pater sit sapientia sicut lumen et Deus.[57]

Bede states several times that Christ was born in order to restore us to the image and likeness of his divinity in which we were created,[58] and the theme of redemption as a refashioning of God's image in the human race is found again and again in Old English literature. Ælfric, talking of the Nativity, says, 'Soðlice men syndon godas gecigede; heald forði, ðu mann, þinne godes wurðscipe wið leahtras; forðan þe God is geworden mann for ðe.'[59] He expands the point in a sermon for Pentecost, where he

---

[56] *CH* I.xx (ed. Thorpe, p. 288); *Homilies*, no. xia (ed. Pope, I, 465).

[57] Augustine, *De Trinitate* VII.iii.5 (ed. Mountain, pp. 253–4, trans. Hill, p. 223): 'Man ought to follow no one but God in his search for bliss, and yet he was unable to perceive God; so by following God made man he would at one and the same time follow one he could perceive and the one he ought to follow ... Thus to conclude, it is not surprising that scripture should be speaking about the Son when it speaks about wisdom, on account of the model which the image who is equal to the Father provides us with that we may be refashioned to the image of God; for we follow the Son by living wisely. Though we must not forget that the Father too is wisdom, just as he is light and God.' See also Augustine, *Enarrationes in Psalmos*, Ps. LII.6 (ed. Dekkers and Fraipont, p. 642): 'Filius enim Dei particeps mortalitatis effectus est, ut mortalis homo fiat particeps divinitatis' and Ps. CXVIII.19.6 (*ibid.*, pp. 1728–9). See also Rom. VIII.28–9.

[58] Bede, *Homeliae* I.7, I.8 and I.15 (ed. Hurst, pp. 50, 57 and 110). See also *Byrhtferth's Enchiridion* (ed. Baker and Lapidge, p. 206): 'Sexta die factus est homo ad imaginem Dei. Sexta etate venit filius Dei et factus est filius hominis, ut nos reformaret ad imaginem Dei', and Ælfric, 'On the Old and New Testament' (ed. Crawford, *Heptateuch*, pp. 22–3).

[59] *CH* I.ii (ed. Thorpe, p. 40): 'Truly, men are called gods, therefore, oh man, guard your divine glory against sins, because God became man for you.' Cf. Ps. LXXXI.6, 'I once said, You too are gods, sons of the Most High', quoted by Christ in John X.34–5.

43

distinguishes between the divinity which was proper to Christ and the divinization of created beings through the Holy Spirit:

On Cristes acennednysse wearð se ælmihtiga Godes Sunu to menniscum men gedon, and on ðisum dæge wurdon geleaffulle men godas, swa swa Crist cwæð: Ic cwæð, ge sind godas, and ge ealle sind bearn þæs Hehstan. Þa gecorenan sind Godes bearn, and eac godas, na gecyndelice, ac ðurh gife þæs Halgan Gastes. An God is gecyndelice on ðrim hadum, Fæder, and his Sunu, þæt is his wisdom, and se Halga Gast, seðe is heora begra lufu and willa. Heora gecynd is untodæledlic, æfre wunigende on anre Godcundnysse. Se ylca cwæð þeahhwæðere be his gecorenum, Ge sint godas. Þurh Cristes menniscnysse wurdon menn alysede fram deofles ðeowte, and ðurh tocyme þæs Halgan Gastes, mennisce men wurdon gedone to godum. Crist underfeng menniscnysse on his tocyme, and men underfengon God þurh neosunge þæs Halgan Gastes.[60]

The Blickling Homilies talk of the exchange by which man, created in the image of God, was restored to his original nature when Christ clothed his divine nature in a human body and became man in order that men should become gods.[61] The point is made more succinctly by Augustine: 'Factus est Deus homo, ut homo fieret deus.'[62]

The second part of the Athanasian Creed defines the basis for this process of salvation: that Christ was perfect God and perfect man, one person, 'not by conversion of the Godhead into flesh but by taking of the

---

[60] *CH* I.xxii (ed. Thorpe, p. 324): 'When Christ was conceived, the almighty Son of God was made man, and on this day believing men were made gods, as Christ said: I said, You are gods, and you are all sons of the most high. The chosen are God's children, and also gods, not by nature but through the gift of the Holy Spirit. There is one God, by nature in three persons, the Father and his Son, that is his Wisdom, and the Holy Spirit who is the love and will of them both. Their nature is indivisible, always living in one divine nature. Yet the same one said of his chosen ones, You are gods. Through Christ's human nature men were freed from slavery to the devil and through the coming of the Holy Spirit humans were made gods. Christ received human nature at his coming to earth and men received God through the coming of the Holy Spirit.' Cf. *Homilies*, nos. i and xxi (ed. Pope I, 211–13 and II, 712).

[61] *Blickling Homilies*, nos. i, ii and v (ed. Morris, pp. 11, 17 and 61). Cf. Augustine, *Sermo clxvi*, iv.4 (PL 38, 909), 'Deus enim deum te vult facere: non natura, sicut est ille quem genuit; sed dono suo et adoptione. Sicut enim ille per humanitatem factus est particeps mortalitatis tuae; sic te per exaltationem facit participem immortalitatis suae', and *Sermo cxcii*, i.1 (PL 38, 1012), 'Deos facturus qui homines erant, homo factus est qui Deus erat.'

[62] Augustine, *Sermo cxxxviii*, 1 (PL 39, 1997).

manhood into God'.[63] This austere statement is very different from the metaphors and symbols which appear so often in early medieval accounts of the redemption. Gregory the Great, for example, likened Christ to a fisherman who caught the greedy fish (the devil) on the hook of his divinity, concealed in the bait of his humanity.[64] In the Blickling Homilies Christ is presented as a king paying a ransom or setting out to do battle against the traitor devil.[65] The poet of *The Dream of the Rood* presents the Crucifixion as a battle after which Christ is weary and needs to rest.[66] The poets of *Christ and Satan* and *Christ I* visualize Christ as a warrior releasing the captives from the prison of hell.[67] But these images do not tackle the question of what actually happened, the reality beneath the metaphors.

The implications of the statement in the Athanasian Creed are explored by Ælfric in relation to four points: first, that Christ was God; secondly, that he was truly man; thirdly, that in his resurrection and ascension his human nature received the glory and immortality which was proper to his divine nature and, finally, that his human body, freed from subjection to death, drew with it the whole of the human race.

The 'proofs' of Christ's divinity were developed during the Arian controversy of the fourth century and the Adoptionist controversy of the eighth.[68] In order to counter the claims of Arius and his followers that Christ had not always existed, and those of the Adoptionists, that Christ had become the son of God at his baptism, orthodox teaching focused on the part played by Christ at the creation of the world. Early commentators linked Christ's words to the Jews, 'I who speak to you am the beginning' (John VIII.25) to the opening words of Genesis: 'In the beginning God created the heavens and the earth' (Gen. I.1).[69] Ælfric says:

---

[63] 'Deus est ex substantia Patris ante saecula genitus, et homo est ex substantia matris in saeculo natus; perfectus Deus, perfectus homo ... unus autem non conversione divinitatis in carnem, sed assumptione humanitatis in Deum' (ed. Mountain, p. 567).

[64] Gregory, *Moralia* XXXIII.ix.17 (ed. Adriaen, pp. 1687–8), followed by Ælfric, *CH* I.xiv (ed. Thorpe, p. 216).

[65] *Blickling Homilies*, nos. i and vi (ed. Morris, pp. 9–11 and 67).

[66] *Dream of the Rood*, 64–5 (ASPR II, 63).

[67] *Christ and Satan*, 385–97 (ASPR I, 148); *Christ I*, 16 and 149–59 (ASPR III, 3 and 7).

[68] For an account of these controversies, see Pelikan, *Christian Tradition* I, 191–210 and III, 52–9.

[69] The Vulgate text, 'Principium qui et loquor vobis' is not preserved in modern translations.

On anginne gesceop     se ælmihtiga Fæder
ðysne middaneard,      swa swa Moyses awrat,
and ðæt angin is       ðæs ælmihtigan Godes sunu
on gastlicum andgite,  swa swa ðæt godspell us segð:
Ego principium qui et loquor vobis.[70]

God created, therefore, through his Son. Three of Ælfric's sermons describe how God, the beginning and the end, creator of everything that is, 'gesceop gesceafta þaða he wolde; þurh his wisdom he geworhte ealle þing, and þurh his willan he hi ealle geliffæste'.[71] Not only that: creation was the work of all three persons of the Trinity, a point revealed by God's words in Genesis, 'Let us make man in our own image, in the likeness of ourselves' (Gen. I.26):

Eft is seo halige Ðrynnys geswutelod on ðisre bec, swa swa is on ðam worde, ðe God cwæð: Uton wyrcean mannan to ure anlicnisse. Mid ðam ðe he cwæð: Uton wyrcean, is seo Ðrynnys gebicnod; mid ðam ðe he cwæð: To ure anlicnysse, is seo soðe annys geswutelod. He ne cwæð na menigfealdlice: To urum anlicnyssum, ac anfealdlice: To ure anlicnysse.[72]

This creation is not to be understood as the work of beings subordinate to the one God, for all three persons of the Trinity are alike in their eternal being:

Næs þeos woruld æt fruman, ac hi geworhte God silf, se þe æfre þurhwunode buton ælcum anginne on his miclan wuldre and on his mægenþrimnisse eall swa mihtig swa he nu ys and eall swa micel on his leohte, for ðan ðe he ys soð leoht and lif and soðfæstnisse, and se ræd wæs æfre on his rædfæstum geþance, þæt he

---

[70] Ælfric, *Exameron Anglice* (ed. Crawford, p. 37): 'In the beginning the almighty Father created this world, as Moses wrote, and that beginning is almighty God's Son in a spiritual sense, as the gospel tells us: I, who speak to you, am the beginning.' See also 'Preface to Genesis' (ed. Crawford, *Heptateuch*, p. 78), a reference I owe to Malcolm Godden. Cf. ps.-Bede, *De sex dierum creatione* and *Quaestiones super Genesim* (PL 93, 208 and 243), and Isidore, *Quaestiones in Vetus Testamentum: in Genesin*, i.2 (PL 83, 209).

[71] *CH* I.i (ed. Thorpe, p. 10): '[God] created those creatures that he wished; through his Wisdom he made all things, and through his Will he gave life to all.' See also *Homilies*, nos. xia and xxi (ed. Pope I, 463–4 and II, 677).

[72] 'Preface to Genesis' (ed. Crawford, *Heptateuch*, p. 78): 'Again, the holy Trinity is revealed in this book, as it is in the word that God spoke: Let us make man in our image. By saying, Let us make, the Trinity is indicated; by saying, In our image, the true unity is revealed. He did not speak in the plural, In our images, but in the singular: In our image.' See also *Exameron Anglice* (ed. Crawford, pp. 58–9).

wircan wolde þa wundorlican gesceafta, be þan ðe he wolde þurh his micclan wisdom þa gesceafta gescippan and þurh his soðan lufe hig liffæstan on þam life, þe hig habbað. Her is seo halige þrinnis on þisum þrim mannum: se ælmihtiga Fæder of nanum oðrum gecumen, and se micla Wisdom of þam wisan Fæder æfre of him anum butan anginne acenned, se þe us alisde of urum þeowte syððan mid þære menniscnisse, þe he of Marian genam; nu is heora begra lufu him bam æfre gemæne, þæt is se Halga Gast, þe ealle þing geliffæst, swa micel and swa mihtig, þæt he mid his gife ealle þa englas onliht, þe eardiað on heofenum, and ealra manna heortan, þe on middanearde libbað, þa þe rihtlice gelifað on þone lifiendan God.[73]

A theme which is closely related to that of the Trinity as creator is that of the twofold birth of Christ: from his Father before all time, and from his mother in human time. Towards the end of his sermon on the creation, Ælfric draws a parallel between God's creation of the world through his Son and his redemption (or re-creation) of the world through the same Son made man:

Ðæt cild is tuwa acenned: he is acenned of þam Fæder on heofonum, buton ælcere meder, and eft þaða he man gewearð, þa wæs he acenned of þam clænan mædene Marian, buton ælcum eorðlicum fæder. God Fæder geworhte mancynn and ealle gesceafta þurh ðone Sunu, and eft, þaða we forwyrhte wæron, þa asende he ðone ylcan Sunu to ure alysednesse.[74]

---

[73] 'On the Old and New Testament' (ed. Crawford, *Heptateuch*, p. 17): 'This world did not exist in the beginning, but God himself made it, he who always existed without any beginning in his great glory and in his power, altogether as mighty as he now is and just as mighty in his light, for he is true light and life and truth, and that plan always existed in his resolved thought, that he would create those wonderful beings, shaping them by his great wisdom and through his true love establishing them in the life which they possess. Here is the holy Trinity in these three persons: the almighty Father, derived from no other, and the great Wisdom of the wise Father, always begotten of him without beginning, he who afterwards freed us from our slavery through the human nature which he took from Mary; now the love, always common to them both, is the Holy Ghost, who gives life to all things, so great and powerful that he through his gift enlightens all the angels who live in heaven, and the hearts of all men who live on earth, those who rightly believe in the living God.'

[74] *CH* I.i (ed. Thorpe, p. 24): 'That Child is born twice: he is born from the Father in heaven without any mother, and again, when he became man, then he was born from the pure maiden Mary, without any earthly father. God the Father created the human race and all created things through the Son, and again, when we were condemned, he sent that same Son to free us.'

He makes the same point, though at rather greater length, in the sermon for the Feast of the Nativity in the second set of Catholic Homilies:

He wæs todæg acenned of ðam halgan mædene Marian mid lichaman and mid sawle, se ðe wæs æfre mid ðam Fæder wunigende on þære godcundnysse. He is tuwa acenned, and ægðer acennednys is wundorlic, and unasecgendlic. He wæs æfre of ðam Fæder acenned, for ðan þe he is þæs Fæder wisdom, þurh ðone he geworhte and gesceop ealle gesceafta. Nu is ðeos acennednys buton anginne, for ðan þe se Fæder wæs æfre God, and his wisdom, þæt is his Sunu, wæs æfre of him acenned, buton ælcere meder. Þeos acennednys þe we nu todæg wurðiað wæs of eorðlicere meder buton ælcum eorðlicum fæder. Se Fæder ðurh hine gesceop us, and eft ða ða we forwyrhte wæron, þa asende he þone ylcan Sunu to ðisum life to ure alysednysse.[75]

The parallel between creation and re-creation is one of the commonplaces of medieval theology and liturgy.[76] Ælfric's treatment of Christ's twofold birth, on the other hand, leads to some more subtle distinctions. He is always careful to stress the indivisibility of Christ's divine and human natures, yet at the same time he emphasizes Mary's role as the source of Christ's humanity. Commenting on Christ's words, 'Fæmne, hwæt is me and ðe to ðan? Ne com gyt min tima',[77] in the story of the turning of water into wine at the marriage at Cana, he points out that Mary's request was for an exercise of Christ's divinity in which she had no part:

Drihten cwæð to his meder, Fæmne, hwæt is me and ðe to ðan? swilce he cwæde, ne wyrcð seo menniscnyss ðe ic of ðe genam þæt tacn þe ðu bitst, ac seo godcundnys þe ic ðe mid geworhte. Þonne min ðrowungtima cymð, þonne geswutelað seo menniscnys hire untrumnysse.[78]

---

[75] *CH* II.i (ed. Godden, p. 3): 'He was born today from the holy maiden Mary with body and soul, he who was always living with the Father in his divine nature. He is born twice, and both births are wonderful and incapable of being described. He was always born from the Father, because he is the Father's Wisdom, through whom he created and shaped all created things. Now this birth is without beginning, because the Father was always God and his Wisdom, that is his Son, was always born from him without any mother. This birth which we celebrate today was from an earthly mother without any earthly father. The Father created us through him and again, when we were condemned, he sent that same Son to this life to free us.'

[76] See Raw, *Crucifixion Iconography*, pp. 175–6.

[77] *CH* II.iv (ed. Godden, p. 29): 'Woman, what is that to you and me? My time has not yet come.'

[78] *CH* II.iv (ed. Godden, p. 30): 'The Lord said to his mother: Woman, what is that to

Ælfric returns to this point in his Palm Sunday homily on the passion when he glosses Christ's words to his mother, 'Woman, this is your son' (John XIX.26) as a reference to himself instead of to St John: 'Efne her hangað nu ðin sunu fæmne. Swilce he cwæde, þis is ðin gecynd, ðus ðrowigendlic, ðe ic of ðe genam.'[79] The reference is important, for it was only through his assumption of human nature that Christ was able to suffer and die.

The reality of Christ's death was crucial to Christian teaching, for if Christ's death was an illusion so too was his resurrection and man's hope of eternal life.[80] Ælfric stresses the reality of Christ's human nature again and again. Towards the end of a sermon for the Feast of the Purification he elaborates on the implications of Luke's statement, 'The child grew to maturity and he was filled with wisdom; and God's favour was with him' (Luke II.40):

He weox and wæs gestrangod on þære menniscnysse, and he ne behofode nanes wæstmes ne nanre strangunge on þære godcundnysse. He æt, and dranc, and slep, and weox on gearum ... He nære na man geðuht, gif he mannes life ne lyfode ... He wæs cild, and weox on þære menniscnysse, and þrowode deað sylfwilles, and aras of deaðe mid þam lichaman þe he ær on þrowode, and astah to heofenum, and wunað nu æfre on godcundnysse and on menniscnysse, an Crist, ægðer ge God ge mann, undeadlic, seðe ær his ðrowunge wæs deadlic. He þrowade, ac he ne ðrowað heononforð næfre eft, ac bið æfre butan ende, ealswa ece on þære menniscnysse swa he is on þære godcundnysse.[81]

you and me? as if he said, The human nature which I received from you does not work the miracle that you ask but the divine nature with which I created you. When the time for my Passion comes, then the human nature will show its weakness.' Cf. Augustine, *In Iohannis evangelium*, viii.9 and cxix.1 (ed. Willems, pp. 87–8 and 658) and *Sermo ccxviii*, x.10 (PL 38, 1086), and Bede, *Homeliae* I.14 (ed. Hurst, p. 97). See Raw, *Crucifixion Iconography*, pp. 103–5.

79  *CH* II.xiv (ed. Godden, p. 146): 'Here hangs your son, woman. As if he said, This is your nature, suffering thus, which I took from you.'

80  See Raw, *Crucifixion Iconography*, p. 107.

81  *CH* I.ix (ed. Thorpe, p. 150): 'He grew and became strong in that human nature, and he needed no growth or strengthening in that divinity. He ate and drank and slept and grew in years ... He would not have been considered human if he had not lived a human life ... He was a child, and grew in his human nature, and suffered death of his own will, and rose from death with the body in which he had previously suffered, and ascended to heaven, and now lives for ever in his divinity and his humanity, one Christ, both God and man, immortal, he who before his passion was mortal. He suffered, but henceforth he will never suffer again, but will always be as eternal in his human nature

In this passage Ælfric develops his account of Christ's earthly existence by considering the nature of his risen body. He rose from the dead in the same body in which he had suffered, and because his human and divine natures were indissolubly linked, his mortal body acquired the immortality proper to the divine. Yet it was still the same body, of the same nature though a different glory. Commenting on the gospel for the First Sunday after Easter (the appearance to Thomas) Ælfric says:

Hwilc wundor is þæt se Hælend mid ecum lichaman come inn, belocenum durum, seðe mid deadlicum lichaman wearð acenned of beclysedum innoðe þæs mædenes? ... Þone lichaman he æteowde to grapigenne, þone ðe he inn brohte beclysedum durum. His lichama wæs grapigendlic, and ðeahhwæðere unbrosnigendlic; he æteowde hine grapigendlicne and unbrosnigendlicne, forðan ðe his lichama wæs þæs ylcan gecyndes ðe he ær wæs, hwæðere þeah oðres wuldres.[82]

He makes the same point in a sermon for the Fourth Sunday after Easter: Christ ate and drank with his disciples after his resurrection; he had feet and hands and tongue; he walked and spoke; his disciples touched him and felt the wounds in his hands and feet.[83] These proofs offered to Thomas and the other disciples were intended to strengthen our faith, and here Ælfric echoes Christ's words to Thomas, 'You believe because you can see me. Happy are those who have not seen and yet believe' (John XX.29). 'We ne gesawon hine, ac we swaðeah gelyfað', he says.[84]

Christ's resurrection, then, was real: it was not a matter of the escape of his divine nature from some imprisonment in the human. Moreover, Christ did not only rise from the dead in the body in which he suffered. He took that same body back to heaven, and so opened heaven to those whose nature he had assumed at his incarnation:

as he is in the divine.' Cf. *CH* II.xv (ed. Godden, p. 154) and Wulfstan, *Homilies*, no. vi (ed. Bethurum, pp. 152–3).

[82] *CH* I.xvi (ed. Thorpe, p. 230): 'What wonder is it that the Saviour, with an eternal body, came in through locked doors, he who with a mortal body was born from the closed womb of the maiden ... He showed that body to be touched, which he brought in through closed doors. His body could be handled and yet it was unable to decay; he showed himself tangible and undecaying, because his body was of the same nature as before, yet of a different glory'; based on Gregory, *Homiliae in evangelia* II.xxvi.1 (PL 76, 1197–8).

[83] *Homilies*, no. vii (ed. Pope I, 346–7).

[84] *Ibid.* (Pope I, 347): 'We did not see him but nonetheless we believe'; cf. *CH* I.xvi and xxi (ed. Thorpe, pp. 234 and 302).

On ðam feowerteogeðan dæge þæs ðe he of deaðe aras
he astah to heofonum to his halgan Fæder,
ætforan his apostolum, ðe him folgodon on life,
mid þære menniscnysse þe he of Marian genam,
and mid þam ylcan lichaman þe he of deaðe arærde.
And we eac wurðiað wurðlice ðone dæg
on þære Gangwucan, for ðan þe he geopenode us
on ðam foresædan dæge infær to heofonum
mid his agenum upstige, gif we hit geearnian wyllað.[85]

At the same time, however, the glorification of Christ's human nature at
his ascension merely revealed what had existed from the beginning in the
mind of God:

Seo Godcundnys wæs mid ðam Fæder ær ðan ðe middaneard gewurde æfre
ælmihtig and seo menniscnys næs ær ðan ðe he hi genam of ðam mædene
MARIAN ac swaðeahhwæðere seo menniscnys wæs æfre forestiht on ðam
godcundan ræde ær middaneardes gesetnysse swa swa Paulus se apostol cwæð:
Qui predestinatus est Filius Dei in virtute. Þæt is se ðe is forestiht. Godes Sunu.
Æfter ðissere forestihtunge wæs seo menniscnys gemærsod mid þam Fæder ær
ðan ðe middaneard wære. Se tima com þæt Crist hæfde lybbende on his Fæder
swiðran þa mærsunge þe he hæfde mid him on forestihtunge his menniscnysse.[86]

A similar point is made in Ælfric's homily for the Feast of St Peter.
Commenting on the verse, 'Nemo ascendit in celum nisi qui de celo

---

[85] *Homilies*, no. xia (ed. Pope I, 469): 'On the fortieth day from his resurrection he
ascended to heaven to his holy Father, before his apostles, who followed him while he
was alive, with the human nature which he took from Mary, and with the same body
that he raised from death. And we also worthily honour that day in Rogationtide
because on that same day he opened the entrance to heaven for us through his own
ascension, if we are willing to earn it.' Cf. *CH* I.i (ed. Thorpe, p. 28), 'Letter to
Wulfgeat' (ed. Assmann, p. 3), *Homilies*, nos. viii and xi (ed. Pope I, 367 and 417), *CH*
II.xxiv (ed. Godden, p. 225) and II.xxii (ed. Godden, p. 211): 'On ðam dæge
[Ascension Day] abær se ælmihtiga Godes Sunu urne lichaman to ðam heofonlican
eðle' ('On that day the almighty Son of God took our body to the heavenly home').

[86] *CH* II.xxii (ed. Godden, p. 209): 'The divine nature was with the Father before the
world was, always almighty, and the human nature did not exist before he took it from
the maiden Mary, but nonetheless the humanity was always pre-ordained in the divine
plan before the creation of the world, as Paul the apostle said: Who was predestined to
be the Son of God in strength. That is the one who was predestined. God's Son.
According to this predestination the humanity was glorified with the Father before the
world was created. The time came that Christ had, living at his Father's right hand, the
glory which he had with him in the predestination of his humanity.'

descendit filius hominis qui est in celo',[87] he remarks that Christ had not yet ascended to heaven when he said this, but what he said was true because of the unity of the two natures in one person, the son of man and the Son of God, born of the Virgin Mary:

Rihtlice is gecweden for ðære annysse þæt se mannes sunu of heofenum astige, and on heofenum wære ær his upstige, for ðan ðe he hæfde on ðære God-cundnysse ðe hine underfeng, þæt þæt he on menniscum gecynde habban ne mihte.[88]

These themes were most clearly articulated in the late Anglo-Saxon period by Ælfric, but they are not peculiar to him. The same themes are found in the Blickling Homilies, texts sometimes considered to be less orthodox than Ælfric's work. The tenth of these homilies, 'Þisses mid-dangeardes ende neah is', links the theme of the imminent end of the world to the need for right belief, defined as belief in God, the Son begotten from him and the Holy Spirit who is coeternal with both.[89] Christ is true man and true God, begotten by God the Father before time began, eternal and almighty.[90] At Christ's incarnation Mary became the mother of her creator and received in her womb the one whom heaven and earth were unable to enclose.[91] Christ's human nature was real: through his incarnation he became able to stand and move from one place to another, yet there was no diminution in his divinity.[92] His divine origin was revealed by God at his baptism and, in fact, he was never absent from heaven in his divinity.[93] He showed his wounds to his disciples as a proof of the reality of his resurrection.[94] At his ascension he took his human nature back to heaven.[95] Finally, and most importantly, at Christ's

---

[87] John III.13: 'No one has gone up to heaven except the one who came down from heaven, the Son of man who is in heaven.'

[88] *CH* II.xxiv (ed. Godden, p. 224): 'It is rightly said because of that unity that the Son of man descended from heaven and was in heaven before his ascension, because he possessed in that divinity by which his human nature was assumed, that which he could not possess in his human nature'; cf. Bede, *Homeliae* II.18 (ed. Hurst, p. 314) and Augustine, *In Iohannis evangelium*, xii.8 (ed. Willems, p. 125).

[89] *Blickling Homilies*, no. x (ed. Morris, p. 111).

[90] *Ibid.*, no. iii (ed. Morris, pp. 31 and 33).

[91] *Ibid.*, nos. i and ix (ed. Morris, pp. 5, 13 and 105).

[92] *Ibid.*, no. ii (ed. Morris, p. 19).

[93] *Ibid.*, nos. iii, vii, xi and xii (ed. Morris, pp. 29, 91, 117, 121, 127 and 131).

[94] *Ibid.*, no. vii (ed. Morris, pp. 89–91).

[95] *Ibid.*, no. xi (ed. Morris, pp. 115–17, 121, 123 and 127).

incarnation God, 'the great and incomprehensible mystery' was made finite: 'on Criste anum is ealles siges fylnes þurhtogen; and þurh þone man þe he on hine sylfne onfeng, þæt is se myccla mægenþrym and se unbegripenlica, se þurh þone man gemedemod wæs mannum to helpe'.[96] The passage echoes the statement in the Acts of the Second Council of Nicaea that 'God the Word circumscribed Himself when He came to us in flesh.'[97]

---

[96] *Ibid.*, no. xv (ed. Morris, p. 179): 'In Christ alone the fullness of all victory is brought about, through the human nature that he accepted; that is the great and incomprehensible mystery which was made finite through that human nature as a help to men'. Cf. Rom. XVI.25, '[Christ] the revelation of a mystery kept secret for endless ages.'

[97] Item 244A–B (trans. Sahas, p. 77).

# 3

# God made visible

The teaching encapsulated in the Blickling homilist's statement that at Christ's incarnation the infinite was made finite[1] was not only central to Christian belief and to the hope of salvation: it provided one of the justifications for religious art.

The iconoclast controversy of the eighth century, which culminated in the condemnation of iconoclasm at the Second Council of Nicaea in 787, was not primarily about idolatry, though accusations of idolatry played a part in it:[2] its main focus was a disagreement about the Incarnation and its implications. Both sides agreed that in Christ the human and divine natures were distinct but, at the same time, inseparable from each other. The iconoclasts, who held that an image must be identical in substance with what it represented, argued that icons could represent only material things and so could not depict the divine nature.[3] They therefore maintained that those who made icons of Christ fell into one of two heresies: either they portrayed only Christ's human nature (which was heretical because it denied his divinity) or they claimed (falsely) to depict his divinity and therefore confused the divine and human natures:[4]

For he has made an icon which he has called 'Christ'. But 'Christ' is a name [indicative] of God as well as man. Consequently, along with describing created

---

[1] *Blickling Homilies*, no. xv (ed. Morris, p. 179); see above, p. 53.

[2] On idolatry, see below, pp. 56–7.

[3] 'They who are quick to make accusations [the iconoclasts] say that "icon" and "prototype" are the same thing ... In the same way also they say that the icon of Christ and Christ himself do not differ from each other in essence', Acts of Nicaea II, item 261A (trans. Sahas, p. 91). See also item 252D-E (*ibid.*, pp. 84–5).

[4] The heresies are, respectively, Nestorianism and Monophysitism. For a discussion of the point, see Barasch, *Icon*, pp. 266–7.

flesh, he has either circumscribed the uncircumscribable character of the Godhead ... or he has confused that unconfused union, falling into the iniquity of confusion ... From those, therefore, who think that they are drawing the icon of Christ, it must be gathered either that the divinity is circumscribable and confused with the flesh or that the body of Christ was without divinity and divided; and also that they ascribe to the flesh a person with a hypostasis of his own – thus, in this respect, identifying themselves with the Nestorian fight against God.[5]

The iconophiles, on the other hand, saw the icon as something quite distinct from the person it represented,[6] resembling its prototype 'only with regard to the name and to the position of the members which can be characterized'.[7] Paintings of human beings, they said, did not separate soul from body even though they could not depict the soul; in the same way, paintings of Christ did not divide his divine and human natures, even though they could not portray the divine essence:

No one, of course, has thought to reproduce with colours his [Christ's] divinity, for *No one*, it says, *has ever seen God*. He is uncircumscribable, invisible and incomprehensible, although circumscribable according to his humanity. For we know Christ to be of two natures, and in two natures, that is, a divine and a human one, without division. The one, therefore, which is uncircumscribable and the one which can be circumscribed are seen in the one Christ.[8]

In depicting Christ, therefore, the iconophiles claimed to be recalling a single, indivisible person in whom the divine and human natures had been united.[9] Far from dividing the person of Christ, they were proclaiming the indivisibility of his divine and human natures and the reality of the Incarnation:

When they [Christians] see in an icon the Virgin giving birth and angels standing around with shepherds, they bring to mind that when God became man He was born for our salvation, and they make a confession, saying: 'He who is

---

[5] Acts of Nicaea II, items 252A + 260A (trans. Sahas, pp. 83 and 90). For the accusation that the iconophiles were introducing a fourth person into the Trinity, see also items 241E, 256B and 261D (*ibid.*, pp. 77, 87 and 92) and cf. Augustine, *Liber de praedestinatione sanctorum*, xv.31 (PL 44, 982–3), quoted below, p. 157.

[6] 'It is quite clear to everyone that "icon" is one thing and "prototype" another; the one is inanimate, the other animate', Acts of Nicaea II, item 261A (trans. Sahas, p. 91); see also item 257D (*ibid.*, p. 89).

[7] *Ibid.*, item 244B (Sahas, p. 77).    [8] *Ibid.*, item 244B (Sahas, p. 77).

[9] *Ibid.*, item 244A–C (Sahas, p. 77).

without flesh, became flesh. The Word assumed density. The uncreated One was made. The impalpable One was touched.' They also confess that He is one and the same, perfect in divinity, and perfect in humanity, truly God and truly man.[10]

An icon was not a portrait, then: it was a statement of belief, first, that God had chosen to become man, to be united in a real sense with his creation, and, secondly, that in doing so he had revealed himself to human sight. Moreover, as a result of this entry of the divine into human existence, all possibility of idolatry had been abolished, for the image of God presented in the person of Christ was given by God himself, unlike the idols against which men were warned in the Old Testament, which derived from the material and sensual ideas of men.[11] This belief that there was a link between the Incarnation and the abolition of idolatry was not confined to the eastern Church. Bede says in a homily for the Feast of the Ascension:

Super nubem quippe levem dominus ascendit ut ingressus Aegyptum eius simulacra subverteret quia *verbum caro factum est et habitavit in nobis* quia immune ab omni sorde iniquitatis corpus adsumpsit in quo mundum ingrediens idolatriae ritum destrueret nigrisque ac tenebrosis gentilium cordibus verum divinitatis lumen aperiret. Per hanc naturae humanae nubem de loco ad locum venire [voluit] qui loco non clauditur.[12]

Ælfric encloses a description of the pagan cults of the Old Testament within an account of the creation of the world by the Trinity, the second person of which came to earth and demonstrated that he was truly God.[13] He makes a similar point in a homily for the Feast of SS Peter and Paul where he interprets Peter's confession, 'You are the Christ, the Son of the living God' (Matt. XVI.16) in relation to the folly of those who honour

[10] *Ibid.*, item 256D–E (Sahas, p. 88).

[11] Torrance, *Trinitarian Faith*, p. 71. See also Nichols, *Art of God Incarnate*, p. 52 and Acts of Nicaea II, item 216A–B (trans. Sahas, p. 57).

[12] Bede, *Homeliae* II.15 (ed. Hurst, p. 286, trans. Martin and Hurst II, 143): 'The Lord ascended upon a swift cloud so that when he entered Egypt he might overturn its idols, when *the Word was made flesh and dwelt among us*. He took upon himself a body immune from all stains of iniquity, and entered the world in it, so that he might destroy the cult of idolatry, and make clear the true light of divinity to the shadowy and dark hearts of the gentiles. He who is not enclosed in a place willed to go from place to place by means of this cloud, his human nature.' Cf. *Homeliae* I.6 (ed. Hurst, p. 44).

[13] *Homilies*, no. xxi (ed. Pope II, 676–712), esp. pp. 677, 704 and 712.

false gods.[14] Through Christ's incarnation, therefore, the visual was 'rehabilitated, rescued from the service of idols, and restored to the worship of one who was, in the words of the Niceno-Constantinopolitan Creed, "Light from Light, true God from true God" '.[15] As John of Damascus said in his treatise justifying icons:

Israel of old did not see God, but 'we all, with unveiled face, behold the glory of the Lord'. We use all our senses to produce worthy images of Him, and we sanctify the noblest of the senses, which is that of sight. For just as words edify the ear, so also the image stimulates the eye. What the book is to the literate, the image is to the illiterate. Just as words speak to the ear, so the image speaks to the sight; it brings us understanding.[16]

The statement that the icon serves as a book for those unable to read recalls Gregory the Great's statements on religious art. In the first of two letters to Serenus, bishop of Marseilles, he praises the recipient for opposing the adoration of paintings but condemns his destruction of them, since they provide a useful substitute for books for those who are unable to read.[17] In a second, longer, letter he reminds Serenus that representations of the lives of saints have traditionally been placed in churches as a means of instruction: Serenus should not prohibit the making of pictures, which rouse those who see them to a feeling of compunction, but he should explain to his congregation that they should adore only the Trinity.[18]

Gregory's statements formed the basis of the Roman Church's attitude to religious art. From the time of Constantine onwards, the popes had encouraged the placing of statues and images in the Roman churches. They consistently supported the iconophiles in the arguments over the legitimacy of religious art and, when the Byzantine Emperor Leo first began to speak against the icons in 726, Pope Gregory II (715–31) immediately condemned his beliefs as heretical and despatched two letters to him refuting his views.[19] Gregory argued that religious pictures create an emotional response as well as reminding the viewer of a person or event: when we see a painting of Christ or his mother, he says, we pray to

---

[14] *CH* I.xxvi (ed. Thorpe, p. 366); cf. Bede, *Homeliae* I.20 (ed. Hurst, p. 142).

[15] Pelikan, *Imago Dei*, p. 99.

[16] John of Damascus, *De imaginibus I*, 16–17 (PG 94, 1248, trans. Anderson, p. 25).

[17] *Ep.* IX.209 (ed. Norberg, p. 768).     [18] *Ep.* XI.10 (ed. Norberg, pp. 873–6).

[19] Duchesne, *Liber pontificalis* I, 409; Mansi, *Sacrorum conciliorum collectio* XII, 959–82.

the one depicted; pictures remind us of the reality of the Incarnation and provide a focus for prayer.[20] This reference to paintings as an adjunct to prayer reminds one of a passage approving the use of portrait images for meditative purposes which was added during the seventh or early eighth century to a letter written by Gregory I to the hermit, Secundinus:

Valde nobis tua postulatio placuit, quia illum in corde tota intentione quaeris, cuius imaginem prae oculis habere desideras, ut visio corporalis cotidiana reddat exsertum et, dum picturam vides, ad illum animo inardescas, cuius imaginem videre desideras. Ab re non facimus, si per visibilia invisibilia demonstramus.[21]

The passage continues:

Scimus quia tu imaginem Salvatoris nostri ideo non petis, ut quasi Deum colas, sed ob recordationem filii Dei in eius amore recalescas, cuius te imaginem videre desideras. Et nos quidem non quasi ante divinitatem ante ipsam prosternimur, sed illum adoramus quem per imaginem aut natum aut passum vel in throno sedentem recordamur. Et dum nos ipsa pictura quasi scriptura ad memoriam filium Dei reducimus, animum nostrum aut de resurrectione laetificat aut de passione emulcat.[22]

It is clear from these passages that the writer considered that pictures were a means of recalling not only Christ's earthly life (his birth and passion) but also his risen and glorified nature: that they could represent the spiritual as well as the material. Opposition to iconoclasm continued under Gregory III (731–41). When he heard of the destruction of images of Christ, Mary and the apostles by Leo and his son Constantine he wrote to the Emperor in the same terms as his predecessor. When his messenger

[20] Mansi, *ibid.* XII, 964, 965 and 968.
[21] *Ep.* IX.148 (ed. Norberg, p. 1110, and trans. Freedberg, *Images*, p. 164): 'Your request [for images] pleases us greatly, since you seek with all your heart and all your intentness Him, whose picture you wish to have before your eyes, so that, being so accustomed to the daily corporeal sight, when you see an image of Him you are inflamed in your soul with love for Him whose picture you wish to see. We do no harm in wishing to show the invisible by means of the visible.'
[22] *Ibid.* (ed. Norberg, pp. 1110–11): 'We know that you do not ask for the image of our Saviour in order to worship it as God, but so that, by remembering the Son of God, you may grow in love for him whose image you wish to see. We do not prostrate ourselves before [the picture] as if before God but we adore the one whom, through the picture, we remember as born, suffering and seated on the throne. And while we recall to memory the Son of God by the same picture as if by scripture, our soul both rejoices in the resurrection and is softened by the passion.'

was detained, so preventing delivery of the letter, he excommunicated those who destroyed, profaned or blasphemed the images of Christ and his saints and condemned those who opposed the veneration of images. When a second letter to Leo, ordering him to restore the images, suffered the same fate as the first, Gregory proceeded to install additional images in the churches of Rome.[23] Pope Stephen III (768–72) anathematized the iconoclast council of 754 and confirmed the veneration of images by the Roman Church.[24] When the Carolingian Church condemned the decisions of the Second Council of Nicaea in a document (the *Libri Carolini*) whose attitude is close to that of the iconoclast council of 754, Pope Hadrian I (772–95) sent Charlemagne a long and detailed refutation of the arguments put forward by his theologians.[25] He drew attention to the long tradition of placing images in churches, making it clear that they were to be venerated, though not worshipped.[26] He recalled the Old Testament images which God commanded Moses to make[27] and the letters of Gregory the Great to Serenus and Secundinus.[28] He referred to the decision of the Sixth Ecumenical Council, the Council in Trullo, that the symbol of the lamb should be replaced by representations of Christ in human form, to remind those who saw them of Christ's birth, sufferings and death.[29] He argued that through pictures we are led from the visible to the invisible[30] and finally, and most strikingly, he approved Basil's statement that the honour paid to the image passes to its prototype.[31] The position of the Roman Church, therefore, was similar to that of the iconophiles: works of art did not simply record past events, nor was their value confined to the instruction of the illiterate or the decoration of

---

[23] Duchesne, *Liber pontificalis* I, 415–19.   [24] *Ibid.* I, 476–7.

[25] MGH Epist. V, 5–57.   [26] *Ibid.*, pp. 15, 44 and 49.

[27] *Ibid.*, pp. 19 and 36.

[28] *Ibid.*, pp. 20, 42–3 and 54–7. Hadrian clearly thought that the passages added to the letter to Secundinus were genuine.

[29] *Ibid.*, p. 32. Canon 82 of the Council in Trullo reads: 'Having thus welcomed these ancient figures and shadows as symbols of the truth transmitted to the Church, we prefer today grace and truth themselves, as a fulfilment of this law. In consequence, and in order to expose to the sight of all, even with the help of painting, what is perfect, we decide that henceforth Christ our God must be represented in his human form instead of the ancient lamb' (trans. Sendler, *Icon*, p. 20).

[30] MGH Epist. V, 56.

[31] *Ibid.*, p. 17; cf. Acts of Nicaea II, item 325E (trans. Sahas, p. 145).

churches; they were a means of raising the mind to God and a reminder of the reality of the Incarnation.

Carolingian theologians viewed religious art in a way which was noticeably different from that of the popes. Their arguments, set out in the *Libri Carolini*, were based on an extremely spiritual and non-material view of worship.[32] Like the iconoclasts, they believed in the primacy of the word.[33] The iconoclast conception of God was the Old Testament one, that he spoke to his people but had no visible form:

*In the Old {Testament} also, where he says to Moses*: Thou shalt not make to thyself an idol, nor likeness of any thing, whatever things are in the heaven above, and whatever are in the earth beneath; *for* in the mountain you heard the sound of words coming from the midst of fire, but you saw no likeness, except the voice.[34]

The iconoclasts admitted that God had chosen to become visible in Christ but argued that this was a temporary dispensation:

Even though we once knew Christ according to the flesh, yet we no longer know him this way, for we walk by faith, not by sight; *and from the same Apostle who said*: So faith comes from what is heard, and what is heard comes by the word of God.[35]

The iconophiles, on the other hand, stressed the change which had taken place at the Incarnation: whereas the patriarchs and prophets had merely heard God's word, Christians were able to see his Word in the person of Christ, the image of God. The shift in emphasis is well put by Hippolytus, in a passage which echoes the opening chapter of the Epistle to the Hebrews:

Vi divina verbis dictis fidem non denegamus. Et haec Deus Logo imperabat. Logus autem loquebatur, per verba convertens hominem ab inobedientia, non vi necessitatis in servitutem redigens, sed ad libertatem voluntario consilio vocans. Hunc Logum posterioribus temporibus mittebat Pater, non amplius per prophetam loqui neque obscure praedicatum subintelligi eum volens, sed ipso visu apparuisse hunc dico, ut mundus eum videns revereretur.[36]

---

[32] For a detailed study of the theory of art set out in the *LC*, see Chazelle, 'Matter, Spirit and Image.'

[33] *LC* II.xxx (ed. Bastgen, pp. 92–5); Chazelle, 'Matter, Spirit and Image', p. 169.

[34] Acts of Nicaea II, item 284C (trans. Sahas, p. 109); the biblical reference is to Deuteronomy IV.12.

[35] *Ibid.*, item 285C (Sahas, p. 111); cf. Rom. X.17.

[36] Hippolytus, *De refutatione omnium haeresum* X.33 (PG 16, 3452, trans. modern Roman

This was not the view of the authors of the *Libri Carolini*. They listed the Old Testament events which were narrated not depicted; they reminded the reader that the gospels talk of books and reading, not of pictures; they described St John, the eye-witness of the gospel events, as the one who wrote about Christ and who was instructed, 'Write down all that you see in a book, and send it to the seven churches' (Apoc. I.11).[37] In addition they believed, like the iconoclasts, that the relationship between an image and its prototype involved an identity of substance: they therefore maintained that images were incapable of representing anything other than the material. It follows from this that pictures could not represent Christ's divine nature but only his external appearance.[38] They could remind the viewer that Christ had once lived on earth but were quite incapable of leading the mind to contemplate spiritual realities including, presumably, the risen and glorified Christ.[39]

By the death of Louis the Pious in 840 the position had changed. When Claudius of Turin attacked the images and relics in his new church as abominations, comparable to statues of pagan gods, he was accused by Jonas of Orleans of resurrecting the Arian and Adoptionist heresies[40] and, by Dungal, of contempt for the Incarnation and Passion of Christ.[41] Both authors were writing at the request of Louis the Pious and addressed their

Breviary, 30 December): 'We do not refuse belief to words spoken by divine power. These God committed to the Word. The Word spoke, and by these words he turned man away from disobedience, not enslaving him by force or necessity, but inviting him to choose freedom of his own accord. In the last days the Father sent the Word. In his plan the Word was no longer to speak through the prophets. He was no longer to be a figure of conjecture, announced in an obscure way. He was to be manifested visibly, so that the world could see him and be saved.'

[37] See above, p. 60, n. 33. Cf. John XX.30–1: 'There were many other signs that Jesus worked and the disciples saw, but they are not recorded in this book. These are recorded so that you may believe that Jesus is the Christ, the Son of God, and that believing this you may have life through his name.'

[38] *LC* I.ii, II.xxvi, III.xv and IV.xiv and xxvii (ed. Bastgen, pp. 13, 85, 135, 199 and 225); Chazelle, 'Matter, Spirit and Image', pp. 172–3.

[39] *LC* IV.ii and xv (ed. Bastgen, pp. 176 and 201); Chazelle, 'Matter, Spirit and Image', pp. 175–6. Note, however, that the dome of Charlemagne's chapel at Aachen was decorated with a mosaic showing the Almighty adored by the twenty-four elders of the Apocalypse: see Hubert, Porcher and Volbach, *Carolingian Art*, p. 11.

[40] Jonas, *De cultu imaginum* (PL 106, 307–9).

[41] Dungal, *Liber* (PL 105, 528).

work to him and to his son, Charles the Bald.[42] Whereas the *Libri Carolini* denied that the images associated with the ark of the covenant and the Tabernacle could be used as precedents for images of Christ and the saints,[43] Jonas argued that likenesses of heavenly beings had been made in the past by Moses and Solomon and, since there had been images in the past which were types of future things, it was surely legitimate to create images of past events.[44] Both Dungal and Jonas drew a clear distinction between the adoration due to God and the veneration offered to images of Christ and the saints; both drew attention to the use of the word *adorare* in the Old Testament and in the liturgy in contexts which imply veneration or respect; both saw attacks on images as attacks on the doctrines of the Incarnation and Resurrection.[45] For Dungal, the veneration of images was a means of showing love and honour to the Saviour and Redeemer of the world and of asking the saints for their prayers;[46] for Jonas, images were an adjunct to prayer.[47]

In contrast to Charlemagne's theologians, the Anglo-Saxons seem never to have shared the iconoclasts' attitude to material things. Bede included a long passage justifying images of Christ and the saints in his *De templo*, written shortly before 731.[48] His information about the rise of iconoclasm probably came from Nothelm, who had recently returned from Rome bringing with him copies of some of Gregory the Great's letters.[49] Nothelm must have been aware of the actions taken by Pope Gregory II against the iconoclasts and it is noticeable that the arguments put forward by Bede in support of images are the traditional ones, found in the papal letters discussed above: the precedent of the Old Testament images which God commanded Moses to make, the value of pictures as a 'living reading' for those who could not read, and the emotional effect produced by religious pictures on those who saw them. Bede's interest in the visual arts and their use has been discussed by George Henderson, who draws

---

[42] *Ibid.* (PL 105, 465) and Jonas, *De cultu imaginum* (PL 106, 305).

[43] *LC* I.xv and xviii–xx (ed. Bastgen, pp. 34–7 and 42–8).

[44] Jonas, *De cultu imaginum* (PL 106, 318).

[45] Dungal, *Liber* (PL 105, 481–2); Jonas, *De cultu imaginum* (PL 106, 319–20 and 331).

[46] Dungal, *Liber* (PL 105, 472 and 527).

[47] Jonas, *De cultu imaginum* (PL 106, 331–2 and 341–4).

[48] Bede, *De templo* II (ed. Hurst, pp. 212–13). See also Meyvaert, 'Church Paintings', pp. 68–9.

[49] Meyvaert, *Bede and Gregory the Great*, pp. 9–10.

attention to his references to the pictures of the Tabernacle and the Temple in Cassiodorus's Codex Grandior, which provided the model for the representation of the Tabernacle in the Codex Amiatinus.[50] Bede notes that Cassiodorus mentions the picture of the Temple in his commentary on the psalms,[51] and Cassiodorus himself says that he placed the picture in his codex because the content of scripture is made clearer by means of a picture.[52] Elsewhere, Bede refers to the way in which an illustrated copy of the life of St Paul helped him to understand the meaning of the reference to 'forty stripes less one' (II Cor. XI.24).[53] In his descriptions of the paintings which Benedict Biscop had brought back to decorate the walls of his churches at Wearmouth and Jarrow, Bede again draws attention to the educational value of pictures, and also to their role as reminders of the Incarnation and of the presence of Christ and his saints:

quatinus intrantes aecclesiam omnes etiam litterarum ignari, quaquaversum intenderent, vel semper amabilem Christi sanctorumque eius, quamvis in imagine, contemplarentur aspectum; vel dominicae incarnationis gratiam vigilantiore mente recolerent; vel extremi discrimen examinis, quasi coram oculis habentes, districtius se ipsi examinare meminissent.[54]

Bede's reference to the Incarnation in relation to painting recalls the iconophile position: that paintings of Christ were themselves assertions of the reality of his human nature.[55] It seems highly likely that this was

---

[50] Henderson, *Bede and the Visual Arts*, pp. 5–6 and 27–8, n. 27; see also Bede, *De tabernaculo* II and *De templo* II (ed. Hurst, pp. 81–2 and 192–3) and Meyvaert, 'Church Paintings', pp. 71–2, n. 7.

[51] *De templo* II (ed. Hurst, p. 192).

[52] Cassiodorus, *Expositio psalmorum* (ed. Adriaen, pp. 789–90): 'Nos enim et tabernaculum, quod eius imago primitus fuit, et templum ipsum fecimus pingi et in corpore pandectae nostrae grandioris fecimus collocari; quatenus, quod scripturae divinae de ipsis textus eloquitur, oculis redditum clarius panderetur'; quoted by Henderson, *Bede and the Visual Arts*, pp. 27–8.

[53] Henderson, *ibid.*, p. 7.

[54] *Historia abbatum*, vi (ed. Plummer, pp. 369–70, trans. Webb and Farmer, p. 191): 'Thus all who entered the church, even those who could not read, were able, whichever way they looked, to contemplate the dear face of Christ and His saints, even if only in a picture, to put themselves more firmly in mind of the Lord's Incarnation and, as they saw the decisive moment of the Last Judgement before their very eyes be brought to examine their conscience with all due severity'; cf. Bede, *Homeliae* I.13 (ed. Hurst, p. 93), and Raw, *Crucifixion Iconography*, pp. 12–13.

[55] See above, p. 55 and also Henderson, *Bede and the Visual Arts*, p. 14.

Bede's belief too, for, like the iconophiles, he places great stress on the Incarnation as a making visible of the divine. The texts which underpin this view come from the writings of St John, who presents Christ not only as the Word of God but the Word made visible: 'The Word was made flesh, he lived among us, and we saw his glory, the glory that is his as the only Son of the Father, full of grace and truth' (John I.14).[56] What the disciples saw in Christ, said St John, was divinity itself:

Something which has existed since the beginning, that we have heard, and we have seen with our own eyes; that we have watched and touched with our hands: the Word, who is life – this is our subject. That life was made visible: we saw it and we are giving our testimony, telling you of the eternal life which was with the Father and has been made visible to us. What we have seen and heard we are telling you so that you too may be in union with us, as we are in union with the Father and with his Son Jesus Christ. We are writing this to you to make our own joy complete. (I John I.1–4)

The role of St John as the disciple who wrote of Christ's divine nature forms a major theme in the writings of the Anglo-Saxon period. Ælfric commented at length on the opening chapter of St John's Gospel in a late sermon for the Feast of the Nativity, based largely on Augustine's commentary on St John's Gospel and on a Christmas homily by Bede.[57] Ælfric draws together material from several different sources in order to elaborate on two of his favourite themes: creation by all three persons of the Trinity and the divine nature of Christ, begotten from God the Father before time began. Whereas St John speaks of God creating through his Word, Ælfric expands the reference into an account of the Trinity, not three gods but one, with one divine nature and power.[58] Christ is not simply the Word through whom God creates: he is the word spoken by the divine Wisdom, a word which men cannot speak or understand.[59] He was already in the world in his divinity and he came to the world in his humanity.[60] He did not lose his divine nature when he became man, yet he was truly man, with a human body and soul.[61] Bede points out that John wrote of the hidden mysteries of Christ's divinity, not about his

---

[56] Quoted in the Acts of Nicaea II, item 244A (trans. Sahas, p. 77).

[57] *Homilies*, no. i (ed. Pope I, 196–225).

[58] *Ibid.* (ed. Pope I, 199–201 and 203–4).

[59] *Ibid.* (ed. Pope I, 203).     [60] *Ibid.* (ed. Pope I, 211).

[61] *Ibid.* (ed. Pope I, 213–14); Ælfric is making the point that Christ's human nature was not an illusion as the Manichaeans had claimed.

human acts.[62] He was especially fitted to do this, for he had leaned on Christ's breast at the Last Supper and absorbed the divine wisdom in a way not open to the other evangelists.[63] Like the eagle, which flies higher than other birds and is able to look into the sun, John, as though flying up to heaven, 'aeternam divinitatis eius potentiam per quam omnia facta sunt ... cognovit ac nobis cognoscendam scribendo contradidit'.[64] Whereas the other evangelists spoke of Christ in time, John spoke of him in eternity:

Ergo alii evangelistae Christum ex tempore natum describunt Iohannes eundem in principio fuisse testatur dicens: *In principio erat verbum*. Alii inter homines eum subito apparuisse commemorant ille ipsum apud Deum semper fuisse declarat dicens: *et verbum erat apud Deum*. Alii eum verum hominem ille verum confirmat esse Deum dicens: *et Deus erat verbum*. Alii eum hominem apud homines temporaliter conversatum ille Deum apud Deum in principio manentem ostendit dicens: *Hoc erat in principio apud Deum*. Alii magnalia quae in homine gessit perhibent ille quod omnem creaturam visibilem et invisibilem per ipsum Deus pater fecerit docet dicens: *Omnia per ipsum facta sunt, et sine ipso factum est nihil*.[65]

Ælfric makes the same points. St John was the one who leaned on Christ's breast at the Last Supper, drinking in the divine wisdom.[66] His symbol of the eagle is a sign of his contemplation of Christ's divine nature.[67] Unlike

---

62  *Homeliae* I.8 and 9 (ed. Hurst, pp. 53 and 62).

63  *Homeliae* I.8 (ed. Hurst, p. 52).

64  *Ibid.* (ed. Hurst, p. 53, trans. Martin and Hurst I, 74): 'recognized the eternal power of [Christ's] divinity, through which all things come into being, and he handed this on in writing for us to learn.'

65  *Ibid.* (ed. Hurst, p. 53, trans. Martin and Hurst I, 74): 'The other evangelists describe Christ born in time; John bears witness that this same [Christ] was in the beginning, saying, *In the beginning was the Word*. The others record his sudden appearance among human beings; John declares that he was always with God, saying, *and the Word was with God*. The others confirm that he is a true human being; John confirms that he is true God, saying, *and the Word was God*. The others [show] that [Christ] was a human being keeping company for a time with human beings; John shows that he was God abiding with God in the beginning, saying, *He was in the beginning with God*. The others testify to the wonders which [Christ] did as a human being; John teaches that God the Father made every creature, visible and invisible, through him, saying, *All things were made through him, and without him nothing was made*.'

66  *Homilies*, no. i (ed. Pope I, 196); see also 'On the Old and New Testament' (ed. Crawford, *Heptateuch*, p. 53) and *LS* I.xv (ed. Skeat I, 330).

67  *Homilies*, no. i (ed. Pope I, 197) and *LS* I.xv (ed. Skeat I, 334). See also O'Reilly, 'St John', p. 167, on the eagle in Anglo-Saxon drawings and paintings of St John.

the other evangelists, who talked primarily of Christ's humanity, St John witnesses above all to Christ's divine nature:

Ða oðre þry godspelleras, Matheus, Marcus, Lucas, awriton æror be Cristes menniscnysse ... He [John] cydde fela be Cristes godcundnysse, hu he ecelice butan angynne of his Fæder acenned is, and mid him rixað on annysse þæs Halgan Gastes, a butan ende. Feawa he awrat be his menniscnysse, forðan þe þa ðry oðre godspelleras genihtsumlice be þam heora bec setton.[68]

Moreover, St John was the great opponent of heresy about Christ's divinity. Bede's Christmas homily treats the opening of St John's Gospel as a refutation, phrase by phrase, of a series of Trinitarian and Christological heresies,[69] and both Bede and Ælfric state that the fourth gospel was written in order to counter claims that Christ did not exist before his birth from Mary:

Þa asprungon gedwolmenn on Godes gelaðunge, and cwædon þæt Crist nære ær he acenned wæs of Marian. Þa bædon ealle þa leodbisceopas ðone halgan apostol þæt he þa feorðan boc gesette, and þæra gedwolmanna dyrstignesse adwæscte.[70]

The same point is made by the artist of the early eleventh-century Eadwig Gospels, who placed a representation of Arius holding a scroll with the words, 'Erat tempus quando non erat', beneath the feet of the evangelist.[71]

The crucial point about St John's Gospel, however, was the link he established between Christ as the Word of God and the image of God. It was this making visible of the Word which was so important and which pervades the writings of both Bede and Ælfric. For both writers, the

---

[68] *CH* I.iv (ed. Thorpe, p. 70): 'The other three evangelists, Matthew, Mark and Luke, had written about Christ's human nature ... John related many things about Christ's divinity, how he is begotten eternally without beginning from his Father, and reigns with him in the unity of the Holy Spirit, ever without end. He wrote little about his human nature because the other three evangelists had written extensively about that in their books.'

[69] *Homeliae* I.8 (ed. Hurst, pp. 53–4); cf. Augustine, *In Iohannis evangelium*, i.11 (ed. Willems, p. 6).

[70] *CH* I.iv (ed. Thorpe, p. 70): 'Then heretics arose in God's church and said that Christ did not exist before he was born of Mary. Then all the diocesan bishops asked the holy apostle to set down the fourth book and crush the boldness of those heretics.' Cf. *LS* I.i (ed. Skeat I, 10) and Bede, *Homeliae* I.9 (ed. Hurst, p. 66). See also O'Reilly, 'St John', p. 180.

[71] Hanover, Kestner Museum, WM xxia 36, 147v, discussed in O'Reilly, 'St John', pp. 178–9 and reprod. pl. 38.

purpose of the Incarnation was to allow humans to see God. Bede, talking of the shepherds in the story of the Nativity, says:

In qua nativitate divina videri ab hominibus non potuit sed ut videri posset *verbum caro factum est et habitavit in nobis. Videamus* ergo, inquiunt, *hoc verbum quod factum est* quia ante quam factum esset hoc videre nequivimus; *quod fecit dominus et ostendit nobis*, quod incarnari fecit dominus et per hoc visibile nobis exhibuit.[72]

Ælfric follows Bede in linking the words of the shepherds, 'Let us see this word which has come to pass', to the opening words of St John's Gospel, 'In the beginning was the word':

Þa hyrdas ða spræcon him betweonan, æfter ðæra engla fram-færelde, Uton gefaran to Bethleem, and geseon þæt word þe geworden is, and God us geswutelode.[73] Eala hu rihtlice hi andetton þone halgan geleafan mid þisum wordum. On frymðe wæs word, and þæt word wæs mid Gode, and þæt word wæs God. Word bið wisdomes geswutelung, and þæt Word, þæt is se Wisdom, is acenned of ðam Ælmihtigum Fæder, butan anginne; forðan ðe he wæs æfre God of Gode, Wisdom of ðam wisan Fæder. Nis he na geworht, forðan ðe he is God, and na gesceaft; ac se Ælmihtiga Fæder gesceop þurh ðone Wisdom ealle gesceafta, and hi ealle ðurh þone Halgan Gast geliffæste. Ne mihte ure mennisce gecynd Crist on ðære godcundlican acennednysse geseon; ac þæt ylce Word wæs geworden flæsc, and wunode on us, þæt we hine geseon mihton. Næs þæt Word to flæsce awend, ac hit wæs mid menniscum flæsce befangen ... Hi cwædon, Uton geseon þæt word þe geworden is, forðan ðe hi ne mihton hit geseon ær ðan ðe hit geflæschamod wæs, and to menn geworden.[74]

---

[72] Bede, *Homeliae* I.7 (ed. Hurst, pp. 47–8, trans. Martin and Hurst I, 67): 'In this divine nativity he [i.e. Christ] could not be seen by human beings, but that he might be seen *the Word was made flesh and dwelt among us*. Therefore they [i.e. the shepherds] said, *"Let us see this Word which has come to be* – for before it came to be we were unable to see this [Word]." [They said,] *"which the Lord has made and shown to us"* – what the Lord made to become flesh and thereby displayed to us in visible [form].' Cf. Bede, *Homeliae* I.4, I.11 and II.12 (ed. Hurst, pp. 28, 73–4 and 264), and Ælfric, *Homilies*, no. viii (ed. Pope I, 367).

[73] Luke II.15 is usually translated, 'Let us ... see this thing that has happened which the Lord has made known to us.' The Latin, however, reads, 'videamus hoc verbum, quod factum est, quod Dominus ostendit nobis.'

[74] *CH* I.ii (ed. Thorpe, p. 40): 'The shepherds then spoke to one another, after the angels' departure, [and said], Let us go to Bethlehem and see the word which has come to pass and which God has shown us. See how rightly they confessed that holy faith with these words, In the beginning was the Word, and that Word was with God, and that Word was God. Words are the expression of wisdom, and that Word, that is Wisdom, is begotten from the almighty Father without any beginning, because he was always God

The shepherds do not merely set out to confirm what the angel has told them; their action is a confession of faith in the Word who was God. Belief in Christ as both God and man is, therefore, bound up with man's ability to see. It is a point to which Ælfric returns again and again. Whereas for the Carolingian Church, the crucial point about the Incarnation was that God, who was impassible, became capable of suffering,[75] for Ælfric, Christ became man in order to suffer and to be seen:

Seo dun þe se Hælend of astah getacnode heofenan rice, of ðam niðer astah se Ælmihtiga Godes Sunu, ðaða he underfeng ure gecynd, and to menniscum men geflæschamod wearð, to ðy þæt he mancynn fram deofles anwealde alysde. He wæs ungesewenlic and unðrowigendlic on his gecynde; þa wearð he gesewenlic on urum gecynde, and þrowigendlic.[76]

He makes the same point in a sermon for the Feast of the Nativity in the second set of Catholic Homilies:

Þa gif he come on ðære godcundnysse buton menniscnysse, þonne ne mihte ure tyddernys aberan his mihte. Ne seo godcundnys ne mihte nan ðing þrowian, for ðan þe heo is unðrowigendlic. Þa genam se ælmihtiga Godes sunu ða menniscnysse of anum mædene, and wearð gesewenlic mann and þrowigendlic.[77]

This emphasis on the visual distinguishes the views of Ælfric and of the late Anglo-Saxon Church quite sharply from those set out in the

from God, Wisdom from the wise Father. He was not created, for he is God and not a creature; but the almighty Father created all created things through that Wisdom and gave life to all through the Holy Spirit. Nor could our human nature see Christ in that divine birth, but that same Word became flesh and lived among us, so that we might see him. The Word was not changed into flesh, but was enclosed in human flesh ... They said, Let us see the word that has come to pass, because they could not see it before it was enclosed in flesh and made man.' Ælfric is drawing on Bede, *Homeliae* I.7 (ed. Hurst, pp. 47–8) and *In Lucam* I.ii.15 (ed. Hurst, p. 53).

[75] Eg. *LC* III.i (ed. Bastgen, p. 107).

[76] *CH* I.viii (ed. Thorpe, p. 120): 'The hill from which the Saviour descended symbolized the kingdom of heaven, from which the almighty Son of God descended when he assumed our nature and became incarnate in order to free mankind from the power of the devil. He was invisible and impassible by nature; then he became visible in our nature and passible.' Cf. Haymo, *Homiliae de tempore*, xix (PL 118, 137): 'ut qui invisibilis erat in suis, visibilis appareret in nostris.'

[77] *CH* II.i (ed. Godden, p. 4): 'Then, if he had come in his divinity without the humanity, our weakness would not have been able to bear his power. Nor could the divine nature suffer, because it is impassible. Then the almighty Son of God took human nature from a maiden and became man, visible and passible.'

*Libri Carolini*. The difference in attitude can be seen particularly clearly in the treatment of the story of the bronze serpent raised up by Moses in the desert (Numbers XXI.4–9). According to the Old Testament account, the Israelites were cured of snake-bite by looking at the image of a snake. In the Book of Wisdom, it is made clear that the cure effected was the result of God's power, not of some magic power inherent in the image (Wisdom XVI.5–14): the episode forms part of a passage contrasting the idolatry of the Egyptians with the true faith of the Israelites (Wisdom XIII.10–XV.19) and the bronze serpent is presented as an example of God's care for his people. Later, however, the bronze serpent becomes an idol to which the Israelites offered sacrifices and which was destroyed by Hezekiah as part of his attack on idolatry (II Kings XVIII.4). When the Byzantine Emperor, Leo, set out to destroy the icons of Constantinople in 726, he claimed to be imitating Hezekiah.[78] In the same way, the *Libri Carolini* focus on the misuse of the serpent image in order to argue that the parallel traditionally drawn between the raising of the serpent in the desert and the raising of Christ on the cross is to be interpreted in a spiritual rather than a literal way: we are to contemplate Christ only in the mind.[79] Bede uses the story of the bronze serpent as a justification for religious art in his *De templo*.[80] Elsewhere, however, he interprets the parallel between the serpent image and Christ's death in a more spiritual way:

sicut illi qui exaltatum pro signo serpentem aeneum aspiciebant sanabantur ad tempus a temporali morte et plaga quam serpentium morsus intulerat ita et qui mysterium dominicae passionis credendo confitendo sinceriter imitando aspiciunt salvantur in perpetuum ab omni morte quam peccando in animo pariter et carne contraxerant.[81]

---

[78] Mansi, *Sacrorum conciliorum collectio* XII, 965.

[79] *LC* I.xviii (ed. Bastgen, p. 43). The reference is to John III.14–15: 'The Son of Man must be lifted up as Moses lifted up the serpent in the desert, so that everyone who believes may have eternal life in him.'

[80] *De Templo* II (ed. Hurst, p. 212).

[81] *Homeliae* II.18 (ed. Hurst, p. 316, trans. Martin and Hurst II, 185): 'Just as those who looked at the bronze serpent which had been lifted up as a sign were cured at that time from temporal death and the wounds which the serpents' bites had caused, so too those who look at the mystery of the Lord's passion by believing, confessing, [and] sincerely imitating it are saved forever from every death they have incurred by sinning in mind and body.'

Ælfric refers to the bronze serpent and its symbolism three times,[82] but he never refers to its destruction, even in his paraphrase of the passage from the Book of Kings which describes how Hezekiah 'abolished the high places, broke the pillars, cut down the sacred poles and smashed the bronze serpent which Moses had made' (II Kings XVIII.4).[83] His main theme is the physical healing given to those who gazed on the serpent fashioned by Moses, and the spiritual healing given to Christians who look to Christ:

> Ða terendan næddran, þe totæron þæt folc,
> syndon ure synna, þe us tosliton wyllað;
> ac we sceolon behealdan ðæs Hælendes þrowunge
> mid soðum geleafan, and we beoð sona hale.
> Ðæt folc on ðam westene wæs þa gehæled
> þurh ða ærenan næddran fram þam andweardan deaðe;
> ac se Hælend sæde þæt þa sceolon habban
> þæt ece lif mid him þe on hine gelyfað.
> Seo gehiwode anlicnys gehælde ða hwilwendlice,
> and þæt soðe þing nu sylð us þæt ece lif.[84]

In the earliest of his three references, however, he adds a comment which reveals that he is interpreting contemplation of Christ's sufferings as contemplation of a crucifix:

Mine gebroðru uton behealdan þone ahangenan Crist, þæt we beon fram ðam ættrigum synnum gehælede. Witodlice swa swa þæt Israhela folc besawon to ðære ærenan næddran, and wurdon gehælede fram ðæra næddrena geslite, swa beoð nu gehælede fram heora synnum þa ðe mid geleafan behealdað Cristes deað and his ærist ... Ðære halgan rode tacn is ure bletsung, and to ðære rode we us gebiddað, na swa ðeah to ðam treowe, ac to ðam Ælmihtigum Drihtne, ðe on ðære halgan rode for us hangode.[85]

[82] *CH* II.xiii (ed. Godden, pp. 135–6) and *Homilies*, nos. xii and xx (ed. Pope I, 488–9 and II, 655–6); for discussion of the sources see Pope II, 664–5.

[83] See *LS* I.xviii (ed. Skeat I, 408).

[84] *Homilies*, no. xx (ed. Pope II, 656): 'The biting serpents, which tore the people, are our sins, which will tear us; but we must gaze on the Saviour's suffering with true faith and we will immediately be healed. The people in the desert were healed from temporal death through the bronze serpent; but the Saviour said that those who believe in him will have eternal life with him. The painted likeness healed the transitory and the true thing now gives us that eternal life.'

[85] *CH* II.xiii (ed. Godden, p. 136): 'My brothers, let us contemplate the crucified Christ so that we may be healed from our poisonous sins. Truly, just as the people of Israel

Further evidence for the way in which the comparison between Christ's death on the cross and the bronze serpent was understood in late Anglo-Saxon England comes from the *Regularis concordia*. During the ceremonies of Holy Week, which commemorated the last days of Christ's life, a candlestick in the shape of a serpent was carried in procession through the church 'as a sign of a certain mystery', almost certainly the raising of Christ on the cross:

Dehinc hora congrua agatur Nona. Qua cantata, ob arcanum cuiusdam mysterii indicium, si ita placuerit induant se fratres et pergant ad ostium ecclesiae ferentes hastam cum imagine serpentis, ibique ignis de silice excutiatur; illo benedicto ab abbate, candela, quae in ore serpentis infixa est, ab illo accendatur. Sicque, aedituo hastam deportante, cuncti fratres chorum ingrediantur unusque dehinc cereus ex illo illuminetur igne.[86]

Clearly, the monks saw no danger in material symbols of this kind.

The emphasis placed by writers such as Bede and Ælfric on the making visible of the divine recalls two features of their outlook: first, the prominent position given by Anglo-Saxon artists to the sense of sight and, secondly, the love of light, apparent in Old English poetry and in Anglo-Saxon jewellery. Their belief that sight was the first of the senses is reflected in two artifacts, both dating from the ninth century: the Fuller Brooch and the Alfred Jewel. The outer border of the Fuller Brooch is decorated with roundels depicting the material world of plants, birds, animals and humans; the central field carries representations of the

---

gazed at the bronze serpent and were healed from the bite of the serpents, so those who, with faith, contemplate Christ's death and resurrection, are now healed from their sins ... The sign of the holy cross is our blessing, and we pray to the cross, not, however, to the wood but to the Almighty Lord who hung for us on the holy cross.' The reference to praying to the cross seems to be Ælfric's own addition; it does not occur in the passages from Augustine and Bede on which he is drawing: Augustine, *In Iohannis evangelium*, xii.11 (ed. Willems, pp. 126–7) and Bede, *Homeliae* II.18 (ed. Hurst, pp. 315–17).

[86] *Regularis concordia*, iv.41 (ed. and trans. Symons, p. 39): 'None shall be said at the proper time; then, as a secret sign of a certain mystery, if it so please, the brethren shall vest and go to the doors of the church bearing with them a staff with the representation of a serpent; there fire shall be struck from flint and blessed by the abbot, after which the candle which is fixed in the mouth of the serpent shall be lit from that fire. And so, the staff being borne by the sacrist, all the brethren shall enter the choir and one candle shall then be lit from that fire.' See also Ælfric, *Epistula*, viii.37 (ed. Nocent, p. 169), and *CH* I.xxxi (ed. Thorpe, p. 474).

ways in which man makes contact with his environment through the senses.[87] No earlier representations of the five senses are known and the brooch is unique in associating the senses with the external world of human, animal, bird and plant life.[88] The meaning of the figures in the central field is conveyed by gesture: taste places his hand in his mouth, smell sniffs at a leaf, hearing raises one hand to his ear and touch places one hand above the other. The figure in the central field, who is larger than the other four and who differs from them in staring out from the brooch towards the viewer, represents sight. A very similar figure decorates the front of the Alfred Jewel and it seems likely that this figure, too, represents sight, something which would be very appropriate if, as is generally thought, the jewel was mounted on a pointer of some kind.[89]

The figure on the front of the Alfred Jewel is clearly a secular figure, as are the representations of taste, smell, hearing and touch on the Fuller Brooch. The central figure on the brooch, however, seems to have a religious significance. The boss at the centre of the brooch gives the impression of a disk clasped between the figure's two hands, like the host in the hands of the priest during the consecration of the mass; the small cross on the figure's clothes confirms this interpretation. Physical sight was constantly interpreted as a symbol of spiritual sight: Gregory the Great, for instance, identifies the blind man of Luke XVIII.35–43 with the human race, 'claritatem supernae lucis ignorans ... sed tamen per Redemptoris sui praesentiam illuminatur, ut internae lucis gaudia iam per desiderium videat'.[90] This inner vision allows one to see through the surface of things to their true nature. Gregory, talking of doubting Thomas, says:

Aliud vidit, aliud credidit. A mortali quippe homine divinitas videri non potuit. Hominem ergo vidit, et Deum confessus est, dicens: *Dominus meus, et Deus meus.*

---

[87] The identification of these figures was first made by Leeds; see Bruce-Mitford, *Aspects of Anglo-Saxon Archaeology*, p. 318.

[88] *Ibid.*, pp. 306–25 and Wilson, *Anglo-Saxon Metalwork*, pp. 91–8.

[89] Bakka, 'The Alfred Jewel', p. 279.

[90] *Homiliae in evangelia* I.ii.1 (PL 76, 1082, trans. Hurst, p. 95): 'ignorant of the brightness of the divine light ... but enlightened by the presence of its Redeemer, to see already the joys of inward light by desire'. See also Augustine, *In Iohannis evangelium*, xxxiv.9 (ed. Willems, pp. 315–16) and Ælfric, *CH* I.x (ed. Thorpe, p. 154).

Videndo ergo credidit, qui considerando verum hominem, hunc Deum, quem videre non poterat, exclamavit.[91]

Discernment was particularly associated with the eucharist, where Christ was contemplated under the appearance of bread and wine, and Ælfric devotes much of one of his Easter homilies to explaining how 'se hlaf and þæt win ðe beoð ðurh sacerda mæssan gehalgode, oðer ðing hi æteowiað menniscum andgitum wiðutan, and oðer ðing hi clypiað wiðinnan geleaffullum modum'.[92] To represent sight holding a host would therefore be an appropriate reminder of the spiritual implications of the senses.

Sight is, of course, dependent on light, and spiritual sight is therefore closely linked to the conception of the divine as light. Christ, the Word and Wisdom of God is, in the words of the Niceno-Constantinopolitan Creed, 'God from God, light from light'.[93] St John says, 'God is light; there is no darkness in him at all' (I John I.5), and of Christ: 'All that came to be had life in him and that life was the light of men, a light that shines in the dark, a light that darkness could not overpower' (John I.4–5). The author of the Epistle to the Hebrews describes Christ as 'the radiant light of God's glory and the perfect copy of his nature' (Heb. I.3), echoing the Book of Wisdom (VII.26), 'She [Wisdom] is a reflection of the eternal light, untarnished mirror of God's active power, image of his goodness.' For Bede, Christ is the invisible Light which was made flesh so that men could recognize the divine image.[94] In the Old English translation of Augustine's *Soliloquia*, God, who is light, is the father of the intelligible light through which humans come to know him: 'Ðu þe æart þæt andgitlice leoht, þurh þe man ongit.'[95] Light is equated with wisdom, or Christ:

---

91 *Homiliae in evangelia* II.xxvi.8 (PL 76, 1202, trans. Hurst, p. 207): 'He saw one thing, and he believed another. Divinity could not be seen by a mortal person. He saw a human being, and he confessed him as God, saying: "*My Lord and my God.*" Seeing he believed. He apprehended a mere man, and testified that this was the invisible God.'

92 *CH* II.xv (ed. Godden, p. 153): 'The bread and the wine that are consecrated through the priest's mass show one thing externally to human understanding and announce another thing internally to believing minds.'

93 Pelikan, *Imago Dei*, pp. 113–15.

94 *Homeliae* I.8 (ed. Hurst, p. 55). Cf. Ælfric, *CH* I.xx (ed. Thorpe, p. 282).

95 *Soliloquies* (ed. Carnicelli, p. 51): 'You who are the intelligible light through which man knows.' See also Ælfric, *CH* I.ix and xx (ed. Thorpe, pp. 150 and 282) and Augustine, *De Trinitate* IV.xx.27 (ed. Mountain, p. 196).

Þu eart fæder soðfestnesse, and wisdomes, and soþes lyfes, and þæs hehstan lyfes, and þara hehstan gesælþe, and þas hehstan goodes, and þara hehstan beorhtnesse, and þæs angitlican leohtes; ðu þe ært feder þæs suna þe us awehte and gyt wrehð of þam slepe ure synna, and us mannað þæt we to þe becumen.[96]

As the sun illuminates the body's eyes, so wisdom illuminates the eyes of the soul, leading it to the eternal sun.[97]

This image of Christ as the light played a major part in the liturgy of Christmas and of Easter. The antiphons for the Christmas season speak again and again of the light which has come into the world: 'Orietur sicut sol Salvator mundi, et descendet in uterum Virginis, sicut imber super gramen, alleluia ... Lux orta est super nos, quia hodie natus est Salvator, alleluia ... Exortum est in tenebris lumen rectis corde, misericors et justus Dominus.'[98] One of the Magnificat antiphons for the period immediately before Christmas talks of Christ as the splendour of light eternal: 'O oriens, splendor lucis aeternae, et sol iustitiae; veni, et illumina sedentes in tenebris et umbra mortis.'[99] The theme of Christ as the manifestation of the uncreated light which is the Godhead pervades the Old English poem known as *Christ I*. God's first act of creation is to separate light from darkness.[100] Gabriel announces to Mary that the Holy Spirit will shed his light on her so that she will bear the Son of God, source of all light.[101] Christ, begotten of the Father before time, comes to shed his light on the human race:

> Eala earendel,    engla beorhtast,
> ofer middangeard    monnum sended,
> ond soðfæsta    sunnan leoma,
> torht ofer tunglas,    þu tida gehwane
> of sylfum þe    symle inlihtes!
> Swa þu, god of gode    gearo acenned,

---

[96] *Soliloquies* (ed. Carnicelli, pp. 50–1): 'You are the Father of truth and wisdom, of the true life and of the highest life, and of the highest blessedness, and of the highest good, and of the highest brightness, and of the intelligible light; you who are Father of the Son who woke us and who still rouses us from the sleep of our sins and warns us to come to you.' Augustine's phrase is 'pater intelligibilis lucis', *Soliloquia* I.i.2 (PL 32, 870).

[97] *Soliloquies* (ed. Carnicelli, p. 78).

[98] *Corpus antiphonalium*, ed. Hesbert I, 32–3 and 38–9 (nos. 17b and 19c) and II, 63 and 68–9 (nos. 18 and 19d). Cf. Ælfric, *CH* I.ii (ed. Thorpe, p. 36).

[99] *Corpus antiphonalium*, ed. Hesbert I, 28–9 (no. 16a) and II, 56–7 (no. 16).

[100] *Christ I*, 224–40 (ASPR III, 9).      [101] *Ibid.*, 203–6 (ASPR III, 8).

```
sunu soþan fæder,        swegles in wuldre
butan anginne      æfre wære,
swa þec nu for þearfum        þin agen geweorc
bideð þurh byldo,        þæt þu þa beorhtan us
sunnan onsende,        ond þe sylf cyme
þæt ðu inleohte        þa þe longe ær,
þrosme beþeahte        ond in þeostrum her,
sæton sinneahtes;        synnum bifealdne
deorc deaþes sceadu        dreogan sceoldan. (Christ I 104–18)¹⁰²
```

The liturgy for the last three days of Holy Week not only talks of the extinction of the divine light through Christ's death and its return at his resurrection: it symbolizes these things through material fire and light. On the last three days of Holy Week, twenty-four candles were lit at the start of the night office and were extinguished one by one during the antiphons and responsories of the office. These candles, extinguished on three consecutive nights, represented the seventy-two hours spent by Christ in the tomb.[103] The Paschal candle, lit from the new fire during the Easter Vigil, symbolized the return of Christ, the Light of the World, and recalled the column of fire in Exodus, one of the Old Testament images of Christ.[104]

In the liturgy, as in the opening verses of St John's Gospel, the light which is Christ is contrasted with the darkness of the world. In the Creed, on the other hand, Christ is portrayed as the light which streams out from the uncreated light of the Godhead, and the emphasis is on the unity of the two.[105] The metaphor of light, therefore, has important consequences

[102] 'Oh rising light, brightest of angels sent to men throughout the world, and true light of the sun, bright above the stars, you constantly enlighten all seasons by your presence. As you, God from God, truly begotten, Son of the true Father, always existed without beginning in the glory of heaven, so now in their need your own creation dares to ask that you should send the bright sun to us, and come yourself, so that you may enlighten those who long since, surrounded by smoke and here in the gloom, have sat during the eternal night; wrapped in sins, have had to endure the dark shadow of death.' On the imagery of this passage, see Cross, 'Coeternal Beam', pp. 72–8.

[103] Ælfric, *Epistula*, viii.33 (ed. Nocent, p. 167). See also Amalarius, *Liber officialis* IV.xxii.1 (ed. Hanssens II, 472).

[104] Ælfric, *Epistula*, ix.46 (ed. Nocent, p. 173); Amalarius, *Liber officialis* I.xviii.1–2 and 6 (ed. Hanssens, II, 111 and 112).

[105] Cf. the comparisons of the Trinity to fire discussed above, pp. 34–5.

for religious art. Whereas the justification of religious art based on the Incarnation applied only to representations of the incarnate Christ, the reference to Christ as light, linked in the Epistle to the Hebrews to his status as the exact image of the Godhead (*charakter tes hypostaseos autou*, Heb. I.3), allows of representations of the invisible and uncircumscribable Godhead through the medium of images of Christ.[106]

[106] Vulgate, 'figura substantiae eius'. The words *figura* and *charakter* refer to the imprint of a seal or die; see Auerbach, 'Figura', p. 15. See also below, pp. 139, 142 and 143.

# 4

# Signs and images

Belief in the Trinity, as opposed to belief in Christ, involved assent to a concept: the paradox of three persons in a single nature. The problems of visualizing such a concept were discussed by Augustine in bk VIII of the *De Trinitate*.[1] Augustine is talking of mental rather than material images, but his argument is equally applicable to drawings or paintings. He contrasts the way in which one can relate the figure of Christ to certain general categories of existence with the impossibility of relating the Trinity to anything other than itself. Belief in gospel events such as the birth of Christ, the raising of Lazarus or Christ's ascension from the Mount of Olives is possible, 'quia secundum specialem generalemque notitiam quae certa nobis est cogitamus'.[2] As regards the Trinity, however, we can have no point of comparison:

Quid igitur de illa excellentia trinitatis sive specialiter sive generaliter novimus quasi multae sint tales trinitates quarum aliquas experti sumus ut per regulam similitudinis impressam vel specialem vel generalem notitiam illam quoque talem esse credamus, atque ita rem quam credimus et nondum novimus ex parilitate rei quam novimus diligamus? Quod utique non ita est ... Hoc ergo diligimus in trinitate, quod deus est. Sed deum nullum alium vidimus aut novimus *quia unus est deus*, ille solus quem nondum vidimus et credendo diligimus.[3]

---

[1] *De Trinitate* VIII.iv.6–v.8 (ed. Mountain, pp. 275–9).

[2] *Ibid.* VIII.v.7 (ed. Mountain, p. 277, trans. Hill, p. 247): 'because we think of them in terms of general and specific notions that we are quite certain of'.

[3] *Ibid.* VIII.v.8 (ed. Mountain, pp. 278–9, trans. Hill, p. 248): 'What then do we know, either generically or specifically, about that transcendent Trinity, as though there were many such trinities and we had experience of some of them, and thus could believe according to a standard of likeness impressed on us or in terms of specific and generic

Early attempts to represent the Trinity either depicted three identical figures (a formula which failed to convey the unity of the Godhead) or suggested the unity without showing the distinction of persons.[4] Only two images, both based on manifestations of the Trinity described in the Bible, were even partially successful. The first was based on the appearance of three men to Abraham (Gen. XVIII.1–8). Grabar gives two examples of this iconography: the mosaics at San Vitale, Ravenna and Santa Maria Maggiore, Rome.[5] The San Vitale mosaic shows three identical, haloed figures seated at table; the mosaic at Santa Maria Maggiore, which shows the arrival of Abraham's visitors, distinguishes the central figure by an oval cloud of light. Grabar interprets this central figure as Christ and the two outer figures as God the Father and God the Holy Spirit. It is possible, however, that the artist was following Irenaeus, who argued that it was the Son of God, accompanied by two angels, who appeared to Abraham.[6] Irenaeus drew a distinction between God's transcendent being and his manifestation of himself in history through his Word and his Wisdom, that is, through his Son and his Spirit,[7] and he therefore held that it was God the Son who spoke to the patriarchs, not God the Father:

It was not the Father of all, who is not visible to the world, it not the creator of all, who said 'heaven is my throne and the earth my footstool, what house shall you build for me, or where is the place of my rest?' (Isaiah LXVI.1), who holds the earth in his fist and the heavens in his palm, it is not he who would stand briefly in a small place and speak with Abraham, but the Word of God, who was always present to the human race, and told and taught human beings in advance what was to come to be concerning God.[8]

Elsewhere he says: 'Inseminatus est ubique in Scripturis eius Filius Dei: aliquando quidem cum Abraham loquens, aliquando cum Noe, dans eis

notions that that trinity is of the same sort, and hence could love the thing we believe and do not yet know from its likeness to what we do know? But this of course is simply not so ... So what we love in the Trinity is what God is. But we have never seen or known another God, because God is one, he alone is God whom we love by believing, even though we have not yet seen him.'

[4] Grabar, *Christian Iconography*, pp. 112–23.     [5] *Ibid.*, pls. 273–4.

[6] *Demonstration of the Apostolic Preaching*, 44 (trans. Robinson, p. 109). Cf. Isidore, *Quaestiones in Vetus Testamentum: in Genesin*, xiv.5–6 (PL 83, 243).

[7] Kelly, *Christian Doctrines*, pp. 104–5.

[8] *Demonstration of the Apostolic Preaching*, 45 (trans. Robinson, pp. 10–11), quoted Minns, *Irenaeus*, p. 42; the text survives only in an Armenian translation.

mensuras; aliquando autem quaerens Adam; aliquando autem Sodomitis inducens iudicium; et rursus cum videretur, et in viam dirigit Jacob, et de rubo loquitur cum Moyse.'[9] Irenaeus does not seem to have thought of these appearances as real manifestations of the *Logos*, however, for he says that Christ spoke to Abraham and Moses, 'in figura ... humana', and that Moses, Elijah and Ezekiel saw 'similitudines claritatis Domini'.[10] In the same way, Pope Leo I, who argued that the Old Testament appearances were of God the Son, not the Father, drew a distinction between these 'outward appearances' and the reality of the Incarnation:

Potuerat quippe omnipotentia Filii Dei sic ad docendos justificandosque homines apparere, quomodo et patriarchis et prophetis in specie carnis apparuit, cum aut luctamen iniit, aut sermonem conservit, cumve officia hospitalitatis non abnuit, vel etiam appositum cibum sumpsit. Sed illae imagines huius hominis erant indices, cuius veritatem ex praecedentium patrum stirpe sumendam significationes mysticae nuntiabant.[11]

Augustine pours scorn on the belief that the *Logos* appeared to men, asking how God's Son, not yet having taken flesh but still in the form of God, could have had his feet washed or sat down to eat.[12] Abraham's three visitors, he said, were an example of God's use of created beings as a sign of his presence: 'cur non hic accipiamus visibiliter insinuatam per

---

[9] *Contra haereses* IV.x.1 (PG 7, 1000, trans. Hill, *Trinity*, p. 40): 'The Son of God is scattered everywhere in the scriptures; sometimes talking to Abraham, sometimes to Noah, giving him the measurements [of the ark], sometimes looking for Adam, sometimes bringing judgement on the men of Sodom; and again when he appeared and guided Jacob on his way, and talked to Moses from the bush.' For discussion of this doctrine of the 'pre-existent Christ', see Hill, *Trinity*, pp. 39–42, and Kelly, *Christian Doctrines*, pp. 106–7.

[10] Irenaeus, *Contra haereses* IV.vii.4 and IV.xx.11 (PG 7, 992 and 1039); see also his statement, 'Adhuc enim invisibile erat Verbum', *ibid.* V.xvi.2 (PG 7, 1167) and the remark that Abraham saw Christ prophetically, *ibid.* V.i.2 (PG 7, 1122).

[11] Leo, *Epistola xxxi*, ii (PL 54, 791–2, trans. modern Roman Breviary, 17 December): 'The almighty Son of God could have come to teach and justify men with only the outward appearance of our humanity, exactly as he appeared to patriarchs and prophets. This he did when he wrestled [with Jacob], or entered into conversation, or when he did not refuse hospitable entertainment, and even partook of the food set before him. Those outward appearances pointed to this man. They had a hidden meaning which proclaimed that his reality would be taken from the stock of his forefathers.'

[12] Augustine, *De Trinitate* II.x.19–xii.22 (ed. Mountain, pp. 105–9). Cf. Bede, *Homeliae* II.21 (ed. Hurst, p. 339), who points out that Christ had no bodily parts in his divine nature.

creaturam visibilem trinitatis aequalitatem atque in tribus personis unam eandemque substantiam?'[13] Ælfric makes a similar point: 'Abraham se heahfæder underfeng þry englas on his gesthuse, on hiwe ðære halgan ðrynnysse, to ðam he spræc swa swa to anum, for ðan ðe seo halige ðrynnyss gecyndelice wunað on anre godcundnysse, æfre an God untodæledlic.'[14]

Pictures of Abraham's three visitors involved the interpretation of an Old Testament event as an image of something which would be fully revealed only in the gospels. The second image, in which the Father is represented by a hand, the Spirit by a dove and the Son by a lamb, draws on a historical event (the baptism of Christ), though without actually representing it. The three elements of the image differ in status. The voice of the Father, heard at Christ's baptism (Matt. III.16–17, Mark I.10–11 and Luke III.21–2), at the Transfiguration (Mark IX.7) and shortly before the Crucifixion (John XII.28), is symbolized by a hand, on the analogy of the many Old Testament references to God's right hand; the motif does not imply that God has a physical form.[15] The dove, which was seen by those present at Christ's baptism, is an example of the use of a created being as a vehicle for the manifestation of the divine. The motif of the lamb, which recalls the passover lamb, John the Baptist's description of Christ as the Lamb of God (John I.29), and the lamb who stands before the throne in the Apocalypse, involves a metaphor.[16] Like the representations of the Abraham episode, this composite motif emphasizes the veiled nature of the divine appearances. But whereas the image of the three men who are, at the same time, one makes some attempt to convey the inner relations of the Trinity, the images of the hand, dove and lamb draw

---

[13]  *Ibid.* II.xi.20 (ed. Mountain, p. 107, trans. Hill, p. 112): 'Why may we not take the episode as a visible intimation by means of visible creations of the equality of the triad, and of the single identity of substance in the three persons?' See also *De videndo Deo*, 23 (ed. Schmaus, p. 16): 'deus, licet non in sua natura, sed in qua voluit specie dignatus est apparere sicut Abrahae'.

[14]  *CH* II.xiii (ed. Godden, p. 133): 'The patriarch, Abraham, received three angels in his guest chamber, as a sign of the holy Trinity, to whom he spoke as though to one, because the holy Trinity exists in one divine nature, always one undivided godhead.' See also 'Preface to Genesis' (ed. Crawford, *Heptateuch*, p. 78).

[15]  Cf. Ælfric, *CH* I.xix (ed. Thorpe, p. 258), Bede, *Homeliae* I.2 (ed. Hurst, p. 12) and Augustine, *De Trinitate* I.i.1–2 (ed. Mountain, pp. 27–9).

[16]  *Ibid.* II.v.10–vi.11 (ed. Mountain, pp. 93–6). See also Ælfric, *CH* II.xv (ed. Godden, pp. 152–3).

attention to external functions appropriated to individual persons of the Trinity. They are unsatisfactory as images of the Trinity since they fail to express either the unity of action of the divine nature in relation to the created world or the relationships of the three persons to one another.[17]

Ælfric draws attention to this unity of action, and to the great gulf between the divine and the human, in his 'De fide catholica':

Nu mage ge, gebroðru, understandan, gif ge wyllað, þæt twa ðing syndon: an is Scyppend, oðer is gesceaft. He is Scyppend seðe gesceop and geworhte ealle ðing of nahte. Þæt is gesceaft þæt se soða Scyppend gesceop. Þæt sind ærest heofonas, and englas þe on heofonum wuniað, and syððan þeos eorðe mid eallum ðam ðe hire on eardiað, and sæ mid eallum ðam þe hyre on swymmað. Nu ealle ðas ðing synd mid anum naman genemnode, gesceaft. Hi næron æfre wunigende, ac God hi gesceop. Þa gesceafta sind fela. An is se Scyppend þe hi ealle gesceop, se ana is Ælmihtig God. He wæs æfre, and æfre he bið þurhwunigende on him sylfum and ðurh hine sylfne. Gif he ongunne and anginn hæfde, butan tweon ne mihte he beon Ælmihtig God; soðlice þæt gesceaft ðe ongann and gesceapen is, næfð nane godcundnysse; forði ælc edwist þætte God nys, þæt is gesceaft; and þæt þe gesceaft nis, þæt is God.[18]

Created beings are distinct from God not only because they are dependent on him, having been formed by him: they are many and various, whereas God is one; they have nothing of the divine in them. They do, however, reflect the divine beauty. The Book of Wisdom tells how, 'through the grandeur and beauty of the creatures we may, by analogy, contemplate their Author' (Wisdom XIII.5), a point echoed by St Paul: 'Ever since God created the world his everlasting power and deity – however invisible – have been there for the mind to see in the things he has made' (Rom.

---

[17] See further below, pp. 106 and 143–4.

[18] Ælfric, *CH* I.xx (ed. Thorpe, p. 276): 'Now you brothers may understand, if you will, that there are two things: one is the Creator, the other is creation. He is the Creator who formed and made all things from nothing. That is creation which the true Creator formed, that is, first, the heavens and angels who live in the heavens, and afterwards this earth with all that lives within it, and the sea with all those things that swim in it. Now all these things are called by the one name, creation. They did not always exist, but God formed them. Those created things are many. The Creator who formed them all is one, he alone is almighty God. He always existed and he will always remain in himself and through himself. If he came into being and had an origin, then without doubt he could not be almighty God; truly that creation that began and was formed has nothing divine about it; therefore every substance that is not God is a creature, and that which is not created, that is God.'

I.20). Augustine frequently quotes Paul's words,[19] linking them specifically to the Trinity:

Oportet igitur ut creatorem *per ea quae facta sunt intellecta conspicientes* trinitatem intellegamus cuius in creatura quomodo dignum est apparet *vestigium*. In illa enim trinitate summa origo est rerum omnium et perfectissima pulchritudo et beatissima delectatio.[20]

Ælfric, too, talks of God's glory as something which is revealed through his works: 'Se ælmihtiga Scippend geswutelode hine sylfne þurh þa micclan weorc ðe he geworhte æt fruman, and wolde þæt ða gesceafta gesawon his mærða.'[21] He makes the same point in the *Hexameron*: 'He geswutelode his mihta ðurh ða gesceafta, and wolde ðæt ða gesceafta gesawon his mærða.'[22] By contemplating created things, therefore, one's mind could rise to contemplation of the invisible realities of which they were a reflection.

The beauty to which Augustine referred was the harmony, order and proportion of a world created by measure, number and weight (Wisdom XI.21).[23] These properties of the created world derive from the archetypal ideas in the mind of God and reflect his triune nature. In contemplating the beauty of creation, therefore, one is concerned with the principles of number and measure rather than their material reality.[24] But in trying to rise above the material, one is faced with the unbridgeable gap between the traces of the divine to be found in created things and the divine nature

---

[19] E.g. *De Trinitate* II.xv.25, IV.xvi.21, XIII.xix.24, XV.i.1 and ii.3 (ed. Mountain, pp. 114, 188, 416, 460 and 462).

[20] *Ibid.* VI.x.12 (ed. Mountain, p. 242 and trans. Hill, p. 213): 'So then, as we direct our gaze at the creator by *understanding the things that are made* (Rom. I.20), we should understand him as triad, whose traces appear in creation in a way that is fitting. In that supreme triad is the source of all things, and the most perfect beauty, and wholly blissful delight.' See also *De civitate Dei* VIII.vi (ed. Dombart and Kalb, pp. 222–4), *Byrhtferth's Enchiridion* (ed. Baker and Lapidge, pp. 6 and 196), Harrison, *Beauty and Revelation*, pp. 97–139, and below, p. 139.

[21] 'On the Old and New Testament' (ed. Crawford, *Heptateuch*, pp. 16–17): 'The almighty Creator manifested himself through the great work which he did in the beginning, and wished that created beings should see his greatness.'

[22] *Exameron Anglice* (ed. Crawford, p. 36): 'He showed his power through created things and wished that creatures should see his greatness.'

[23] Harrison, *Beauty and Revelation*, pp. 101–12.

[24] Augustine, *De Genesi ad litteram* IV.iv (ed. Zycha, pp. 100–1).

itself. God, the source of measure, number and weight, is himself above any such concepts:

We sprecað ymbe God, deaðlice be Undeaðlicum, tyddre be Ælmihtigum, earmingas be Mildheortum; ac hwa mæg weorðfullice sprecan be ðam ðe is unasecgendlic? He is butan gemete, forðy ðe he is æghwær. He is butan getele, forðon ðe he is æfre. He is butan hefe, forðon þe he hylt ealle gesceafta butan geswince; and he hi ealle gelogode on þam ðrim ðingum, þæt is on gemete, and on getele, and on hefe. Ac wite ge þæt nan man ne mæg fullice embe God sprecan, þonne we furðon þa gesceafta þe he gesceop ne magon asmeagan, ne areccan ... Hwylc wundor is, gif se Ælmihtiga God is unasecgendlic and unbefangenlic, seðe æghwær is eall, and nahwar todæled?[25]

Ælfric maintains that humans are quite incapable of crossing that gap and understanding or even speaking intelligibly about God. The author of the Old English poem known as *Prayer* goes even further. Drawing, perhaps, on St Paul's prayer in the Epistle to the Ephesians (Ephes. III.14–21) and Zophar's rebuke to Job (Job XI.7–9), the poet moves from an expression of man's inability to understand the mystery of God to wonder at God's understanding of himself:

> Ne mæg þe aherian    hæleða ænig;
> þeh us gesomnie    geond sidne grund,
> men ofer moldan,    geond ealne middaneard,
> ne mage we næfre asæcgan,    ne þæt soðe witan,
> hu þu æðele eart,    ece drihten.
> Ne þeah engla werod    up on heofenum
> snotra tosomne    sæcgan ongunnon,
> ne magon hy næfre areccan,    ne þæt gerim wytan,

[25] Ælfric, *CH* I.xx (ed. Thorpe, p. 286): 'We speak about God, mortals about the immortal, the weak about the almighty, wretched about the merciful; but who can adequately speak of the one who is unspeakable? He is without measure, for he is everywhere. He is without number for he is eternal. He is without weight for he holds all creation without labour; and he established everything through those three things, that is, by measure, number and weight. But you must know that no man can adequately speak about God when we cannot even think about or reckon the things that he created ... What wonder is it if almighty God is indescribable and uncircumscribable, who is everywhere entire and nowhere divided?' Cf. Hippolytus, *Sermo in sancta Theophania*, ii: 'Qui ubique praesens est nec usquam abest, incomprehensibilis angelis et ab hominum conspectu remotus' (PG 10, 854), Augustine, *De Genesi ad litteram* IV.iii (ed. Zycha, p. 99), and John Scotus, *Periphyseon* III (ed. Sheldon-Williams, p. 58).

hu þu mære eart,       mihtig drihten.
Ac is wunder mycel,       wealdend engla,
gif þu hit sylfa wast,       sigores ealdor,
hu þu mære eart,       mihtig and mægenstrang,
ealra kyninga kyning,       Crist lifiende,
ealra worulda scippend,       wealdend engla,
ealra dugeþa duguð,       drihten hælend.       (*Prayer* 30–44)[26]

The *vestigia Dei*, apparent in creation as a whole, are to be distinguished from the divine image imprinted on the human race at its
creation.[27] In the *De Genesi ad litteram* Augustine applied St Paul's words
in the Epistle to the Romans to creation generally. In the final book of
the *De Trinitate* he gradually narrows his definition of 'the things he
[God] has made' until he reaches the image of the Trinity in the human
soul.[28] He argues, first, that statements about the Creator based on
inferences from his creation must apply to the one divine nature, whose
actions are inseparable, and therefore cannot help in understanding the
Trinity.[29] Only an image based on relationship can do this. Secondly, he
makes a distinction between knowledge (*scientia*) and wisdom (*sapientia*).[30] Wisdom, which involves an actual sharing in God himself, is
won by contemplating what is eternal, namely the image according to

---

[26] ASPR VI, 95, and Raw, *Art and Background*, pp. 124–6: 'Nor can any hero praise you;
though he summon us men from across the broad deep, over the earth, from the whole
world, we can never say or know the truth, how noble you are, eternal lord. Nor indeed
can the armies of angels up in heaven, the company of wise ones, begin to say, nor can
they ever reckon or compute how famous you are, mighty lord. But it is a great
wonder, ruler of angels, lord of victory, if you yourself know how famous you are,
mighty and strong, king of all kings, living Christ, creator of all worlds, lord of angels,
glory of all glories, lord and saviour.' For the idea that God cannot understand himself
– that is, he does not know *what* he is, because he is not a *what* – see John Scotus,
*Periphyseon* II (ed. Sheldon-Williams, pp. 140–8, 152 and 162–4).

[27] For creation as mirroring the divine, see Augustine, *De Trinitate* VI.x.12, XV.i.1 and
ii.3 (ed. Mountain, pp. 242–3, 460 and 462), and *Confessiones* X.vi.10 (ed. Verheijen,
p. 160); for man as the image of God see *De Trinitate* IX.i.1–v.8 and XV.xxii.42 (ed.
Mountain, pp. 292–301 and 519–20); see also *De Trinitate* XV.xx.39 (ed. Mountain,
pp. 516–17).

[28] *De Trinitate* XV.i.1 (ed. Mountain, p. 460, trans. Hill, p. 395): 'In pursuance of our
plan to train the reader, *in the things that have been made* (Rom. I.20), for getting to know
him by whom they were made, we came eventually to his image.'

[29] *Ibid.* XV.iv.6–vii.13 (ed. Mountain, pp. 467–79).

[30] *Ibid.* XII.xv.25, XIII.i.2 and XIV.viii.11 (Mountain, pp. 379–80, 381–2 and 435–8).

which man was created.[31] As St Paul says, 'You have put on a new self which will progress towards true knowledge the more it is renewed in the image of its creator' (Col. III.10) and 'We, with our unveiled faces reflecting like mirrors the brightness of the Lord, all grow brighter and brighter as we are turned into the image that we reflect' (II Cor. III.18). For Augustine, this mirror was the human mind. Commenting on St Paul's statement, 'Now we are seeing a dim reflection in a mirror; but then we shall be seeing face to face' (I Cor. XIII.12), he says: 'Quale sit et quod sit hoc speculum si quaeramus, profecto illud occurrit quod in speculo nisi imago non cernitur. Hoc ergo facere conati sumus ut per hanc imaginem quod nos sumus videremus utcumque a quo facti sumus tamquam *per speculum*.'[32]

The link between redemption and contemplation described by St Paul was embodied in one of the most common of early medieval allegories, that of the earthly and heavenly cities. Paul contrasted the earthly city of Jerusalem with the heavenly one, the true home of Christians (Gal. IV.21–31). Later writers exploited the etymology of the names Jerusalem and Sion. Jerusalem means vision of peace, an appropriate name for the heavenly city.[33] Sion is normally interpreted to mean contemplation. Hilary, for example, says: 'nominis Sion interpretatio est speculatio' and 'mons Sion mons speculationis est'.[34] Isidore says, 'Ipsa est et Sion, quae Hebraice interpretatur speculatio, eo quod in sublimi constructa sit, et de longe venientia contempletur. Hierusalem [autem] pacifica in nostro sermone transfertur.'[35] Augustine interprets Sion as a symbol of the Church, which looks forward to the age to come. Commenting on Psalm XLIV, he identifies the queen who stands at Christ's right as follows: 'Ipsa est Sion spiritaliter; quod nomen Latine interpretatum speculatio est; speculatur enim futuri saeculi magnum bonum, quoniam illuc dirigitur

---

[31] *Ibid.* XV.iii.5 (ed. Mountain, pp. 466–7).

[32] *Ibid.* XV.viii.14 (ed. Mountain, p. 479, trans. Hill, p. 405): 'If we ask what kind of mirror this might be, the thought occurs to us that the only thing ever seen in a mirror is an image. So what we have been trying to do is somehow to see him by whom we were made by means of this image which we ourselves are, as through a mirror.'

[33] *Blickling Homilies*, no. vi (ed. Morris, pp. 79–81).

[34] Hilary, *Tractatus super Psalmos*, Ps. CXXIV.3 and 4 (ed. Zingerle, p. 599).

[35] Isidore, *Etymologiae* XV.i.5 (ed. Lindsay): 'She is Sion, which in Hebrew means looking, because she is built on high and is contemplated by those coming from afar. Jerusalem in our language means peaceful.'

eius intentio.'[36] Ælfric interprets the name in the same way. Talking of Christ's entry to Jerusalem, he says:

Sion is an dun, and heo is gecweden, Sceawungstow; and Hierusalem, Sibbe gesihð. Siones dohtor is seo gelaðung geleaffulra manna, þe belimpð to ðære heofonlican Hierusalem, on þære is symle sibbe gesihð, butan ælcere sace, to ðære us gebrincð se Hælend, gif we him gelæstað.[37]

The monastic life, characterized by its focus on the heavenly Jerusalem, was described as 'vita speculativa' in contrast to the 'vita negotiativa' of lay people.[38] It was therefore concerned with seeing. Augustine, however, was quite clear that the direct contemplation of the divine which humans seek is only possible through the intellect: physical sight and the spiritual sight which derives from it are useless from this point of view.[39] In the *De videndo Deo*, he distinguishes between physical and mental sight, contrasting things that happened, which are perceptible through the senses and are transmitted by witnesses, with faith in a God who is unseen and can be contemplated only with the eyes of the mind (*oculi mentis*).[40] In his *De civitate Dei*, he points out that we do not understand the inner image of the Trinity through the external senses or via the immaterial images derived from them.[41] At the same time, his comparison of the Trinity to the soul's activities of remembering, understanding and willing, and his claim that God is present in the human memory, suggests that there is some resemblance between the way in which one remembers and contemplation of the Godhead.[42]

Augustine discussed human memory at length in the *Confessiones*,

[36] *De civitate Dei* XVII.xvi (ed. Dombart and Kalb, p. 581, trans. Bettenson, p. 747): 'This queen is Sion, in the spiritual sense. The name Sion means contemplation; for she contemplates the great blessing of the age to come, since all her striving is directed to that end.' See also *Enarrationes in Psalmos*, lxiv.3 (ed. Dekkers and Fraipont, p. 825).

[37] Ælfric, *CH* I.xiv (ed. Thorpe, p. 210): 'Sion is a hill, and it is interpreted, Place of contemplation; and Jerusalem is called Vision of peace. Sion's daughter is the assembly of believing men, which belongs to the heavenly Jerusalem, in which there is the constant sight of peace without any conflict, to which our Saviour will bring us if we follow him.'

[38] Leclercq, 'Vocabulaire monastique', pp. 84–5 and 93–9.

[39] Chazelle, 'Matter, Spirit and Image', p. 175, Augustine, *De Genesi ad litteram* XII.vi–xiv (ed. Zycha, pp. 386–400) and *LC* III.xxvi (ed. Bastgen, pp. 160–1).

[40] *De videndo Deo* (ed. Schmaus, pp. 9, 24 and 33).

[41] Augustine, *De civitate Dei* XI.xxvi (ed. Dombart and Kalb, p. 345).

[42] *De Trinitate* XIV.xi.14 (ed. Mountain, pp. 441–2). As Augustine recognized, he was

describing it first as a storehouse for images conveyed to it by the senses, each sense-impression entering through a different gate and being stored in a separate place. In addition, memory contains things such as facts, feelings and general laws and principles, which are perceptible only through the mind. Because animals, too, are able to remember things, Augustine tries to find God by passing beyond memory but concludes that this is impossible because he cannot find or recognize something of which he has no memory. Yet God is not present in the memory as the image of some material thing, or as an emotion, nor is he part of the human mind and its self-awareness. Augustine concludes, therefore, that his awareness of God must come from God himself.[43] The memory of God and the image of God are therefore both imprints which derive from God.

This link between the divine image and the images within the memory, is expressed in a metaphor used for both: the imprint of a seal on wax or the stamp on a coin. Augustine, talking of sense impressions, says:

Neque enim cum anulus cerae imprimitur ideo nulla imago facta est quia non discernitur nisi cum fuerit separata. Sed quoniam post ceram separatam manet quod factum est ut videri possit, propterea facile persuadetur quod inerat iam cerae forma impressa ex anulo et antequam ab illa separaretur. Si autem liquido humori adiungeretur anulus, eo detracto nihil imaginis appareret. Nec ideo tamen discernere ratio non deberet fuisse in illo humore antequam detraheretur anuli formam factam ex anulo, quae distinguenda est ab ea forma quae in anulo est unde ista facta est quae detracto anulo non erit, quamvis illa in anulo maneat unde ista facta est.[44]

Memories are essentially mental images which can be scanned and read by

---

using the word 'memory' in an unusual way, to imply a kind of self-awareness rather than the recollection of things from the past.

[43] *Confessiones* X.viii–xxvi (ed. Verheijen, pp. 161–75).

[44] *De Trinitate* XI.ii.3 (ed. Mountain, pp. 336–7, trans. Hill, pp. 305–6): 'When a signet ring is imprinted in wax, it does not mean that there is no image of it just because it cannot be made out until the wax is removed. But when the wax is removed, what took place in it remains and can be seen, and so one is easily persuaded that the form impressed by the ring was in the wax even before it was removed from it. If the ring however is put to the surface of a liquid, no image of it appears when it is taken away. Still, that does not mean one cannot infer by reason that before the ring was taken away its form was in the liquid and there derived from the ring; and that this form is to be distinguished from the form which is in the ring, from which this one is derived that will cease to be when the ring is taken away, even though that one which produced this one will remain in the ring.'

the eye of the mind: 'Quae vestigia tamquam imprimuntur memoriae quando haec quae foris sunt corporalia sentiuntur ut etiam cum absunt ista, praesto sint tamen imagines eorum cogitantibus.'[45] This visual element is true of memories however they were formed. Augustine, for example, says:

Ad oculos enim proprie videre pertinet. Utimur autem hoc verbo etiam in ceteris sensibus, cum eos ad cognoscendum intendimus. Neque enim dicimus: audi quid rutilet, aut: olefac quam niteat, aut: gusta quam splendeat, aut: palpa quam fulgeat: videri enim dicuntur haec omnia. Dicimus autem non solum: vide quid luceat, quod soli oculi sentire possunt, sed etiam: vide quid sonet, vide quid oleat, vide quid sapiat, vide quam durum sit.[46]

The one example of a reference to the ear of the mind rather than the eye of the mind is the opening words of the Benedictine Rule: 'Obsculta, O fili, praecepta magistri et inclina aurem cordis tui.'[47]

Just as memories are considered as imprints which, like the imprints of a seal, preserve the form of the prototype, so it is with the divine image in Christ and in the human soul. Augustine distinguishes the perfect image, namely Christ, from the imperfect one seen in the human soul by comparing them to the king's image in his son and on a coin.[48] Bede, too, used the image of the coin in his commentary on the tribute money of

---

[45] *Ibid.* X.viii.11 (ed. Mountain, p. 325, trans. Hill, p. 295): 'These traces are as it were imprinted on the memory when these bodily things outside are perceived by the senses, so that even when these things themselves are absent their images are available to be thought about.' See also *ibid.* XI.ii.3, XI.ii.6–iv.7 (ed. Mountain, pp. 336 and 339–43).

[46] Augustine, *Confessiones* X.xxxv.54 (ed. Verheijen, p. 184, trans. Pine-Coffin, pp. 241–2): 'Although, correctly speaking, to see is the proper function of the eyes, we use the word of the other senses too, when we employ them to acquire knowledge. We do not say "Hear how it glows", "Smell how bright it is", "Taste how it shines", or "Feel how it glitters", because these are all things which we say that we see. Yet we not only say "See how it shines" when we are speaking of something which only the eyes can perceive, but we also say "See how loud it is", "See how it smells", "See how it tastes", and "See how hard it is".' See also *De videndo Deo*, 7 (ed. Schmaus, p. 8) and *De Trinitate* XI.i.1 (ed. Mountain, p. 334).

[47] *Benedicti regula* (ed. Hanslik, p. 1). See also Carruthers, *Book of Memory*, pp. 16–17, 21 and 27.

[48] Augustine, *Sermo ix*, viii.9 (PL 38, 82). See also his discussion of *imago*, *aequalitas* and *similitudo*, *De diversis quaestionibus*, l, li and lxxiv (ed. Mutzenbecher, pp. 77–82 and 213–14).

Mark XII.17: 'Quemadmodum Caesar a vobis exigit impressionem imaginis suae sic et Deus ut quemadmodum illi redditur nummus sic Deo anima lumine vultus eius illustrata atque signata.'[49] For Dionysius, the metaphor of the seal implies the equal participation of each of the three persons of the Trinity in the one Godhead:

This is unified and one and common to the whole divinity, that the entire wholeness is participated in by each of those who participate in it; none participates in only a part ... Take the example of a seal. There are numerous impressions of the seal and these all have a share in the original prototype; it is the same whole seal in each of the impressions and none participates in only a part.[50]

And just as the seal gives itself totally each time it is used, even though its imprint may differ according to the substance which receives it, so the divine image remains the same even in an alien substance such as human nature.[51]

Because memories were considered as visual traces, however they originated, techniques of memorization tended to rely on visual patterns. The written arts of memory are all later than the Anglo-Saxon period but there are many indications that similar techniques existed at this time.[52] Alcuin talks of storing figures in the treasury of the mind; Ælfric drew on this material in his *Lives of the Saints*.[53] The poem *Widsith* begins, 'Widsið maðolade, wordhord onleac' and the poet of *The Wanderer* (13–14) says that it is a noble custom in a man 'þæt he his ferðlocan fæste binde, healde his hordcofan'.[54] Byrhtferth compares himself to the bee gathering nectar, a common metaphor for memorization.[55] The poet of *The Order of the World* (19–20) tells his reader or listener, 'bewritan in gewitte wordhordes

---

[49] Bede, *In Marcum*, xii (ed. Hurst, p. 588): 'Just as Caesar demands from us the imprint of his image, so too will God; just as the coin is surrendered to the one, so God must receive back the soul adorned and sealed with the light of his countenance.' See also *Homeliae* I.6 (ed. Hurst, pp. 38–9).

[50] Ps.-Dionysius, *The Divine Names*, ii.5 (trans. Luibheid, p. 62).

[51] *Ibid.*, ii.6 (trans. Luibheid, p. 63).

[52] Carruthers, *Book of Memory*, p. 144. See also Raw, 'Verbal Icons', pp. 132–4.

[53] *De animae ratione*, vii (PL 101, 642) and *LS* I.i (ed. Skeat I, 18 and 24). See Godden, 'Anglo-Saxons on the Mind', pp. 273 and 279.

[54] ASPR III, 149: 'Widsith spoke, unlocked his word-hoard', and *ibid.*, p. 134, 'that he should bind fast his heart, hold fast the treasury of his mind'.

[55] *Byrhtferth's Enchiridion* (ed. Baker and Lapidge, p. 128).

cræft, fæstnian ferðsefan'.[56] Alfred talks of learning through visual signs in his translation of Augustine's *Soliloquia*: 'Ða eagan me gebrodton on þam angytte. Ac siðþan ic hyt þa ongyten hæfde, þa forlet ic þa sceawunga mid þam eagum and þohte; forði me þuhte þæt ic his mæahte micle mare geþencan ðonne ic his mahte geseon, siððan þa eagan hyt ætfæstnodon minum ingeþance.'[57] The Blickling homilist describes how the material traces of Christ's ascension, in particular the imprint of his feet, act as prompts to the memory.[58]

One very common method of memorizing a series of items consisted in placing them against an image of a building or landscape.[59] Other mnemonic devices were diagrams such as those in Byrhtferth's *Enchiridion*,[60] the drawing of the paschal hand in the Leofric Missal,[61] or the arrangement of references in the canon tables at the beginning of gospel-books.[62] Finally, pictures acted as mnemonics. The drawings in the Utrecht Psalter, which illustrate the text phrase by phrase, can remind one of the words of the psalms.[63] The idea that pictures prompt the memory was accepted even by the authors of the *Libri Carolini*, who were in general opposed to any form of religious art.[64] The belief that pictures might help the viewer recall the presence of God, on the other hand, was specifically condemned: God was everywhere, they said, and there was no need for images of him; Christ, too, should be present in one's heart and there should be no need to recall him.[65] According to the *Libri Carolini*, then, pictures lead to memory, though not to God; their main function is to record historical events.[66]

[56] ASPR III, 164: 'write the word-hoard's craft in the mind, fasten it within the thought'. See Lerer, *Literacy and Power*, pp. 114–15.

[57] Alfred, *Soliloquies* (ed. Carnicelli, p. 61): 'The eyes brought me understanding. But after I had perceived those things, I abandoned looking with my eyes and thought; because it seemed to me that I could understand much more of it than I could see once the eyes had fastened it in my mind.'

[58] *Blickling Homilies*, no. xi (ed. Morris, pp. 125–9).

[59] Carruthers, *Book of Memory*, pp. 71–9.

[60] See the diagrams in the edition of Baker and Lapidge.

[61] Oxford, Bodleian Library, Bodley 579, 49r (reprod. Temple, *Anglo-Saxon Manuscripts*, pl. 54).

[62] Carruthers, *Book of Memory*, pp. 139 and 248.     [63] *Ibid.* pp. 226–7.

[64] *LC* III.xvi and IV.ii (ed. Bastgen, pp. 138 and 176).

[65] *Ibid.* III.xv and IV.ii (ed. Bastgen, pp. 135 and 176); see also II.xii and II.xxii (Bastgen, pp. 73 and 81).

[66] *Ibid.* II.xxvii and III.xxiii (ed. Bastgen, pp. 88–9 and 153).

Augustine, who is usually remembered for his statement that pictures and writing are grasped in different ways,[67] was more ambivalent. The walls of his basilica at Hippo were decorated with paintings, including one of the stoning of Stephen and the conversion of Paul which he used as the focus of a sermon.[68] The picture was accompanied by an inscription which allowed all who saw it to learn as if from a book.[69] Elsewhere he talks of the contrast between dark and light shades in paintings, or of the way in which a painter selects the right colours to depict a human face.[70] He was well aware of the beauty of artistic creations but he saw them as temptations which distract the mind from the divine beauty.[71] Yet at the same time he thanks God for human creation:

At ego, deus meus et decus meum, etiam hinc tibi dico hymnum et sacrifico laudem sanctificatori meo, quoniam pulchra traiecta per animas in manus artificiosas ab illa pulchritudine veniunt, quae super animas est, cui suspirat anima mea die ac nocte. Sed pulchritudinem exteriorum operatores et sectatores inde trahunt approbandi modum, non autem inde trahunt utendi modum.[72]

In the *Soliloquia* he groups paintings and portraits together with the images seen in a mirror and the figures seen in dreams. He distinguishes between the natural image in the mirror and the artificial one in the painting but at the same time he sees a resemblance between them. Both are both true and false: true images but false men.[73] Since he compares the

---

[67] Augustine, *In Iohannis evangelium*, xxiv.2 (ed. Willems, pp. 244–5). For discussion of this passage and Ælfric's translation of it, see Gameson, 'Script and Picture', pp. 85–6 and 90–1.

[68] *Sermo cccxvi*, v (PL 38, 1434).      [69] Augustine, *Sermo cccxix*, viii (PL 38, 1442).

[70] *De civitate Dei* XI.xxiii (ed. Dombart and Kalb, p. 342), *Epistola xxix*, 11 (PL 33, 120), and *Sermo cxxv* (PL 38, 692–3). On the contrast between light and dark, see also Ælfric, *CH* I.xxiii (ed. Thorpe, p. 334).

[71] *Confessiones* X.xxxiv.51 (ed. Verheijen, p. 182).

[72] *Ibid.* X.xxxiv.53 (ed. Verheijen, pp. 183–4, trans. Pine-Coffin, p. 241): 'But, O my God, my Glory, for these things too I offer you a hymn of thanksgiving. I make a sacrifice of praise to him who sanctifies me, for the beauty which flows through men's minds into their skilful hands comes from that Beauty which is above their souls and for which my soul sighs all day and night. And it is from this same supreme Beauty that men who make things of beauty and love it in its outward forms derive the principle by which they judge it: but they do not accept the same principle to guide them in the use they make of it.'

[73] Augustine, *Soliloquia* II.vi.11–x.18 (PL 32, 889–93).

divine image in the human soul to a reflection in a mirror,[74] it is at least possible that he could have accepted a painted image of the Trinity, but, like the image in the soul, it would have been an imperfect image:[75] a symbol rather than a portrait.

Augustine's understanding of signs or symbols was that they had no direct connection with something beyond themselves: they were merely triggers which prompted mental processes.[76] Other writers saw signs differently. Pseudo-Dionysius, the Areopagite, whose works were translated into Latin by John Scotus in the ninth century, and whose theory of a hierarchy of images influenced John of Damascus's defence of images, took a different view.[77] The stress placed by Dionysius on God's absolute transcendence and unknowability means that he considered not only visible forms but also names and concepts as inadequate expressions of the reality.[78] It was precisely because God was unknowable, even through the intellect, that images of all kinds were necessary. For Dionysius, as for St Paul, God reveals himself through his creation which exhibits a hierarchy of forms.[79] Dionysius defines hierarchy (one of his key terms) as follows:

A hierarchy is a sacred order, a state of understanding and an activity approximating as closely as possible to the divine. And it is uplifted to the imitation of God in proportion to the enlightenments divinely given to it ... The goal of a hierarchy, then, is to enable beings to be as like as possible to God and to be at one with him. A hierarchy ... is forever looking directly at the comeliness of God. A hierarchy bears in itself the mark of God. Hierarchy causes its members to be images of God in all respects, to be clear and spotless mirrors reflecting the glow of primordial light and indeed of God himself.[80]

Talking of the ecclesiastical hierarchy, which itself is an image of the celestial one, he says:

---

[74] See above, p. 85.     [75] See above, p. 36.

[76] Augustine, *De doctrina christiana* II.i.1–iii.4 (ed. Martin, pp. 32–4).

[77] Barasch, *Icon*, pp. 158–82, and Chenu, *Nature, Man and Society*, pp. 124–7.

[78] Dionysius, *The Divine Names*, i.1–2 and ix.1–10, *The Mystical Theology* and *The Celestial Hierarchy*, ii.3 (trans. Luibheid, pp. 49–50, 115–19, 135–41 and 149). Cf. Augustine's statement that the divine image in the human soul is merely an image, and not to be confused with the reality: *De Trinitate* XV.xxiii.44 (ed. Mountain, p. 522), quoted above, p. 36.

[79] *The Divine Names*, iv.4, *The Celestial Hierarchy*, i.3 and *Letter Nine*, 2 (trans. Luibheid, pp. 75, 146 and 284). See also McGinn, *Foundations of Mysticism*, p. 161.

[80] *The Celestial Hierarchy*, iii.1–2 (trans. Luibheid, pp. 153–4).

Using images derived from the senses they spoke of the transcendent. They passed on something united in a variegation and plurality. Of necessity they made human what was divine. They put material on what was immaterial. In their written and unwritten initiations, they brought the transcendent down to our level. As they had been commanded to do they did this for us, not simply because of the profane from whom the symbols were to be kept out of reach, but because, as I have already stated, our own hierarchy is itself symbolical and adapted to what we are. In a divine fashion it needs perceptible things to lift us up into the domain of conceptions.[81]

Even material and incongruous symbols are useful in lifting the mind to the immaterial; they may even be better than conceptual images, since there is less likelihood of their being confused with the reality:

Using matter, one may be lifted up to the immaterial archetypes. Of course one must be careful to use the similarities as dissimilarities, as discussed, to avoid one-to-one correspondences, to make the appropriate adjustments as one remembers the great divide between the intelligible and the perceptible ... The mysterious theologians employ these things not only to make known the ranks of heaven but also to reveal something of God himself ... They honor the dissimilar shape so that the divine things remain inaccessible to the profane and so that all those with a real wish to see the sacred imagery may not dwell on the types as true.[82]

Dionysius does not talk of works of art as images of the divine. However, he does draw a parallel between the contemplative, fixing his gaze on God, and the artist who keeps his eye on his subject: in both cases, the result is the creation of an exact image of the original, either through a material work of art or an image within the mind.[83] Moreover, as Dionysius's translator, John Scotus, said several times, God is an artist and humans, who create works of art, are also images of the Creator and therefore sharers in his artistic work:

Nam quemadmodum filium artem omnipotentis artificis vocitamus – nec immerito quoniam in ipso, [sua] quippe sapientia, artifex omnipotens pater ipse omnia quaecumque voluit fecit aeternaliterque et incommutabiliter custodit – ita etiam humanus intellectus quodcumque de deo deque omnium rerum principiis

---

[81] *The Ecclesiastical Hierarchy*, i.5 (trans. Luibheid, p. 199); see also *ibid.*, i.2 (Luibheid, p. 197) and *The Celestial Hierarchy*, ii.2–3 and ii.5 (Luibheid, pp. 148–9 and 152–3).

[82] *The Celestial Hierarchy*, ii.4–5 (trans. Luibheid, p. 152). See also *Letter Nine* (*ibid.*, pp. 280–8), and cf. Augustine, *De doctrina christiana* III.vi.10–ix.13 (ed. Martin, pp. 83–6).

[83] *The Ecclesiastical Hierarchy*, iv.3 (trans. Luibheid, pp. 225–6).

purissime incunctanterque percipit veluti in quadam arte sua, in ratione dico, mirabili quadam operatione scientiae creat per cognitionem inque secretissimis ipsius sinibus recondit per memoriam.[84]

Like John, the writers of the Anglo-Saxon period frequently described God's creation of the world through the metaphor of an artist or craftsman. In *Christ I* God is portrayed as an architect who will come to earth and rebuild the ruined house of mankind:

> Nu is þam weorce þearf
> þæt se cræftga cume     ond se cyning sylfa,
> ond þonne gebete,     nu gebrosnad is,
> hus under hrofe.               (*Christ I* 11–14)[85]

The created world is God's jewelled and ornamented work.[86] Augustine, too, compares the beauty of the created world to the colours on a painter's palette which will be applied to a painting.[87]

For Augustine, the aim was to rise above these sense impressions to a purely intellectual apprehension of the divine. For Dionysius, on the other hand, the divine nature was so completely other that humans needed the support of material images: 'The heavenly beings, because of their intelligence, have their own permitted conceptions of God. For us, on the other hand, it is by way of the perceptible images that we are uplifted as far as we can be to the contemplation of what is divine.'[88] This statement,

---

[84] John Scotus, *Periphyseon* II (ed. and trans. Sheldon-Williams, pp. 120–1): 'As we call the Son the art of the almighty Artist, and not unreasonably, since in Him, as in [His] Wisdom, the almighty Artist, the Father Himself, has made all things whatsoever He desired and preserves [them] eternally and immutably in Him, so also the human intellect, through the act of knowing, creates, by a wonderful operation of its science, whatsoever it most clearly and unambiguously receives from God, and from the principles of all things in its art, as it were, I mean, in its reason, and by means of the memory stores [it] in its most secret recesses.' See also *ibid.* I (p. 64) and III (pp. 64 and 116–18).

[85] ASPR III, 3: 'Now it is necessary for the work that the craftsman should come and the king himself and make good what is now ruined, the house beneath its roof.'

[86] *Menologium* 207 (ASPR VI, 54), *Christ II* 692 and *Guthlac* 1212 (ASPR III, 22 and 83), and *Genesis* 956 and 2191 (ASPR I, 31 and 66).

[87] Augustine, *De diversis quaestionibus*, xlv (ed. Mutzenbecher, p. 67) and *Sermo cxxv* (PL 38, 692–3); see Harrison, *Beauty and Revelation*, pp. 138–9.

[88] *Ecclesiastical Hierarchy*, i.2 (trans. Luibheid, p. 197). For discussion, see Freedberg, *Images*, pp. 164–6.

together with the Dionysian concept of hierarchy, underlies the justification of images in the writings of John of Damascus.

In the third of his orations in defence of icons, John argues that the icon, in the sense of a painting, forms the sixth and final stage in a series of images of the divine.[89] The primary image is Christ, the perfect copy of God's nature; (Heb. I.3); below this comes man, created in the image and likeness of God (Gen. I.26–7). These images were very different, however: the first, eternal and invisible, sharing the divine nature, the second, visible and temporal, an image through grace and adoption. To bridge this gulf between creator and created, John inserted a further set of images: the archetypal ideas in the mind of God.[90] He is drawing here on Dionysius, who says: 'We give the name of "exemplar" to those principles which pre-exist as a unity in God and which produce the essences of things. Theology calls them predefining, divine and good acts of will which determine and create things and in accordance with which the Transcendent One predefined and brought into being everything that is.'[91] The influence of Dionysius is seen again in John's fourth class of images, 'the shadows and forms and types of invisible and bodiless things which are described by the Scriptures in physical terms. These', says John, 'give us a faint apprehension of God and the angels where otherwise we would have none, because it is impossible for us to think immaterial things unless we can envision analogous shapes'.[92] John's fifth group of images is, again, biblical: the types and prefigurations of the Old Testament. These five groups of images are all examples of imprints of the divine. In linking religious paintings to this sequence, therefore, John asserts that they, too, have some real relationship to the divine; they are not mere signs.

Anglo-Saxon literature does not include a detailed and coherent theory of images comparable to that of John of Damascus or to the very different view set out in the *Libri Carolini*.[93] It seems unlikely, however, that they were unaware of the arguments about religious art which were taking

---

[89] *De imaginibus III*, 18–23 (PG 94, 1337–44, trans. Anderson, pp. 74–8).

[90] *Ibid.*, 19 (PG 94, 1340, trans. Anderson, pp. 75–6). See also *De imaginibus I*, 10 (PG 94, 1240–1, trans. Anderson, pp. 19–20).

[91] *The Divine Names*, v.8 (trans. Luibheid, p. 102).

[92] *De imaginibus III*, 21 (PG 94, 1341, trans. Anderson, p. 76). Cf. Dionysius, *Ecclesiastical Hierarchy*, i (trans. Luibheid, pp. 195–200).

[93] For the latter, see Chazelle, 'Matter, Spirit and Image'.

place in the East and in the Carolingian empire. They were certainly familiar with image theology, for the nature of the divine image in Christ and in man forms a major theme in the writings of Ælfric.[94] They were also familiar with the concept that created things derived from the archetypal images in God's mind. The idea is found in the writings of both Boethius and Gregory the Great,[95] and Ælfric talks several times of God as a craftsman creating from the ideas in his mind. In a homily on the opening verses of St John's Gospel he says:

> Ðu sceawast þa heofonan and sunnan and monan;
> hi synd on þam cræfte, we cweðað nu swutelicor,
> on þam Godes wisdome, þe is witodlice lif.[96]

The Old Testament images which form John of Damascus's fourth and fifth categories – the use of words referring to material items to symbolize God and the use of Old Testament types – are basic to Ælfric's exposition of scripture.[97] It is also possible that Ælfric knew something of Dionysius's ideas via the writings of John Scotus. John's Homily on the Prologue to St John's Gospel was included in three Anglo-Saxon copies of Paul the Deacon's Homiliary,[98] and the ideas in his *Periphyseon* attracted a good deal of attention on the Continent, particularly at Corbie, which had links with Æthelwold's monastery at Abingdon and could therefore have provided a route for their transmission to England.[99]

For John of Damascus, as for Dionysius, physical forms were necessary

---

[94] See above, pp. 35–8.

[95] *Philosophiae consolatio* IV.vi.12 (ed. Bieler, p. 80) and the Old English version of Gregory's Dialogues, IV.vi (ed. Hecht, pp. 269–70), a reference I owe to Malcolm Godden.

[96] *Homilies*, no. i (ed. Pope I, 208): 'You look at the heavens and the sun and the moon; they exist in the [artist's] conception, as we will now say more clearly, in the Wisdom of God which is truly life.' Cf. Ælfric, 'On the Old and New Testament' (ed. Crawford, *Heptateuch*, p. 17): 'Se ræd wæs æfre on his rædfæstum geþance, þæt he wircan wolde þa wundorlican gesceafta.' The lines are probably based on Augustine, *In Ioannis evangelium*, i.17 (ed. Willems, p. 10): 'Terram vides; est in arte terra. Caelum vides; est in arte caelum. Solem et lunam vides; sunt et ista in arte', see Pope, *Homilies* I, 208 and 224. See also Raw, 'Verbal Icons', p. 138.

[97] See esp. *CH* I.xxv (ed. Thorpe, p. 358).

[98] Gneuss, 'Preliminary List', nos. 16, 424 and 763 (James Cross, private communication); Ritzke-Rutherford, *Light and Darkness*, pp. 124–9, suggests that Ælfric also knew John's *Periphyseon*.

[99] On the influence of John Scotus, see Marenbon, *Circle of Alcuin*, pp. 88, 97–8 and

because human nature cannot grasp what is divine except through images and analogies:

Visible things are corporeal models which provide a vague understanding of intangible things. Holy Scripture describes God and the angels as having descriptive form, and the same blessed Dionysius teaches us why. Anyone would say that our inability immediately to direct our thoughts to contemplation of higher things makes it necessary that familiar everyday media be utilized to give suitable form to what is formless, and make visible what cannot be depicted, so that we are able to construct understandable analogies.[100]

The passage from Dionysius to which John refers comes in *The Divine Names*:

We now grasp these things in the best way we can, and as they come to us, wrapped in the sacred veils of that love towards humanity with which scripture and hierarchical traditions cover the truths of the mind with things derived from the realm of the senses. And so it is that the Transcendent is clothed in the terms of being, with shape and form on things which have neither, and numerous symbols are employed to convey the varied attributes of what is an imageless and supra-natural simplicity.[101]

These material images of the divine, then, are both an example of God's love and a form of knowledge.[102]

When John of Damascus quoted Gregory of Nyssa's statement, 'The beauty of divinity cannot be pictured with beautiful forms or bold colours, but is perceived in unutterable blessedness, in virtue of its excellence. Therefore human forms are what painters transfer to the canvas using various colours, adding suitable and harmonious tints to the image, trying with precision to capture in the image the beauty of its archetype',[103] he was thinking of paintings of Christ. But, in this system of symbols which could stand in place of the invisible God, representations of Christ, the perfect image of God, could act as signs in the same way as the common

---

100–1. Æthelwold invited monks from Corbie to teach the chant at Abingdon; see *Wulfstan of Winchester*, ed. Lapidge and Winterbottom, p. lxxxiii.

100  *De imaginibus I*, 11 (PG 94, 1241, trans. Anderson, p. 20).

101  *The Divine Names*, i.4 (trans. Luibheid, p. 52).

102  *De imaginibus III*, 17 (PG 94, 1337, trans. Anderson, p. 74).

103  *De imaginibus I* (PG 94, 1269, trans. Anderson, p. 40). The passage is from Gregory's *De hominis opificio*, v (PG 44, 137); see also the translation by John Scotus (ed. Cappuyns, pp. 213–14).

device of the *dextera Dei*. The distinction is one which would have been well understood by Eusebius of Caesarea, who criticized Constantia for asking him to send her an image of Christ and yet spoke with approval of a statue showing Christ as the Good Shepherd.[104] The word used by Eusebius for the first kind of representation is *charakter*, a term derived from the imprint of a die on a coin or of a seal on wax; when used of a painting it implies that it derives in some direct way from its model. The figure of the Good Shepherd, on the other hand, is described as a *symbolon*, a symbol.[105] Like the verbal symbols described by Dionysius, it helps us to understand what we believe. It does not simply mediate between the divine and the human: it forces the observer to reflect on the relationship between the symbol and what it symbolizes. Whereas representations of gospel events stir the memory, the image of Christ which is also an image of the Godhead provokes reflection on the theology of the Incarnation and of the God who is at the same time One and Three. It structures and directs our thoughts.

[104] Barasch, *Icon*, pp. 143–55.    [105] *Ibid.*, pp. 152–3, and above, p. 76.

# 5

# God in history

The distinction drawn by Eusebius between portrait-images and symbolic representations (which included narrative pictures as well as symbols in the strict sense)[1] corresponds to a distinction between different forms of revelation. The portrait-image implies a presence, a relationship with a person, which corresponds to God's revelation of himself in the person of his Son. The narrative picture recalls God's interventions in history. Symbolic representations correspond to various indirect forms of revelation: the prophecies of the Old Testament; figures such as Abraham and Joshua, and events like the crossing of the Red Sea or the water struck from the rock, whose deeper meaning became apparent only at a later date; material objects like the dove at Christ's baptism or the fire of Pentecost; the liturgy and the sacraments.[2] The distinction between these different modes of revelation is reflected in the poetry of the Anglo-Saxons and in late Anglo-Saxon manuscript art. The verse adaptations of parts of Genesis, Exodus and Daniel in the Cædmon Manuscript, Junius 11 in the Bodleian Library, are primarily narrative works which recount biblical history from the creation of the world, via the covenants with Noah and Abraham and the Exodus from Egypt, to the exile in Babylon.[3] By contrast, the poem *Christ and Satan*, which forms the second part of the manuscript, focuses on a post-Resurrection world in which the human race confronts its destiny in a choice between heaven and hell; here, the creation of the world, Satan's rebellion against God, his expulsion from heaven and man's fall, which were described in narrative form in the first

[1] Barasch, *Icon*, pp. 148–55; see also above, p. 98.
[2] For an account of different forms of revelation, see Nichols, *Art of God Incarnate*, pp. 107–12.
[3] Oxford, Bodleian Library, Junius 11, pp. 1–212 (ASPR I, 3–132).

part of the manuscript (*Genesis* 1–938), are merely reminiscences on the part of Satan.[4] Other Old English poems on New Testament subjects are similar.[5] *Christ I*,[6] for example, does not tell the story of the Nativity; instead, it relates Christ's birth in time to the longing of the patriarchs and prophets for the coming of the Messiah, to the longing of the Church during the liturgical season of Advent, to praise of the Trinity and to celebration of the wonderful exchange by which the creator of the world became man, expressed in the antiphon: 'O admirabile commercium! Creator generis humani, animatum corpus sumens, de virgine nasci dignatus est; et procedens homo sine semine, largitus est nobis suam deitatem.'[7] The poem *The Dream of the Rood*[8] places Christ's death at the centre of redemption history and relates the cross, the tree of life, to the dreamer's need for forgiveness and protection. It is a meditation on the relationship of Christ's death to God's eternal plan, rather than an account of Christ's passion. In *The Descent into Hell*[9] Christ's resurrection is set within the medieval context of the Easter liturgy and its baptismal symbolism. *Christ II*[10] presents Christ's return to heaven at his ascension as both a promise and a warning to his followers.

Manuscript decoration follows a similar pattern. The vernacular versions of parts of the Old Testament in Junius 11 and Cotton Claudius B. iv are accompanied by extensive sets of narrative illustrations;[11] most Anglo-Saxon gospelbooks, on the other hand, are illustrated with evangelist portraits, with images of Christ, saints and angels placed above the canon tables, or with pictures of the Crucifixion or of the enthroned Christ. Only two gospelbooks and gospel-lectionaries from late Anglo-Saxon England contain narrative scenes: the Boulogne Gospels includes a small group of pictures of the Annunciation, Visitation and Nativity at the beginning of St Matthew's Gospel while the Getty fragments are probably the remains

---

[4] Junius 11, pp. 213–29 (*ibid.*, pp. 135–58).

[5] Raw, 'Biblical Literature', pp. 227–32.

[6] ASPR III, 3–15, and Burlin, *Old English Advent*.

[7] *Corpus antiphonalium*, ed. Hesbert I, 60–1 (no. 23b) and II, 94–5 (no. 23b): 'O wonderful exchange: the Creator of the human race, taking a living body, deigns to be born of a Virgin; and becoming man without human seed, has bestowed on us his divinity.'

[8] ASPR II, 61–5.

[9] ASPR III, 219–23. For discussion, see Raw, 'Why does the River Jordan Stand Still?'

[10] ASPR III, 15–27.

[11] Reprod. Gollancz, *Cædmon Manuscript* and *Hexateuch*, ed. Dodwell and Clemoes.

of a fully illustrated gospel-lectionary, comparable to the lavishly illustrated gospelbooks produced in Ottonian Germany.[12] Anglo-Saxon
manuscripts do, of course, include examples of scenes from the gospels but
they are found in liturgical manuscripts rather than in gospelbooks, in
particular the Benedictional of Æthelwold and the Bury and Tiberius
Psalters.[13]

Pictures of gospel events record things which were visible to those who
were present at the time. But whereas Christ had a form, a material
existence which could be pictured, the God of the Old Testament had no
form, no physical existence. John of Damascus says: 'How can the invisible
be depicted? How does one picture the inconceivable? How can one draw
what is limitless, immeasurable, infinite? How can a form be given to the
formless? How does one paint the bodiless? How can you describe what is
a mystery?'[14] Yet the Old Testament talks of God walking in the garden
with Adam, telling Noah how to build the ark or conferring with
Abraham, as though it were describing a material being. Moses and his
companions are said to have seen 'the God of Israel beneath whose feet
there was, it seemed, a sapphire pavement' (Exodus XXIV.10) and Moses
himself talked with God face to face, as a man talks to his friend (Exodus
XXXIII.11). Isaiah saw the Lord seated on his throne, surrounded by
seraphs (Isaiah VI.1–3), Daniel watched as one 'like a son of man'
approached 'the one of great age' who was seated on the throne (Daniel
VII.9–14) and, in New Testament passages based on these descriptions, St
John is said to have seen God enthroned in heaven (Apoc. IV.2–V.14 and
XX.11–12).

Augustine discussed these different kinds of vision in the *De Genesi ad*

---

12 Boulogne, Bibliothèque municipale, 11, and Malibu, California, J. Paul Getty
Museum, 9 (reprod. Ohlgren, *Textual Illustration*, pls. 5.1–28, and Temple, *Anglo-
Saxon Manuscripts*, pls. 173–6). For examples of Ottonian gospel illustrations, see Mayr-
Harting, *Ottonian Book Illumination* I, 57–117 and II, 70–83, Trier, Stadtbibliothek, 24
(reprod. Schiel, *Codex Egberti*) and Munich, Bayerische Staatsbibliothek, Clm. 4453
(reprod. Dressler, Mütherich and Beumann, *Das Evangeliar Ottos III*).

13 BL, Additional 49598 (colour reproductions of all miniatures in Deshman, *Benedic-
tional*), Vatican, Biblioteca Apostolica Vaticana, Regin. lat. 12 (reprod. Ohlgren,
*Textual Illustration*, pls. 3.1–49), and BL, Cotton Tiberius C. vi (reprod. Wormald,
*Collected Writings* I, pls. 124–54).

14 *De imaginibus I*, 8 (PG 94, 1237–40, trans. Anderson, p. 18). See also *ibid.*, 4, 7 and 16
and *De imaginibus II*, 7 (PG 94, 1236–7, 1245 and 1288, Anderson, pp. 16–17, 23
and 54).

*litteram* and concluded that Moses saw some material object which acted as a sign of something else, while Isaiah and John saw what he calls, 'spiritual visions': that is, mental images which lead to intellectual understanding.[15] In the *De Trinitate* he concludes, after lengthy and detailed consideration, that the Old Testament appearances of God were symbols of the divine; they were not manifestations of the divine persons themselves.[16] His conclusion is similar to that of John of Damascus, who held that Old Testament figures such as Abraham, Moses or Isaiah saw images of God, not the divine essence.[17] John contrasts this seeing with that of the New Testament: 'I have seen God in human form, and my soul has been saved. I gaze upon the image of God, as Jacob did (Gen. XXXII.30), but in a different way. For he only saw with spiritual sight what was promised to come in the future, while the memory of Him who became visible in the flesh is burned into my soul.'[18]

The question of the appearances of God to the patriarchs has clear implications for religious art. The artists of the Vienna Genesis and of the eleventh- and twelfth-century Greek Octateuchs represented the God of the Old Testament symbolically, by the *dextera Dei*; the artists of the sixth-century Cotton Genesis, on the other hand, showed him in human form, first as a curly-haired youth holding a cross-staff and, later, as an older, bearded figure.[19] Weitzmann and Kessler interpret these figures as conveying a theological distinction: the curly-haired youth in the creation scenes represents the Christ-*Logos*, God's agent in creation; the bearded figure of the later scenes represents God the Father, the author of the 'covenantal relationships' with the patriarchs.[20] This distinction is not maintained in later versions of the Cotton cycle of pictures: the artist of the Salerno antependium consistently shows the God of the Old Testament as a bearded figure, holding a scroll;[21] the artists of the Carolingian Bibles, on the other hand, represent the creator as a long-haired, beardless figure,

---

[15] *De Genesi ad litteram* XII.iv and x–xii (ed. Zycha, pp. 383–4 and 392–7).

[16] Augustine, *De Trinitate* II.vii.12–xviii.35 and III.x.27 (ed. Mountain, pp. 96–126 and 158). See also *De videndo Deo*, 13–14 and 18–19 (ed. Schmaus, pp. 10–11 and 12–14), and above, pp. 79–80.

[17] *De imaginibus II*, 20, and *III*, 24–6 (PG 94, 1308 and 1344–5, trans. Anderson, pp. 65 and 78–82).

[18] *De imaginibus I*, 22 (PG 94, 1256, trans. Anderson, pp. 30–1).

[19] Weitzmann and Kessler, *Cotton Genesis*, pp. 41–2.     [20] *Ibid.*, p. 37.

[21] E.g. Weitzmann and Kessler, *ibid.*, pls. 9, 13, 15 and 18.

holding a scroll or staff but without any specifically Christological features such as a cruciferous nimbus or cross-staff.[22] The throned figure of Ezekiel's vision which forms the frontispiece to the books of the Prophets in the San Callisto Bible is similar,[23] whereas the Christ of the gospel frontispieces in the Vivian and San Callisto Bibles is portrayed as bearded,[24] and it is possible that the artists were making a distinction between the incarnate Christ (bearded) and the Godhead (beardless).

Anglo-Saxon artists seem to have had no coherent method of depicting the God of the Old Testament. The illustrations to the Old English Hexateuch, Cotton Claudius B. iv, indicate God's presence by the *dextera Dei*, by a bearded figure and, occasionally, by a youthful, beardless figure. Some figures have a cruciferous nimbus, some a plain one and some, none at all; in two places (3v and 7v) the bearded figure carries a cross-staff, a motif usually associated with youthful, Christ-type images. The first artist of Junius 11 represents the Almighty both with and without a beard, sometimes with a cruciferous nimbus, sometimes with no nimbus at all. The second artist, who illustrates parts of the stories of Noah and Abraham, invariably represents God as a beardless, curly-haired youth.[25] It is possible that he was copying the model of the pictures more faithfully than the first artist, but, if this is the case, it implies a model where God was portrayed as a Christ-like figure throughout the Genesis story.[26]

There is some support for this hypothesis about the model of the Junius 11 drawings in the picture of the burial of Moses in Cotton Claudius B. iv. The Bible states that God buried Moses: 'There in the land of Moab, Moses the servant of Yahweh died as Yahweh decreed; he buried him in the valley, in the land of Moab, opposite Beth-peor; but to this day no one has ever found his grave' (Deuteronomy XXXIV.5–6). The text of the Old English Hexateuch manuscript follows the Bible account, as does Ælfric in his treatise on the Old and New Testament: 'Moises se mæra, mid þam þe he wæs on ylde hundtwentig wintra, ða gewat he of life, and

22 BL, Additional 10546, 5v, Paris, BN, fonds latin 1, 10v and Rome, San Paolo fuori le Mura, Bible, 8v (reprod. Kessler, *Illustrated Bibles*, pls. 1, 3 and 4).

23 San Paolo fuori le Mura, Bible, 117r (reprod. Kessler, *ibid.*, pl. 70).

24 BN, fonds latin 1, 329v and San Paolo fuori le Mura, Bible, 259v (reprod. Kessler, *ibid.*, pls. 49–50).

25 Junius 11, pp. 73–88.

26 For the evidence that both artists were copying from the same model, see Raw, 'Probable Derivation', pp. 137–9.

God silf hine bebirigde.'[27] In Jewish legends an angel was substituted for the figure of God, a detail preserved in the illustrations to the Octateuchs and in the frontispiece to Deuteronomy in the Carolingian San Callisto Bible.[28] The illustration of the death of Moses in the Old English Hexateuch manuscript is closely related to the San Callisto painting but with one major change: Moses is led up the mountain and laid in his grave by a youthful, beardless figure with a cruciferous nimbus.[29]

But despite these examples of what is usually thought of as a Christ-type figure, it seems very unlikely that the Anglo-Saxons believed that the Old Testament appearances were of Christ rather than God the Father. Ælfric, in fact, seems to imply the contrary. Almighty God, he says, revealed the mysteries of the creation to Moses on Mount Sinai and dictated the first five books of the Old Testament to him; Christ then revealed the spiritual meaning of these things to his disciples.[30] Ælfric stresses the deep spiritual meaning of the Old Testament,[31] yet in some ways he presents it in a very literal way. In his 'De initio creaturae' and in his treatise 'On the Old and New Testament' he follows the Bible in describing God forming Adam with his hands, locking Noah and his family into the ark, coming down from heaven to inspect the tower of Babel, and burying Moses.[32] His only reference to an Old Testament appearance of God the Son seems to be that in the story of Nebuchadnezzar and the three children in the fiery furnace, where he interprets the fourth figure in the furnace, described in the Bible as an angel (Daniel III.25–92), as God the Son: 'Se feorða is gelic Godes bearne. Þa geseah se

---

[27] Ælfric, 'On the Old and New Testament' (ed. Crawford, *Heptateuch*, p. 31): 'When the renowned Moses was a hundred and twenty years old, he left this life and God himself buried him.' For the text of Deuteronomy XXXIV.5–6, see Crawford, p. 375.

[28] San Paolo fuori le Mura, Bible, 50 (lxviiii)v (reprod. Mütherich and Gaehde, *Carolingian Painting*, pl. 43). For discussion of the scene, see Gaehde, 'Carolingian Interpretations', pp. 371–5.

[29] BL, Cotton Claudius B. iv, 139v (reprod. Dodwell and Clemoes).

[30] *Exameron Anglice* (ed. Crawford, pp. 34–5).

[31] Ælfric, 'Preface to Genesis' (ed. Crawford, *Heptateuch*, pp. 77 and 79).

[32] *CH* I.i (ed. Thorpe, pp. 16, 20 and 22); 'On the Old and New Testament' (ed. Crawford, *Heptateuch*, pp. 20, 24–5 and 31). The illustrations in both Claudius B. iv and Junius 11 depict God in an equally material way: placing the sun and moon in the sky, drawing Eve from Adam's side, closing the door of the ark or descending a ladder to view the tower at Babel (Claudius B. iv, 3r, 6v and 19r; Junius 11, pp. 9, 66 and 68).

hæðena cyning þone lifigendan Godes sunu, and he hine gecneow ðurh Godes onwrigenysse.'[33] The expansion of the Latin, 'et species quarti similis filio Dei', into a vision of Christ suggests more than simple mechanical following of the word 'similis', though Ælfric need not have thought of an actual appearance of a 'pre-existent' Christ: when he talks of Isaiah's vision of God he describes it as a spiritual vision.[34] At the same time, however, he sees both Old and New Testaments as revelations of the Trinity:

> Eall seo ealde gesetnyss     ðe we ær embe spræcon
> and se Hælend sylf     on his halgan godspelle
> cyðað ða halgan ðrynnysse     on soðre annysse,
> ænne ælmihtigne God     æfre unbegunnenne,
> se ðe næfre ne geendað.[35]

The prime example of this revelation was God's creation of the world through his wisdom and his will: words symbolizing the Son and the Holy Spirit.[36] The artist of the Old English Hexateuch, who depicted the creation in a very literal way, showed a single figure who could be either God the Father or God the Son; other artists attempted to portray creation by all three persons of the Trinity. The first artist of the Cædmon Manuscript compressed the story of creation into three images which form a kind of triptych.[37] These drawings have a different format from the narrative illustrations which surround them and probably derive from a different source.[38] The central image (p. 7) shows a bearded figure, enclosed in a mandorla and holding a book in the left hand while blessing with the right; below are plants, a bird and a stag, symbolizing the creation of plants, animals and birds on the third, fifth and sixth days of

---

[33] *CH* II.i (ed. Godden, p. 10): 'The fourth is like the Son of God. Then the heathen king saw the Son of the living God, and recognized him through God's revelation.' In *CH* I.xxxvii (Thorpe, p. 570), on the other hand, he describes the fourth figure as an angel.

[34] 'On the Old and New Testament' (ed. Crawford, *Heptateuch*, pp. 68–9): 'on his gastlican gesihðe'.

[35] Ælfric, *Exameron Anglice* (ed. Crawford, p. 40): 'All the Old Testament, about which we spoke before, and the Saviour himself in his holy gospel, speak of the holy Trinity and true Unity, one almighty God, without beginning, who will never end.'

[36] 'On the Old and New Testament' (ed. Crawford, *Heptateuch*, p. 17) and *CH* I.i (ed. Thorpe, p. 10).

[37] Junius 11, pp. 6–7 (reprod. Gollancz, *Cædmon Manuscript*).

[38] Raw, 'Probable Derivation', pp. 136–7.

creation (Gen. I.11–12, 20–1 and 24). The two outer scenes[39] show a youthful, beardless figure with no mandorla but accompanied by an angel holding a bowl from which light pours down. Christ is regularly described as the light of God,[40] and it seems likely that the pictures are intended to represent creation by the Trinity, the central figure representing God the Father, and the two outer figures God the Son and God the Holy Spirit.

Other artists represented the creation of the world in purely diagrammatic form. In a drawing in the Tiberius Psalter (pl. Ib) the world is shown as a circle; above is a head, surrounded by a jewelled fillet and a cruciferous nimbus and with twin trumpets emerging from its mouth; to the sides of the world-circle are two hands, one of which holds compasses and scales. Within the circle is a representation of the separation of the waters above and below the firmament and of the Spirit, in the form of a dove, moving on the waters (Gen. I.2 and 6–8). A drawing in the Royal Bible is similar, though here the hands holding scales and compasses are placed within the circle of the world.[41] A third example of the iconography, though without the dove, appears in the Bury Psalter, opposite Psalm LX, where it illustrates the prayer of Hezekiah,[42] and a diminished version is seen above the canon tables in the Eadwig Gospels, where a hand holding compasses and scales appears opposite a representation of God in the form of a human bust with a cross behind the head.[43] These drawings illustrate God's creation through number, measure and weight:

Who was it measured the water of the sea in the hollow of his hand and calculated the dimensions of the heavens, gauged the whole earth to the bushel, weighed the mountains in scales, the hills in a balance? (Isaiah XL.12)[44]

Measure is symbolized by the compasses and weight by the scales,

---

[39] Pl. Ia and Junius 11, p. 7 (reprod. Gollancz, *Caedmon Manuscript*).

[40] See above, p. 73.

[41] BL, Royal 1. E. VII, 1v (reprod. Temple, *Anglo-Saxon Manuscripts*, pl. 319). On the iconography, see Heimann, 'Three Illustrations', pp. 46–56.

[42] Biblioteca Apostolica Vaticana, Regin. lat. 12, 68v (reprod. Ohlgren, *Textual Illustration*, pl. 3.21). For Hezekiah, see II Kings XX.4–6 and Isaiah XXXVIII.4–6.

[43] Hanover, Kestner Museum, WM xxia 36, 9v and 10r (reprod. Ohlgren, *Textual Illustration*, pls. 8.1–2).

[44] See also Wisdom XI.21, 'You ordered all things by measure, number, weight'; quoted by Byrhtferth (*Byrhtferth's Enchiridion*, ed. Baker and Lapidge, pp. 6 and 196) and by Ælfric, *CH* I.xx (ed. Thorpe, p. 286). As Heimann notes ('Three Illustrations', p. 48), the passage from Wisdom is also used by Augustine, Isidore and Hrabanus.

suggesting that the two horns which emerge from God's mouth must represent number.[45] But God also created through his word, that is, through Christ, the Word of God, or, as the Psalms say:

> By the word of Yahweh the heavens were made,
> their whole array by the breath of his mouth.     (Ps. XXXII.6)

Ælfric quotes this verse with reference to creation by the Trinity in his homily on the opening of St John's Gospel,[46] and the idea is echoed in the Advent antiphon, 'O Sapientia, quae ex ore Altissimi prodisti, attingens a fine usque ad finem, fortiter suaviter disponensque omnia.'[47] These diagrams, therefore, illustrate creation by the Trinity, God the Father being shown in human form, God the Son as the Word proceeding from his mouth, and the Holy Spirit by the traditional symbol of the dove.

It is noteworthy that the Tiberius creation image occurs in a psalter rather than a copy of Genesis, though the related image in the Royal 1. E. VII Bible does preface the text of Genesis. Whereas the Book of Genesis was considered primarily as history, though with a strong typological dimension, the psalter was classified as prophecy and everything in it was read with reference to Christ.[48] It is natural, therefore, that both the Bury Psalter and the Harley copy of the Utrecht Psalter should include numerous representations of gospel events, which act as a commentary on and interpretation of the psalter text.[49] In addition, both manuscripts include vivid depictions of God intervening in human affairs to save the righteous or afflict the wicked. The artists of the Harley Psalter usually represent him as a Christ-like figure with a cruciferous nimbus, though sometimes only the *dextera Dei* is shown. In the Bury Psalter God appears in various guises. An illustration to Psalm VIII.6, 'You have made him little less than a god, you have crowned him with glory and splendour' (25r) shows a bearded figure with cruciferous nimbus crowning a young man. On 32r a similar figure girds a sword on to a younger, haloed man,

---

[45] Heimann, *ibid.*, p. 52.

[46] *Homilies*, no. i (ed. Pope I, 200–1). The verse is also quoted by Jerome in relation to Isaiah XL.12: *In Esaiam* XI (ed. Adriaen, p. 461).

[47] *Corpus antiphonalium*, ed. Hesbert I, 28–9 (no. 16a) and II, 56–7 (no. 16): 'O Wisdom, who came from the mouth of the Most High, reaching from end to end and ordering all things mightily and sweetly.'

[48] *Enarrationes in Psalmos*, Ps. XCVIII (ed. Dekkers and Fraipont II, 1378).

[49] Regin. lat. 12 and BL, Harley 603 (both fully reproduced in Ohlgren, *Textual Illustration*, pls. 3.1–49 and 2.1–102).

illustrating the verse, 'This God who girds me with strength and makes my way without blame' (Ps. XVII.33). Psalm XII.4, 'Give my eyes light, or I shall sleep in death' (28r) is illustrated by a youthful, Christ-like figure with cross-staff and cruciferous nimbus, who thrusts a torch down over the head of the psalmist. In the drawing of the Crucifixion (35r), God the Father is represented by the *dextera Dei* extended over Christ's head. On the following folio, by contrast, he is symbolized by a youthful, halo-less figure who emerges from a mandorla to hand shield and spear to the psalmist below. The representation of the *rex gloriae* of Psalm XXIII.8, usually interpreted as a reference to Christ's triumphal entry into heaven at the Ascension, shows a crowned figure, armed with shield and spear, with no obvious Christological attributes (37v). Similarly, the blessing figure whom the psalmist addresses on 69v (Ps. LXII.2) is clearly intended to represent the God for whom the psalmist thirsts, yet the figure has no halo or mandorla. The same is true of the figure on 81r, who stands on a coiled dragon and holds symbols of day and night to illustrate the words, 'God, my king from the first ... you crushed Leviathan's heads ... you are master of day and night, you instituted light and sun' (Ps. LXXIII.12–16).[50] As was the case with the illustrations to the Genesis texts described earlier, the artist of the Bury Psalter seems to have seen no need to distinguish between God the Father and God the Son, possibly because, like Augustine, he believed that all Old Testament appearances were symbolic and that it is unnecessary to decide whether they were manifestations of one of the divine persons rather than another.[51]

There can be no such confusion over the identity of the figures in the gospel scenes of the Benedictional of Æthelwold, the Sacramentary of Robert of Jumièges and the Tiberius Psalter. The Sacramentary contains three short narrative sequences of scenes, associated with the masses for the Nativity, Epiphany and Holy Saturday, in addition to representations of the Ascension and Pentecost; it may also have included illustrations, now lost, for Palm Sunday and the Feast of the Purification.[52] The first group of scenes includes representations of the annunciation to the shepherds and of the flight into Egypt as well as one of the scene at the manger. The illustrations for the Feast of Epiphany show Herod consulting the priests

---

[50] Ohlgren, *ibid.*, pls. 3.5, 3.11, 3.7, 3.12, 3.13, 3.14, 3.22 and 3.30.

[51] See above, p. 102.

[52] Rouen, Bibliothèque municipale, Y. 6 [274] (reprod. Temple, *Anglo-Saxon Manuscripts*, pls. 237–40, and *Missal of Robert of Jumièges*, ed. Wilson).

and scribes, the journey of the Magi and the angel's warning as well as the
scene of the Adoration itself. The pictures for Holy Saturday show the
betrayal of Christ and the deposition from the cross in addition to the
more usual scenes of the Crucifixion and the Maries at the tomb.[53]
Whereas the gospel scenes in the Harley and Bury Psalters acted as a form
of commentary, drawing attention to the prophetic meaning of the text,
the scenes in the Sacramentary link the events taking place in the church
to events from the past, allowing those who see them to take part in the
gospel events, at least in imagination. They therefore have a meditative
function rather than an exegetical one.

The paintings in the Benedictional of Æthelwold serve a similar
purpose in that they link liturgical commemoration to historical event,
but they lack the narrative context of the pictures in the Sacramentary and
the choice and arrangement of the pictures suggests that, in addition to
the royal and monastic themes to which Robert Deshman has drawn
attention,[54] there is an emphasis on the events in which Christ's divine
nature was manifested: the Annunciation, the Adoration of the Magi, the
Baptism, the presentation in the Temple, the appearance to Thomas and
the Ascension.[55] In contrast, there are no representations of the temptation
of Christ, the Last Supper, the washing of the disciples' feet, the arrest of
Christ or his death on the cross, even though the text of the blessings
mentions these events.[56] It is possible that the artists of the Benedictional
did not have access to pictures of these scenes, but this seems unlikely
since they are illustrated in the Drogo Sacramentary, which provides
parallels to many details in the Benedictional.[57] Examples were certainly

[53] Rouen, Bibliothèque municipale, Y. 6 [274], 32v–33r, 36v–37r and 71r–72v (all
reprod. in Wilson, *Missal of Robert of Jumièges*).

[54] Deshman, *Benedictional*, pp. 170–214.

[55] BL, Additional 49598, 5v, 24v, 25r, 34v, 56v and 64v (Deshman, *Benedictional*, pls. 8,
18–20 and 24–5). On the events of Christ's life as signs, see Ælfric, *CH* I.vii and ix
(ed. Thorpe, pp. 104, 136 and 144–6).

[56] The relevant texts in the Benedictional are at 41r–42r (Quadragesima and 1 in Lent,
the temptation), 46r–48v (Palm Sunday, with a reference to the Passion) and 48v–49v
(Maundy Thursday, with references to the meal and the washing of feet), ptd Warner
and Wilson, *Benedictional*, pp. 14–15 and 17–19.

[57] BN, fonds latin 9428, 41r (Quadragesima, the three temptations), 43v (Palm Sunday,
Crucifixion) and 44v (Maundy Thursday, the Last Supper and the arrest). For a
complete facsimile, see Koehler and Mütherich, *Drogo-Sakramentar*.

available later in the Anglo-Saxon period and were used by the artists of the Sacramentary of Robert of Jumièges and of the Tiberius Psalter.[58]

The artists of the Benedictional drew attention to the significance of the gospel events as theophanies through two main symbols. The first is the cloud which envelops Gabriel and Mary in the Benedictional's illustration of the Annunciation (5v) and which Deshman sees as a reminiscence of the cloud through which God manifested himself in his Old Testament appearances. This theme of the divine storm-cloud is taken up again in the painting of the Second Coming (pl. III) where Christ is shown coming in the clouds, with rays of light streaming from his body.[59] The second symbol is the mandorla. The motif is common in representations of the Ascension or of Christ enthroned in heaven but the Benedictional is unusual in depicting Christ within a mandorla at the Baptism and the appearance to Thomas.[60] The second of these pictures illustrates the disciple's recognition of Christ's divine nature when, having placed his hand in Christ's wounds, he exclaims, 'My Lord and my God' (John XX.28), and the mandorla indicates that Christ was both human and divine, though his divine nature was invisible except to the eyes of faith.[61] Epiphany was pre-eminently a celebration of God's manifestation,[62] and Ælfric speaks of a three-fold revelation: to the kings, at the Baptism and at the marriage at Cana. The kings, he says, knew Christ to be man when they asked about his birth, to be a king when they referred to him as such and to be God when they prayed to him, knowledge reflected in their gifts of gold for a king, frankincense for God and myrrh for one who was mortal.[63] The symbolism of the Baptism, and of the Benedictional's picture of it, is more complex. In most early representations of the

---

[58] Rouen, Bibliothèque municipale, Y. 6 [274] (reprod. Wilson, *Missal of Robert of Jumièges*) and London, BL, Cotton Tiberius C. vi (reprod. Wormald, *Collected Writings* I, pls. 124–54). The St Augustine's Gospels, CCCC 286, 125r, also contains an extensive series of passion pictures, including the Last Supper, the washing of the feet and the betrayal by Judas (Wormald, *ibid.*, pl. 1 and Henderson, *Losses and Lacunae*, pp. 15–23).

[59] Deshman, *Benedictional*, pp. 10–19 and 66–9.

[60] Folios 25r and 56v (reprod. Deshman, *Benedictional*, pls. 19 and 24). The mandorla appears in the Baptism scene on the Brunswick Casket (Deshman, fig. 34) but not in the scene with Thomas in the Tiberius Psalter, Tiberius C. vi, 14v (reprod. Wormald, *Collected Writings* I, pl. 140).

[61] See above, p. 72.      [62] Ælfric, *CH* I.vii (ed. Thorpe, p. 104).

[63] *Ibid.* (ed. Thorpe, pp. 106–8 and 116); cf. *Laterculus Malalianus*, 5 and 6 (ed.

Baptism, Christ's divine nature is indicated by the inclusion of the dove of the Holy Spirit and sometimes the *dextera Dei*, symbolizing the voice which came from heaven.[64] There was another sign, however, which is of importance for the painting in the Benedictional. In a homily for Epiphany, Gregory the Great listed the occasions on which dumb creation acknowledged Christ's divinity; Ælfric drew on this passage in two of the first set of Catholic Homilies.[65] The author of the Vercelli Epiphany homily added another sign to those listed by Gregory: the River Jordan stood still.[66] The motif derives from the antiphons and responsories for the Feast of Epiphany which link Christ's baptism to the parting of the waters at the Exodus and at the crossing of the River Jordan into the promised land:

Hodie coeli aperti sunt et mare dulce factum est, terra exsultat, montes et colles laetantur, quia a Joanne in Jordane Christus baptizatus est.
V.A. Quid est tibi mare quod fugisti, et tu Jordanis quia conversus es retrorsum? Quia a Joanne in Jordane Christus baptizatus est.
V.B. Mare vidit et fugit, Jordanis conversus est retrorsum. Quia a Joanne in Jordane Christus baptizatus est.[67]

The painting of the Baptism in the Benedictional of Æthelwold shows the

---

Stevenson, pp. 126 and 128). For the Adoration of the Magi (Benedictional, 24v, Deshman, pl. 18) as a manifestation of the Trinity, see below, p. 141.

[64] Ælfric, *CH* II.iii (ed. Godden, p. 22), quoted above, p. 41, and Bede, *Homeliae* I.12 (ed. Hurst, pp. 83–4). For the iconography of the Baptism, see Schiller, *Christian Iconography* I, 127–43.

[65] Gregory, *Homiliae in evangelia* I.x.2 (PL 76, 1111) and Ælfric, *CH* I.vii and xv (ed. Thorpe, pp. 108 and 228). See above, p. 26.

[66] *Vercelli Homilies*, no. xvi (ed. Scragg, pp. 269–70). The reference is to Ps. CXIII.3–5; for discussion, see Raw, 'Why does the River Jordan Stand Still?', pp. 40–3. Schiller, *Christian Iconography* I, 134–5, draws attention to various representations (pls. 358, 360 and 361) in which the personification of the Jordan is shown turning away from the scene to recall the prophecy, though she does not mention the hill of water seen in the Benedictional's picture.

[67] *Corpus antiphonalium*, ed. Hesbert I, 64 (no. 24b), 71 (no. 25b), II, 105 (no. 24c): 'Today the skies are opened and the sea is made sweet, the earth exults, mountains and hills rejoice, because Christ is baptized by John in the Jordan. Why did you flee, oh sea, and why did you turn back oh Jordan? Because Christ is baptized by John in the Jordan. The sea saw and fled, Jordan turned back. Because Christ is baptized by John in the Jordan.' Versicles A and B are alternatives found in different manuscripts.

River Jordan standing up in a hill as a sign of Christ's divine nature, manifested to the world.[68]

The paintings in the Benedictional, therefore, allow those looking at them to share in the gospel manifestations of the divine. This making present of events from the past is seen again in the series of drawings which preface the Tiberius C. vi psalter, most of which are accompanied by inscriptions beginning with the word 'hic'; the drawing of Thomas, for example, is inscribed, 'Hic Thomas qui dicitur Didimus non credidit quod Iesus surrexisset a mortuis et extendens Iesus brachium suum Thomas tetigit vulneram eius et stitiam credidit' (14v).[69] Some details in these inscriptions suggest that the gospel scenes may have been copied from a liturgical manuscript. The picture of the entry to Jerusalem (11r) is labelled, 'Hic aequitavit Iesus Cristus in Palma Dominica' and that of the washing of the feet (11v), 'Hic fecit Ihesus mandatum cum discipulis suis', possibly referring to the tradition that Christ's life exemplified the various grades of ordination, from door-keeper to bishop, and that he acted as a subdeacon when he washed his disciples' feet.[70] The combination of scenes from the gospels with scenes from the life of David, however, implies that, whatever the source of some individual pictures may have been, the picture cycle in the Tiberius manuscript as a whole was designed for a psalter. David was traditionally interpreted as a type of Christ[71] and, as Kathleen Openshaw has pointed out, there seems to have been an insular tradition of marking the three main divisions of the psalter by paintings of the Crucifixion and of David's fight with the lion and his defeat of Goliath.[72] A similar linking of David and Christ can be seen in the Durham Cassiodorus, whose artist depicted David with a cruciferous

---

[68] A passage in the commentaries from Canterbury refers to the Jordan standing up in a hill: Bischoff and Lapidge, *Biblical Commentaries*, pp. 392–3 (no. 23).

[69] Reprod. Wormald, *Collected Writings* I, pls. 124–54.

[70] *Laterculus Malalianus*, 19 (ed. Stevenson, p. 148).

[71] Raw, *Crucifixion Iconography*, pp. 34 and 86–7, Openshaw, 'Christ and Satan', pp. 15–17, and 'Symbolic Illustration'.

[72] Openshaw, 'Symbolic Illustration', pp. 42–8. Insular influence on the Tiberius picture cycle is supported by the presence of insular spellings in the inscriptions to the pictures of the death of Goliath (8v) and that of doubting Thomas (14v), noted by Wormald, *Collected Writings* I, 128.

nimbus and standing on a double-headed serpent in imitation of scenes of Christ above the asp and the basilisk.[73]

Kathleen Openshaw has argued that the scenes of the temptation of Christ, the Crucifixion and the Harrowing of Hell in the Tiberius manuscript, together with the prophetic images of David's fight with the lion and his defeat of Goliath, should be interpreted as symbols of the conflict between good and evil, or between God and the devil, a view supported by some early psalter commentaries and by the penitential texts which are placed, together with the Psalter Prefaces, between the main picture cycle and the text of the psalter in the Tiberius manuscript.[74] The conception of the Christian life as a battle against evil, a participation in the long war between God and Satan which began before the creation of the world and will end only with the end of time, is a common one, exemplified, for example, in the Old English poem, *Christ and Satan*.[75] It is plausible that the drawings in the Tiberius Psalter served as a focus for meditation on this theme though, as Openshaw recognizes, this is not their only theme, for the gospel scenes and their Old Testament prototypes are framed by pictures of the creation of the world (pl. Ib) and of Michael fighting the dragon (16r).[76] A parallel to this placing of scenes from Christ's life within world history, and to the emphasis on Christ's passion, death and resurrection, can be seen in a prayer in the Book of Cerne and in a sequence of private prayers in the Book of Nunnaminster.[77] Both manuscripts include the gospel accounts of Christ's passion.[78] The prayer in the Book of Cerne opens with a reference to the creation: 'Domine Iesu Christe, adoro te quando dixisti ante saecula: "Fiat lux" – et facta est lux. Lux tuum fiat in me salus.' The prayer continues with references to the condemnation of Adam, the saving of Noah and the crossing of the Red Sea, followed by Christ's birth, baptism, ministry and passion, and ending

---

[73] Durham, Cathedral Library, B. II. 30, 81v and 172v; Openshaw, 'Symbolic Illustration', pp. 48–51.

[74] BL, Cotton Tiberius C. vi, 19r–28r; Openshaw, 'Christ and Satan', pp. 17–32.

[75] Raw, 'Biblical Literature', pp. 231–2; see also the Old English *Prayer* 11–15 (ASPR VI, 94–5).

[76] Openshaw, 'Symbolic Illustration', p. 57. For discussion of the creation picture, see above, p. 106.

[77] Raw, *Crucifixion Iconography*, pp. 57–9, *Book of Cerne*, ed. Kuypers, pp. 114–17 (no. 19) and *Book of Nunnaminster*, ed. Birch, pp. 61–81.

[78] *Book of Cerne*, ed. Kuypers, pp. 5–79 (all four gospels); *Book of Nunnaminster*, ed. Birch, pp. 39–57 (Mark, Luke and John).

with his ascension into heaven and return as judge. The prayers in the Book of Nunnaminster move from the creation of the angels and praise of God, the Creator and Redeemer of man, to reminders of the main events of Christ's life, ending with a prayer on the future judgement. Again, the main focus of the prayers is Christ's passion, death and resurrection.

Whereas most of the preliminary drawings in the Tiberius manuscript (7v–16r) represent events, and are identified by narrative inscriptions, the pictures which mark the divisions of the manuscript are iconic. Two represent David: the first, showing David playing the psaltery (17v), is associated with a series of drawings of musical instruments mentioned in the Bible; the second (30v) shows David with his musicians, and is placed opposite Psalm I as a frontispiece to the text of the psalms. The pictures at the other major divisions of the psalter show a tonsured ecclesiastic, possibly St Jerome,[79] at Psalm LI (71v), a drawing of Christ trampling the asp and the basilisk at Psalm CI (114v) and a symbolic representation of the Trinity[80] at Psalm CIX (pl.XIa). Finally, a painting of Christ enthroned between angels (pl. II) is placed before the Psalter Prefaces.

The drawing of Christ above the beasts derives from the text of Psalm XC.13, 'You will tread on lion and adder, trample on savage lions and dragons', though it does not necessarily illustrate this verse. The motif is a common one, found in the Utrecht and Stuttgart Psalters and, in England, in the Crowland, Winchcombe and Bury St Edmunds Psalters.[81] The scene also features in the decoration to the canon tables in the Arenberg Gospels.[82] The artists of the Bury Psalter placed the scene in the margin next to Psalm XC but in the Crowland, Tiberius and Winchcombe Psalters the link between text and picture is broken and the motif is used to mark one of the divisions of the Psalter: Psalm LI in the Crowland Psalter, Psalm CI in Tiberius and Psalm CIX in the Winchcombe Psalter. Kathleen Openshaw relates the scene of Christ above the beasts in the Tiberius Psalter to the theme of the defeat of evil which she sees as

[79] Wormald, *Collected Writings* I, 126.      [80] Discussed below, p. 144.

[81] Utrecht, Universiteitsbibliothek 32, 36r and 53v (reprod. van der Horst and Engelbregt, *Utrecht-Psalter*); Stuttgart, Württembergische Landesbibliothek, Cod. Bibl. fol. 23, 107v (reprod. Hoffmann, *Der Stuttgarter Bilderpsalter*); Oxford, Bodleian Library, Douce 296, 40r (reprod. Temple, *Anglo-Saxon Manuscripts*, pl. 259); CUL, Ff. 1. 23, 195v (reprod. Ohlgren, *Catalogue*, pl. 30) and Regin. lat. 12, 98r (reprod. Ohlgren, *Textual Illustration*, pl. 3.39).

[82] NY, Pierpont Morgan Library, 869, 13v (reprod. Ohlgren, *Textual Illustration*, pl. 6.9).

permeating the preliminary pictures in the manuscript.[83] She notes that the gospel accounts of the temptation of Christ describe the devil as quoting Psalm XC, and draws attention to the representation of Christ trampling the asp and basilisk in the temptation scenes in the Odbert Psalter.[84] As further evidence of the assimilation of Psalm XC to Christ's life she refers to an eleventh-century Easter homily whose author interprets the psalm verse as a prophecy of the defeat of the devil during Christ's harrowing of hell.[85] Jane Rosenthal, in her discussion of the decoration of the canon tables in the Arenberg Gospels, compares the representation of Christ above the beasts which forms the final item in the series (13v) to a detail of the illustration to Psalm LXIV in the Utrecht Psalter (36r), in which the motif of Christ trampling the beasts is associated with a representation of the dead rising from their tombs to illustrate the verse, 'All flesh must come to you with all its sins' (Ps. LXIV.3). Rosenthal argues on the basis of this comparison that the scene in the Arenberg manuscript must represent the Last Judgement.[86] The drawing in the Utrecht Psalter does not necessarily depict the judgement, however: it could equally well illustrate the dead rising from their tombs at the time of Christ's death (Matt. XXVII.51–3), and Christ's defeat of the devil at the Harrowing of Hell. Grabar considered that the motif was a way of representing the Resurrection: a symbolic alternative to the gospel episodes of the women at the tomb or of doubting Thomas, and to the story of Christ's release of the patriarchs and prophets from hell.[87]

In considering the meaning of the various representations of Christ above the beasts, it is important to remember that they are not textual illustrations nor do they depict events: they are symbols which bring

---

83 Openshaw, 'Christ and Satan', pp. 25–9.

84 Boulogne, Bibliothèque municipale, 20, 101r (reprod. Openshaw, 'Christ and Satan', pl. 11b). Augustine, *Enarrationes in Psalmos*, Ps. XC, I.1 (ed. Dekkers and Fraipont II, 1254) states that the psalm is about the temptation of Christ, though he does not interpret the reference to the lion and dragon in this way; Ælfric, *CH* I.xi (ed. Thorpe, p. 170) applies the psalm verse to humans, not to Christ; cf. *Blickling Homilies*, no. iii (ed. Morris, p. 29).

85 Openshaw, 'Christ and Satan', p. 26; the homily is in Oxford, Bodleian Library, Junius 121.

86 Rosenthal, 'Canon Tables', pp. 270–2.

87 Grabar, *Christian Iconography*, pp. xlviii and 123–6. All three episodes are, of course, depicted in the series of narrative drawings prefixed to the text of the Tiberius Psalter, 13v–14v (reprod. Wormald, *Collected Writings* I, pls. 138–40).

together the prophecies of Genesis III.15 and Psalm XC.13[88] and which recall one facet of Christ's being, namely his power over evil. Christ's defeat of the devil is not part of a sequence of historical events; it is something present from the beginning and independent of human time.

This timelessness and, in a sense, ambiguity, is seen again in the remaining painting in the Tiberius manuscript, that of Christ with angels (pl. II). The small cross held by the throned figure indicates that this is the risen and glorified Christ; the two trumpeting angels to his sides suggest that the scene shows the Last Judgement. The horn in Christ's right hand may be a symbol of the horn of salvation mentioned in the Canticle of Zechariah: 'Benedictus Dominus Deus Israel, quia visitavit et fecit redemptionem plebis suae; et erexit cornu salutis nobis in domo David pueri sui' (Luke I.68–9).[89] Bede, commenting on St Luke's Gospel, says that the horn symbolizes the kingdom ruled over by Christ which was prefigured by the horn of oil with which David and Solomon were anointed as rulers.[90] A drawing of David anointed by Samuel appears in the preliminary series of pictures in the Tiberius manuscript (9v), followed (10r) by a drawing of David enthroned as king. The inscription to this second scene reads, 'Hic venit Sanctus Spiritus ad David regem et locutus est cum eo'; the Holy Spirit is represented as a dove perched on the sceptre in David's left hand to draw attention to the divine inspiration behind the psalms. The picture has a further meaning, however. Above the king's head a hand emerges from a cloud, holding a horn from which oil pours down.[91] The physical anointing by Samuel has become a heavenly one, conferred by God, and the scene as a whole, with its combination of throned, kingly figure, dove and hand, becomes a typological image of the anointing of Christ depicted in the baptism scenes of the Brunswick

---

[88] Cf. *Quaestiones super Genesim* (ptd under Bede, *dubia et spuria*, PL 93, 282): 'Illud quod subiunctum est, *Ipsa conteret caput tuum, et tu insidiaberis calcaneo eius* (Gen. III.15): hoc de fructu ventris Mariae, qui est Christus, intelligitur, id est, Tu eum supplantabis, ut moriatur: ille autem victor resurget, et caput tuum conteret, quod est mors. Sicut et David dixerat ex persona Patris ad Filium: *Super aspidem et basiliscum ambulabis, et conculcabis leonem et draconem.*' Isidore, too, links Genesis III.15 with Ps. XC.13, *Quaestiones in Vetus Testamentum*, v.7 (PL 83, 221). See also below, pp. 161–2.

[89] 'Blessed be the Lord, the God of Israel! He has visited his people and redeemed them. He has raised up for us a mighty Saviour in the house of David his servant.'

[90] Bede, *In Lucam*, i.69 (ed. Hurst, p. 42).

[91] Wormald, *Collected Writings* I, 132, describes the object as a trumpet but a horn seems more likely in view of the similarities to the horn on the previous page.

116

Casket and the Benedictional of Æthelwold[92] and described in the opening chapter of the Epistle to the Hebrews: 'To his Son he says: *God, your throne shall last for ever and ever*; and: *his royal sceptre is the sceptre of virtue; virtue you love as much as you hate wickedness. This is why God, your God, has anointed you with the oil of gladness, above all your rivals*' (Heb. I.8–9 and Ps. XLIV.8). A further parallel to the horn held in Christ's hand in the Tiberius picture comes in the Canticle of Habbakuk, sung at Lauds each Friday: 'Splendor eius ut lux erit, cornua in manibus eius, ibi abscondita est fortitudo eius.'[93] Jerome interprets the horns in the Lord's hands in two different ways.[94] First, they symbolize the 'vexilla et tropaea crucis', hanging on which Christ's divine nature (his *fortitudo*) was hidden. Secondly, they are a symbol of kingship, as in a verse in the First Book of Samuel: 'Sublimabit cornu Christi sui.'[95] Bede has a similar interpretation: the horns symbolize the horns of the cross and also Christ's role as 'Rex regum et dominus dominantium' (Apoc. XIX.16).[96] Both writers, then, link the symbol of the horn with Christ's death on the cross as does the painting in the Tiberius Psalter, but they also imply a link with the Second Coming. The passage from Paul's Epistle to Timothy, quoted by Bede in relation to the horns in God's hands, speaks of 'the Appearing of our Lord Jesus Christ':

> who at the due time will be revealed
> by God, the blessed and only Ruler of all,
> the King of kings and the Lord of lords,
> who alone is immortal,
> whose home is in inaccessible light,
> whom no man has seen and no man is able to see.
>
> (I Tim. VI.14–16)

Here it is God the Father who rules, but in the Apocalypse the words 'King of kings and Lord of lords' are transferred to Christ, the Word of

---

92 BL, Additional 49598, 25r, and Brunswick, Herzog Anton-Ulrich Museum, Brunswick Casket (reprod. Deshman, *Benedictional*, pl. 19 and fig. 34). Cf. Ælfric, *CH* II.i (ed. Godden, p. 7).

93 Hab. III.4: 'His brightness is like the day, rays flash from his hands, that is where his power lies hidden.'

94 Jerome, *In Abacuc* II.iii.4 (ed. Adriaen, pp. 624–5).

95 I Samuel II.10, 'Yahweh judges the ends of the earth, he endows his king with power, he exalts the horn of his Anointed.'

96 Bede, *In canticum Abacuc*, iii.4 (ed. Hudson, p. 388).

God (Apoc. XIX.16), as in the painting of the Second Coming in the Benedictional of Æthelwold (pl. III). Jerome draws attention to this assimilation of Father and Son when he says in his commentary on the horns of Habbakuk's canticle, 'post ascensionem ad caelos ... incipiat Filius esse quod Pater est'.[97] He also notes that the Hebrew text of the Canticle of Habbakuk reads 'in manu', not 'in manibus', and points out that Christ is the right hand of God (*manum Dei fortem*) and that all the kingdoms of heaven are in this hand.[98] Bede's commentary also suggests an explanation of the angel with two priests at the foot of the Tiberius drawing. Commenting on the verse, 'Deus a Libano veniet et sanctus de monte umbroso et condenso' (Hab. III.3), a verse he links with one from Isaiah (II.3), 'De Sion exibit lex, et Verbum Domini de Hierusalem', he explains that God came from Lebanon at the Incarnation, when he scattered the seeds of faith not only through the apostles but also through their successors in the Church.[99] Bede goes on to quote from Psalm XVIII.5, 'Their voice goes out through all the earth, and their message to the ends of the world', a text used as antiphon and responsory for the feasts of apostles and, in at least one case, for the Feast of All Saints.[100] The same verse was quoted by St Paul in the Epistle to the Romans (X.18) in his account of how 'faith comes from what is preached, and what is preached comes from the word of Christ' (Rom. X.17). The image of the angel and the two priests holding a scroll is suggestive of this preaching role of the Church.

The pictures in the Tiberius Psalter, then, do three things. First, they make the gospel events present to those studying them. Secondly, they show the unity of Old and New Testaments and, by implication, the coherence of God's plan for the world. Thirdly, they make Christ present, not as an actor in history but as the God who is outside history. The pictures in the two Old Testament manuscripts reminded those studying them of God's revelation of himself through his interventions in history; the paintings in the Sacramentary of Robert of Jumièges and the

---

[97] Jerome, *In Abacuc* II.iii.4 (ed. Adriaen, p. 625); cf. John XVII.5, 'Et nunc clarifica me tu, Pater, apud temetipsum claritate, quam habui, priusquam mundus esset, apud te.'

[98] Jerome, *ibid.* II.iii.4 (ed. Adriaen, pp. 625–6).

[99] Bede, *In canticum Abacuc*, iii.3 (ed. Hudson, p. 385).

[100] *Corpus antiphonalium*, ed. Hesbert I, 320 (no. 115b, All Saints), I, 348–9 and II, 654–5 (no. 122a, Common of Apostles); the same antiphons and responsories occur on the feasts of individual apostles.

Benedictional of Æthelwold linked these interventions to their commemoration in the liturgy; the pictures in the Psalter go beyond this, to define revelation in terms of encounter with a person. Moreover, this view of what belief entails implies a changed understanding of what prayer, and specifically meditation, is about. Whereas pictures of events invite meditation, portrait-images invite contemplation. Meditation involves our effort; contemplation involves God's initiative. The distinction is similar to that drawn between reading, in which God speaks to us, and prayer, when we speak to God.[101] Paradoxically, however, the situation is reversed. In meditative reading, and in the rather similar meditative reading of pictures of gospel events, the effort comes from the human side; in the prayer of contemplation, to which the portrait-image relates, we wait for God to speak.

[101] See *Vercelli Homilies*, no. iii (ed. Scragg, p. 82) and below, p. 169.

# 6

# Christ, the icon of God

Although in one sense the throned or standing figures of Christ which throng the pages of Anglo-Saxon manuscripts are portraits, they are not so in any realistic way. Augustine drew attention to the fact that people visualize biblical characters, including Christ, in many different guises, none of which relates to the reality or is even relevant to a belief which is concerned with Christ's nature, not his individual appearance:

Nam et ipsius facies dominicae carnis innumerabilium cogitationum diversitate variatur et fingitur, quae tamen una erat quaecumque erat. Neque in fide nostra quam de domino Iesu Christo habemus illud salubre est quod sibi animus fingit longe fortasse aliter quam res habet, sed illud quod secundum speciem de homine cogitamus; habemus enim quasi regulariter infixam naturae humanae notitiam secundum quam quidquid tale aspicimus statim hominem esse cognoscimus vel hominis formam.[1]

What matters in art is not Christ's appearance but the details which are used to create a variety of meanings out of basic seated or standing figures: motifs like crowns or a cross-staff, accompanying figures such as seraphs, and inscriptions which link image to text. Just as the gospels present different and sometimes contradictory pictures of Christ, so it is with art: the many different ways of representing Christ are attempts to grasp the

[1] Augustine, *De Trinitate* VIII.iv.7 (ed. Mountain, p. 276, trans. Hill, p. 246): 'Even the physical face of the Lord is pictured with infinite variety by countless imaginations, though whatever it was like he certainly only had one. Nor as regards the faith we have in the Lord Jesus Christ is it in the least relevant to salvation what our imaginations picture him like, which is probably quite different from the reality. What does matter is that we think of him specifically as a man; for we have embedded in us as it were a standard notion of the nature of man, by which whenever we see some such thing we immediately recognize it as a man, or at least as the shape of a man.'

complexity of revelation, to understand what Christ was.[2] And pictures do not merely reflect our differing views of Christ: they determine our conception of him.[3]

The well-known drawing of Dunstan at the feet of Christ (pl. IV) shows how a representation of the risen Christ like that in a manuscript at St John's College, Oxford, could be varied by the addition of extra figures and inscriptions.[4] The Dunstan drawing shows a standing figure of Christ, his feet concealed behind a cloud. In his right hand he holds a rod inscribed, 'Virga recta est, virga regni tui' (Ps. XLIV.7); in his left hand is a book or tablet inscribed, 'Venite, filii, audite me, timorem Domini docebo vos' (Ps. XXXIII.12). To his left, and on a much smaller scale, is the kneeling figure of a monk. This figure, together with the inscription identifying it as Dunstan, is based on a picture from the *De laudibus sanctae crucis* showing Hrabanus Maurus adoring the cross.[5] However, Dunstan, unlike Hrabanus, does not raise his hands in prayer: instead, he covers his face. Mildred Budny has associated the scene with representations of the Transfiguration, where the three disciples cover their faces,[6] but there are other, and better, explanations of the scene.

The verse from Psalm XXXIII inscribed on Christ's book occurs in the Prologue to the Benedictine Rule. Benedict begins with an exhortation: 'Obsculta o fili, praecepta magistri.'[7] After drawing attention to the urgent need to serve God, he continues:

Exurgamus ergo tandem aliquando excitante nos scriptura ac dicente: *Hora est iam nos de somno surgere*; et apertis oculis nostris ad deificum lumen adtonitis auribus audiamus, divina cotidie clamans quid nos admonet vox dicens: *Hodie si vocem eius audieritis, nolite obdurare corda vestra*; et iterum: *Qui habet aures audiendi, audiat, quid*

---

[2] Matthews, *The Clash of Gods*, pp. 98 and 141–2; Nichols, *Art of God Incarnate*, pp. 114–15.

[3] Matthews, *ibid.*, pp. 10–11.

[4] Oxford, St John's College, 28, 2r (reprod. Temple, *Anglo-Saxon Manuscripts*, pl. 42). For discussion of the Dunstan drawing, see d'Alverny, 'Le symbolisme de la sagesse', Gneuss, 'Dunstan', Higgitt, 'Glastonbury, Dunstan, Monasticism' and Budny, 'St Dunstan's Classbook'.

[5] Hrabanus Maurus, *De laudibus sanctae crucis* I.xxviii (PL 107, 261–4). See Gneuss, 'Dunstan', pp. 146–8, and Alexander, 'Benedictional', p. 175.

[6] Budny, 'St Dunstan's Classbook', p. 134.

[7] These words are inscribed on the book offered to St Benedict by the monks of Canterbury in a picture in London, BL, Arundel 155, 133r (reprod. Temple, *Anglo-Saxon Manuscripts*, pl. 213).

*spiritus dicat ecclesiis.* Et quid dicit? *Venite, filii, audite me, timorem domini docebo vos. Currite, dum lumen vitae habetis, ne tenebrae mortis vos comprehendant.*[8]

The inscription on the book, then, draws attention to the monastic vocation of the kneeling figure and, in particular, to the need to turn to Christ before death overtakes one. In addition, the passage from the Rule in which the verse from Psalm XXXIII is embedded reminds the monk, who is shading his eyes, that he should open them to the divine light which makes those contemplating it divine. The light, of course, is Christ who said, 'I am the light of the world; anyone who follows me will not be walking in the dark; he will have the light of life' (John VIII.12).[9]

The passage from Psalm XLIV, from which the inscription on the rod held by Christ is taken, has messianic associations.[10] Ælfric links the passage to Isaiah's prophecy that the Messiah would make all that was crooked straight: 'Ðwyrnyssa beoð gerihte, þonne ðwyrlicra manna heortan, þe beoð ðurh unrihtwisnysse hocas awegde, eft ðurh regolsticcan ðære soðan rihtwisnysse beoð geemnode.'[11] Bede sees the rod as a symbol of Christ's priesthood, linking it to Aaron's rod, which was placed with the manna in the Ark:

Virga Aaron quae excisa fronduerat potestas est invicta sacerdotii illius de qua dicit propheta: *Virga aequitatis virga regni tui.* Quae postquam ad tempus per mortem visa est esse succisa illucescente mane resurrectionis vivacius refloruisse

---

[8] *Benedicti regula*, Prol. (ed. Hanslik, p. 3): 'Then let us rise at last, as Scripture stirs us, saying: Now is the time for us to rise from sleep. And having opened our eyes to the divine light, let us hear with wondering ears how the divine voice admonishes us daily, saying: Today, if you hear his voice, do not harden your hearts. And again: He who has ears to hear, let him hear what the Spirit says to the churches. And what does it say? Come, my sons, hear me: I will teach you the fear of the Lord. Run while you have the light of life, lest the shadows of death take hold of you.'

[9] The text from St John VIII.12 is inscribed in abbreviated form on the book held by Christ in the earliest of the Tours representations of Christ in Majesty, Stuttgart, Württembergische Landesbibliothek, H.B. II, 40, 1v; see Kessler, *Illustrated Bibles*, pp. 36–9 and pl. 51; the inscription behind Christ's head in this painting refers to him as the creator of the world. On Christ as light, see also above, pp. 73–6.

[10] See Heb. I.8–9 and above, p. 117.

[11] Ælfric, *CH* I.xxv (ed. Thorpe, p. 362): 'The crooked is made straight when the hearts of evil men, which are made crooked through the hooks of unrighteousness, are made straight again through the ruling-sticks of true righteousness.' Cf. Isaiah XL.3–4, quoted in Luke III.4–6, and Augustine, *Enarrationes in Psalmos*, Ps. XLIV.17 (ed. Dekkers and Fraipont I, 505).

inventa est ac perpetuo inviolabilis atque immarcescibilis permansura esse innotuit. *Christus* enim *surgens a mortuis iam non moritur, mors illi ultra non dominabitur* ... Verbi ipsamque carnem post passionem mortis resurrectione glorificatam et aeterna regis ac pontificis dignitate sublimatam monstravit.[12]

Paschasius Radbertus notes that the Hebrew text of Psalm XLIV refers to a sceptre – a symbol of kingship – rather than a rod.[13] Kingship, however, involves justice. He therefore interprets the throne (*sedes*) and sceptre (*sceptrum aequitatis vel virga directionis*) of Psalm XLIV.7 as symbols of judgement and of Christ's love of justice, which will be shown when he returns to judge the world.[14] Augustine makes a similar point, linking the rod of Psalm XLIV with the rod of iron of Psalm II.9:

> He has told me, You are my son,
> today I have become your father.
> Ask and I will give you the nations for your heritage,
> the ends of the earth for your domain.
> With iron sceptre you will break them,
> shatter them like potter's ware.                          (Ps. II.7–9)[15]

This judgement theme may explain the way in which Christ is represented in the Dunstan drawing, with the lower part of his body hidden in clouds. At his trial, Christ told the High Priest, 'You will see *the Son of Man seated at the right hand of the Power* and *coming on the clouds of heaven*' (Matt. XXVI.64, Mark XIV.62). The reference is to a messianic prophecy in the Book of Daniel, 'I saw, coming on the clouds of heaven, one like a son of man' (Dan. VII.13), a verse echoed in the opening chapter of the

---

[12] Bede, *De tabernaculo* I (ed. Hurst, p. 17, trans. Holder, p. 16): 'Aaron's rod that budded although cut off [from the tree] is the invincible power of his [Christ's] priesthood, concerning which the prophet says: *The rod of your kingdom is a rod of equity*. Even after it seemed for the time being to have been cut off through death, in the dawn of the resurrection morn it was found to have blossomed again all the more vigorously, and it became clear that it would remain forever imperishable and unfading. For *Christ rising from the dead will never die again: death no longer has dominion over him* ... It showed that after the passion of death the same flesh would be glorified in the resurrection and lifted up to the eternal dignity of a king and priest.'

[13] Paschasius, *Expositio* II.xliv.7 (ed. Paulus, p. 61).

[14] *Ibid.*, II.xliv.7 (ed. Paulus, pp. 61–3).

[15] Augustine, *Enarrationes in Psalmos*, Ps. XLIV.17–18 (ed. Dekkers and Fraipont I, 505–7). See also Ambrosius Autpertus, *Expositio in apocalypsin* V.xii.5a (ed. Weber I, 451), who links the verse from Ps. XLIV to Apoc. II.26–8.

Apocalypse: 'It is he who *is coming on the clouds*; everyone will see him, even *those who pierced him*' (Apoc. I.7).

The theme of Christ's return as judge is a common one in Old English literature and Anglo-Saxon art. Two paintings inserted among the preliminary material in the Athelstan Psalter represent Christ enthroned as judge (pls. VIIa–b).[16] The first, placed before the calendar, depicts Christ seated within a mandorla, a book in his left hand; behind his throne are the symbols of the passion: the spear, sponge and cross. In the background are choirs of angels, patriarchs, prophets and apostles. The second shows the enthroned Christ holding a small cross in his left hand and raising his right arm to show the wound in his side; to the sides of his head are the symbols *alpha* and *omega*. Around him, and enclosed in an outer mandorla, are choirs of martyrs, confessors and virgins; the corners of the picture are filled by figures of angels and at the upper corners of the frame are four heads, possibly representing the four winds. In the first of the two paintings Mary appears among the apostles in the lower register, a detail which links the scene with representations of the Ascension and recalls the words of the two men in white, 'This same Jesus will come back in the same way as you have seen him go there' (Acts I.11). The inclusion of the instruments of the passion in this painting and the display of the wound in Christ's side in the other is in accordance with a tradition taken over by Anglo-Saxon poets and homilists from Caesarius of Arles in which Christ reminds the human race of his passion and displays his wounds as a sign of reproach.[17]

The richness of meaning conveyed by the two paintings in the Athelstan Psalter appears again in the frontispiece to a collection of homilies which shows Christ seated in a mandorla, an open book on his left knee and his right hand raised in blessing (pl. VIII). The subject of the drawing is usually defined as Christ the judge, but the inscriptions on the book and clothes of the figure show that this is a quite inadequate description of the picture's meaning. The words 'Iustus Iudex' on Christ's breast indicate that he is not merely a judge but a just judge. The words are applied in the psalms to the God who protects the virtuous when they

---

[16] For discussion of the manuscript, see Wormald, *Collected Writings* I, p. 79, Alexander, 'Benedictional', pp. 170–2, Deshman, 'Anglo-Saxon Art', pp. 176–83, Lapidge, 'Metrical Calendar', pp. 342–8 and Keynes, 'Athelstan's Books', pp. 193–6.

[17] Caesarius, *Sermo lvii*, 4 (ed. Morin I, 253–4). For discussion of the theme of the showing of the wounds, see Raw, *Crucifixion Iconography*, pp. 38–9 and 65–6.

are attacked: 'Iustum adiutorium meum a Domino, qui salvos facit rectos corde. Deus iudex iustus, fortis et patiens, nunquid irascitur per singulos dies?' (Ps. VII.11–12).[18] The Messiah is described as the one who 'judges the wretched with integrity, and with equity gives a verdict for the poor of the land' (Isaiah XI.4);[19] his judgement is concerned with justice for the poor rather than condemnation of the wicked. When, therefore, God's Word, whose name is Faithful and True, is described in the Apocalypse as a 'judge with integrity, a warrior for justice' (Apoc. XIX.11), the implication is that Christ protects the oppressed. Protection, like judgement, is associated with kingship, a point made through the second inscription on Christ's clothes, 'Rex Regum'. The title is taken from the words written on the cloak and thigh of the Word of God in the Apocalypse: 'The King of kings and the Lord of lords' (Apoc. XIX.16); the complete text, 'Rex regum et Dominus dominantium', is inscribed on Christ's robe in the painting of the Second Coming in the Benedictional of Æthelwold (pl. III). The Apocalyptic linking of the titles of judge and king influenced at least two late eleventh-century texts: a hymn by Berengarius of Tours (*ob.* 1088) begins, 'Iuste iudex Iesu Christe, regum rex et domine' and a prayer by Anselm of Lucca, intended for recitation before receiving communion, addresses Christ as 'rex regum, iuste iudex'.[20]

The inscription on Christ's book in the homilies manuscript adds further layers of meaning to the picture. On the left-hand leaf are the words, 'Ego sum qui de morte surrexi, ego vivo in eternum' echoing Christ's words in St John's vision, 'Noli timere; ego sum primus et novissimus: et vivus et fui mortuus, et ecce sum vivens in saecula saeculorum' (Apoc. I.17–18). On the right-hand leaf are the words, 'lux mundi; ego venio in die iudicii'. The words are, of course, a reminder of Christ's return as judge but, more importantly, they define Christ as the one who is both light and life.[21] The picture as a whole, then, reminds those contemplating it that Christ, who has risen from the dead, is no

---

[18] 'My help comes from the Lord, who saves those who are true of heart. God is a just judge, strong and patient; is he not provoked daily?' (my translation).

[19] Vulgate, 'Iudicabit in iustitia pauperes et arguet in aequitate pro mansuetis terrae.'

[20] Ptd Bestul, *Durham Book of Devotions*, pp. 53–4 and Wilmart, 'Cinq textes de prière', pp. 49–57.

[21] See John I.4–5 and 9 and VIII.12, and above, p. 122 with reference to Dunstan.

severe judge; rather he is the one who saves the poor and gives life and light to his followers.

A drawing in the Winchcombe Psalter offers a different view of the judgement.[22] The manuscript contains four drawings: a picture of David at Psalm I (4v), one of the Crucifixion at Psalm LI (88r), a drawing of Christ with angels at Psalm CI (171r) and one of Christ above the beasts at Psalm CIX (195v). As George Henderson has pointed out, the enthroned figure on 171r holds a scroll inscribed, 'Ego sum Deus qui reddo unicuique iuxta sua opera.'[23] Here Christ's justice is related to human actions as in the closing words of the Athanasian Creed.[24]

In these two drawings, as in that of Dunstan with Christ, the nature of Christ's relationship to the viewer is conveyed through the inscriptions. The meaning of the figures above the canon tables in the Trinity, Pembroke and Harley Gospels, by contrast, is expressed visually.[25] The relationship, too, is different. Whereas the drawings in the Dunstan Classbook (pl. IV), the collection of homilies (pl. VIII) and the Winchcombe Psalter remind those who look at them that Christ is still present to those living in this world, the figures in the three gospel-books, like the paintings at the beginning of the Athelstan Psalter, allow a glimpse of the next. The vision of heaven offered for contemplation resembles that in St John's vision (Apoc. VII.9–12), where God is enthroned among the saints and angels. Ælfric elaborated on this passage from the Apocalypse in a homily for the Feast of All Saints.[26] Just as the paintings in the Athelstan Psalter (pls. VIIa–b) show Christ surrounded by the choirs of angels, patriarchs, prophets, apostles, martyrs, confessors and virgins, so Ælfric expands the biblical reference to the 'huge number, impossible to count, of people from every nation, race, tribe and language' into a description of the nine orders of angels, the patriarchs, prophets and apostles, the martyrs whose sufferings have brought them a glorious crown, confessors (defined as priests, hermits and monks) and, finally, the great company of virgins,

---

[22] CUL, Ff. 1. 23, 171r (reprod. Temple, *Anglo-Saxon Manuscripts*, pl. 253).

[23] Henderson, 'Idiosyncrasy', pp. 241–2. Henderson gives several parallels to the text: Prov. XXIV.12, Matt. XVI.27, Rom. II.5–6 and Apoc. XXII.12, 'Ecce venio cito, et merces mea mecum est, reddere unicuique secundum opera sua.'

[24] See above, p. 32.

[25] Cambridge, Trinity College B. 10. 4, Cambridge, Pembroke College 301 and BL, Harley 76 (reprod. Ohlgren, *Textual Illustration*, pls. 7.1–24, 9.1–23 and 10.1–15).

[26] Ælfric, *CH* I.xxxvi (ed. Thorpe, pp. 538–48).

of whom the greatest is Mary, Mother of God and Temple of the Holy Spirit, who alone is raised to God's throne. We honour these saints, Ælfric says, in the hope that, through their intercession, we may come to the eternal feast which they already enjoy.[27]

The decoration of the canon tables in the Trinity, Pembroke and Harley manuscripts suggests that there was an agreed view of how heaven should be represented. Angels holding books, scrolls, orbs, sceptres and trumpets feature prominently in their decoration. In the Trinity Gospels a major theme is the royalty of Christ. The angels who face each other across the canon tables hold orbs and sceptres, as do the two angels who stand to the sides of a blessing figure of Christ, and the royal theme is reiterated in the full-page painting of Christ wearing a fleur-de-lis crown which stands before the gospel text.[28] In the Pembroke Gospels, on the other hand, the angels hold scales and trumpet in an allusion to the judgement.[29] In all three manuscripts a picture of Mary, holding a palm branch or a flowering rod and accompanied by two female saints, is placed next to one of Christ accompanied by angels.[30] In the Trinity and Pembroke manuscripts, she also holds a book, a symbol of wisdom. The flowering rod recalls both the rod of Jesse (Isaiah XI.1–10) and the rod of Aaron (Numbers XVII.23–8). Christ was addressed as 'radix Iesse' in one of the antiphons said at the Magnificat in the days immediately before Christmas and the text from Isaiah, 'Egredietur virga de radice Jesse', formed one of the responses during Advent.[31] Jerome interprets the rod as a symbol of Mary and its flower as Christ:

Nos autem virgam de radice Iesse sanctam Mariam virginem intellegamus, quae nullum habuit sibi fruticem cohaerentem: de qua et supra legimus: *Ecce virgo concipiet et pariet filium*. Et florem Dominum Salvatorem, qui dicit in Cantico canticorum: *Ego flos campi et lilium convallium*.[32]

---

[27] For discussion of the choirs of saints in the Benedictional of Æthelwold in relation to intercession, particularly at the judgement, see Deshman, *Benedictional*, pp. 146–58.

[28] Cambridge, Trinity College B. 10. 4, 10v–11r, 13r and 16v (reprod. Ohlgren, *Textual Illustration*, pls. 7.4–5, 7.9 and 7.16).

[29] Cambridge, Pembroke College 301, 3r–v (reprod. Ohlgren, *Textual Illustration*, pls. 9.4–5).

[30] Trinity B. 10. 4, 12v-13r, Pembroke 301, 2r–v and Harley 76, 8v–9r (reprod. Ohlgren, *Textual Illustration*, pls. 7.8–9, 9.2–3 and 10.6–7).

[31] *Corpus antiphonalium*, ed. Hesbert I, 28–9 (no. 16a), III, 197, and IV, 164.

[32] Jerome, *In Esaiam* IV.xi.1 (ed. Adriaen, p. 147): 'We interpret the rod from the root of Jesse as Saint Mary the Virgin, to whom no plant could be compared, of whom we read above,

The flowering rod of Aaron was interpreted in a similar way, either as Christ, who says 'Ego flos campi', or as Mary, of whom it is said, 'Exiet virga de radice Iesse'.[33] Whereas the rod of Jesse draws attention to Christ's descent from David and embodies a Messianic allusion, the palm branch is a symbol of victory or of martyrdom; when held by Mary it recalls Simeon's prophecy (Luke II.35) that a sword would pierce her heart.[34] In addition to the figures of Christ and Mary, the Trinity Gospels include representations of two saints in mass vestments, the first holding a scroll and the second a book (11v–12r). Comparison with the Pembroke and Harley manuscripts suggests that the figures may represent SS Peter and Paul. In the Harley Gospels Peter, holding his keys and a book, faces Paul across the page opening (7v–8r). In the Pembroke Gospels (4r–5v), as in the Benedictional of Æthelwold, Peter and Paul are grouped with the other ten apostles;[35] a further six male saints appear on the following four pages (6r–7v). Peter and Paul appear again, standing one on each side of Christ, above the canon tables in the Arenberg Gospels and before the reading for the Vigil of Christmas (Matt. I.18–21), on the opening page of a gospel-lectionary.[36]

Two gospel-books have a more complex decorative scheme.[37] In the Boulogne Gospels the comparatively simple decoration of the canon tables with representations of Christ among the evangelists, angels, evangelist symbols, the *dextera Dei* and the *Agnus Dei*, is expanded into elaborately decorated openings to each of the four gospels. St Matthew's Gospel is preceded by a picture of God the creator (pl. IX), followed by representations of the evangelist and of the ancestors of Christ from Abraham to Jacob, listed by Matthew at the beginning of his gospel (10v–11v, Matt. I.1–16). These, in turn, are followed by scenes of the Annunciation,

Behold a virgin shall conceive and bear a son. And the flower is our Lord and Saviour, who says in the Song of Songs, I am the flower of the field and the lily of the valleys.'

33  Ælfric, *CH* II.i (ed. Godden, p. 4) and ps.-Bede, *Quaestiones super numeros*, xv (PL 93, 402).

34  See below, p. 165.

35  Additional 49598, 2v–4r (reprod. Deshman, *Benedictional*, pls. 4–7).

36  NY, Pierpont Morgan Library, 869, 12r (reprod. Ohlgren, *Textual Illustration*, pl. 6.6) and Florence, Biblioteca Medicea-Laurenziana, Plut. XVII.20, 1r (reprod. Temple, *Anglo-Saxon Manuscripts*, pl. 232).

37  Boulogne, Bibliothèque municipale, 11 and NY, Pierpont Morgan Library, 869 (reprod. Ohlgren, *Textual Illustration*, pls. 5.1–28 and 6.1–17).

Visitation, Nativity and annunciation to the shepherds (11v–12r) based on part of St Luke's Gospel (Luke I.26–56 and II.6–20). For St Mark, the artist showed the evangelist with his symbol of the lion (55v), followed by a drawing of Christ enthroned between angels (56r); below are the seated figures of John the Baptist and the prophet Isaiah, holding scrolls inscribed with Isaiah's prophecy, quoted at the beginning of Mark's Gospel (Mark I.3 and Isaiah XL.3). For the opening of St Luke's Gospel the artist chose the traditional scene of the angel's appearance to Zechariah (62r, Luke I.5–22) to accompany the writing figure of the evangelist (61v). The initial page to St John's Gospel (107v) shows Christ enthroned in a mandorla and accompanied by two angels; to the sides of his head are the letters *alpha* and *omega* and the upper part of the page carries the inscription, 'principium finisque Patris Verbum Deus hic est'.[38]

In the Arenberg Gospels, all the drawings, apart from the evangelist portraits and the picture of the Crucifixion which precedes the canon tables, are of heavenly scenes; there are no pictures of gospel events, as there are in the Boulogne Gospels, and the figures belong to the same timeless existence as the saints and angels of the Trinity, Pembroke and Harley Gospels.[39] In addition to the picture of Christ with Peter and Paul mentioned above, the drawing of Christ above the beasts discussed in ch. 5, and the pictures of the Virgin and Child and of the Virgin with the Trinity discussed in ch. 7,[40] the Arenberg canon tables include two unusual representations of Christ. In the first (12v), he holds an open book and a disk bearing the figure of a lamb (or, more accurately, a horned ram) and is accompanied by two unidentified saints; in the second (13r), he holds a cross-staff and an open book and is accompanied by two seraphs.

Jane Rosenthal identifies the disk in the first drawing as a paten, and interprets the scene as a representation of Christ as the eternal priest of the Epistle to the Hebrews, standing in the midst of the church and offering the sacrifice of the mass.[41] The disk is not necessarily a paten, however, nor is the motif of the lamb necessarily a symbol of the eucharist. On three

---

[38] For discussion of the pictures on 10r and 107v, see below, pp. 136–40.

[39] This view of the pictures differs from that of Jane Rosenthal, who sees them as images of four historical periods: Rosenthal, 'Canon Tables', p. 279.

[40] Above, pp. 128 and 114–15, and below, pp. 163–7.

[41] Rosenthal, 'Canon Tables', pp. 252–62; for the paten, see Barb, '*Mensa sacra*', p. 46, and Elbern, 'Der eucharistische Kelch', pp. 183–5.

of the sixth-century Monza ampullae a series of twelve medallion portraits of the apostles surrounds the central scene;[42] on others, a bust of Christ enclosed in a medallion is placed above a cross.[43] A similar motif appears in the sixth-century mosaic of the Transfiguration at Sant'Apollinare in Classe, Ravenna and a seventh-century mosaic in the apse of San Stefano Rotondo, Rome.[44] In both continental and Anglo-Saxon art, the symbols of the evangelists are frequently enclosed in circular frames, as are the symbols of sun and moon in Crucifixion pictures.[45] A painting of the Trinity executed by an English artist working at Fleury encloses both Lamb and Dove in circular frames.[46] Representations of a lamb framed in a medallion are frequent. St John the Baptist holds a disk with a lamb on the front panel of the sixth-century ivory throne of Maximian in Ravenna.[47] A Merovingian Sacramentary in the Vatican Library contains a painting of a cross with a disk containing a lamb at the centre.[48] The ninth-century Trier Apocalypse includes six examples of a lamb enclosed in a circular frame and surrounded by the four animals which symbolize the evangelists.[49] The miniature for the Feast of All Saints in the Sacramentary of Robert of Jumièges depicts a crowd of the blessed acclaiming the lamb, who is enclosed in a circular frame supported by two angels.[50] In all these cases the circular frame serves to separate what it encloses from the rest of the scene, to show that what is being depicted is an image within an image.

The practice of representing Christ in the symbolic form of a lamb derives from the metaphor used of him by John the Baptist: 'Look, there is the lamb of God that takes away the sin of the world' (John I.29). This

[42] Ampullae 3, 12 and 13 (reprod. Grabar, *Ampoules*, pls. IX, XXIII and XXV).
[43] Ampullae 6 and 8 (*ibid.*, pls. XII and XIII).
[44] Reprod. Grabar, *Byzantium*, pl. 153 and Oakeshott, *Mosaics of Rome*, pl. 91.
[45] E.g. Aachen altar-frontal of *c.* 1020 (reprod. Lasko, *Ars sacra*, pl. 131), gold and ivory crucifix in the Victoria and Albert Museum, London, BL, Arundel 60, 12v, and CUL, Ff. 1. 23, 88r (reprod. Raw, *Crucifixion Iconography*, pls. IVb, IX and X).
[46] Paris, BN, lat. 6401, 159r (reprod. Temple, *Anglo-Saxon Manuscripts*, pl. 95).
[47] Reprod. Grabar, *Byzantium*, pl. 334.
[48] Biblioteca Apostolica Vaticana, Regin. lat. 316, 3v (reprod. Hubert, Porcher and Volbach, *Dark Ages*, pl. 175).
[49] Trier, Stadtbibliothek, 31, 17v, 18v, 19v, 20v, 23r and 24r (reprod. Laufner and Klein, *Trierer Apokalypse*).
[50] Rouen, Bibliothèque municipale, Y. 6 [274], 158v (reprod. Wilson, *Missal of Robert of Jumièges*).

metaphor, which asserts that Christ fulfilled the Old Testament prophecies about the lamb led to slaughter, was developed by the author of the Apocalypse in the scenes of the lamb standing before the throne, the adoration of the lamb, the lamb leading the redeemed to the living waters and the lamb standing on Mount Zion.[51] The lamb image belongs to Christ in virtue of his death on the cross, which replaced the sacrifices of the Old Testament and, in particular, the passover lamb of Exodus XII.3.[52] It has a eucharistic significance, for the body of Christ, sacrificed on the cross, formed the food for the communion which replaced the passover meal,[53] but it also has other associations: with Old Testament prophecy, New Testament reality, and the eternal present of heaven where Christ continues to offer himself to God (Heb. VII.23–5). In some representations of the *Agnus Dei* the eucharistic significance is made clear through other motifs. The paintings of the adoration of the lamb which illustrate the Feast of All Saints in three sacramentaries from Fulda, for example, show Ecclesia holding a chalice to the lamb's side.[54] Ecclesia appears again in a painting of the lamb with angels and evangelist symbols in a lectionary from Fulda,[55] and on the back of the portable altar known as the Heinrichsportatile.[56] The Anglo-Saxon portable altar in the Musée de Cluny, decorated with a crucifix, figures of angels, Mary, John and evangelist symbols, also includes a representation of a lamb in a circular frame.[57] The drawing in the Arenberg Gospels, however, does not include a chalice, a figure of Ecclesia or representations of any of the Old Testament prefigurations of Christ's sacrificial death and it is therefore worth considering whether it might have some other meaning.

An early eleventh-century gospelbook which belonged to Bernward of Hildesheim includes a painting of a figure with a cruciferous nimbus, throned on a globe and accompanied by two seraphs; in his right hand is a disk with a figure of a lamb; in his left hand is a book inscribed 'Vita';

51  Isaiah LIII.7 and Jeremiah XI.19; Apoc. V.6, VII.9–12, VII.17 and XIV.1. For discussion of the image of a ram, see below, p. 163.

52  *CH* I.xxii (ed. Thorpe, p. 312) and II.iii and xv (ed. Godden, pp. 21 and 151).

53  *CH* I.xxxviii (ed. Thorpe, p. 590).

54  Bamberg, Staatsbibliothek, Cod. lit. 1, 165v, Udine, Archivio Capitolare, 1, 66v and Göttingen, Universitätsbibliothek, Cod. theol. 231, 111r (reprod. Mayr-Harting, *Ottonian Book Illumination* II, pls. XIV, XV and 94).

55  Aschaffenburg, Hofbibliothek, 2, 1v (reprod. Mayr-Harting, *ibid*. II, pl. IX).

56  Reprod. Lasko, *Ars sacra*, pl. 129.

57  Okasha and O'Reilly, 'Anglo-Saxon Portable Altar' and *Golden Age*, pp. 92–3 (no. 76).

below is the infant Christ in the manger, and below again, figures of Oceanus and Gaia, the latter holding figures of Adam and Eve beneath the Tree of Knowledge.[58] The painting is one of a group of pictures placed before St John's Gospel and Tschan considered that it illustrates the words, 'The Word was with God' and 'The Word was made flesh' (John I.1 and 14): in the upper part of the painting the Word, in the form of a lamb, is shown with God the Father; in the lower section, the incarnate Word lies in the manger. The lamb, however, is touching the book and Gertrud Schiller rightly identifies the upper part of the painting with the scene in the Apocalypse where the Lamb comes and takes the book from the hand of the One sitting on the throne, whom she identifies as God the Father (Apoc. V.7).[59] A very similar image of a throned figure holding a book and a lamb enclosed in a circular frame occurs in an early twelfth-century manuscript referred to by Paul Meyvaert in connection with the figure holding a lamb on the eighth-century Ruthwell Cross.[60] This, too, is an Apocalyptic scene, though Meyvaert identifies the throned figure as Christ rather than God the Father.[61] In the Arenberg drawing Christ holds an open book in his right hand; the lamb grasps a second, closed book but does not touch the open one. Early commentators understood the opening of the book in the Apocalypse as a symbol of the fulfilment of the Old Testament promises by the New Testament. Haymo of Auxerre says:

Liber autem in dextera sedentis Vetus et Novum Testamentum significat ... Idcirco autem Vetus et Novum Testamentum unus liber appellatur, quia nec Novum a Vetere, nec Vetus a Novo valet disiungi, sed quidquid praedictum est in Vetere, completum constat in Novo. Nam Vetus Testamentum nuntius est et velamen Novi, Novum vero revelatio et adimpletio est Veteris.[62]

---

[58] Hildesheim, Cathedral Treasury, 18, 174r (reprod. Tschan, *Bernward* III, pl. 73).

[59] Schiller, *Christian Iconography* I, 8–9.

[60] Ghent, Bibliothèque de l'Université, 92, 88r; Meyvaert, 'New Perspective', pp. 112–25, pl. 57.

[61] Meyvaert, *ibid.*, p. 124.

[62] Haymo, *Expositio in Apocalypsin* II.v (PL 117, 1013): 'The book in the right hand of the one sitting [on the throne] symbolizes the Old and New Testament ... For the Old and New Testaments constitute one book, because the New is not separated from the Old or the Old from the New, but whatever is prophesied in the Old is completed in the New. For the Old Testament is the messenger and veil of the New, while the New Testament is the unveiling and completion of the Old.' The passage is quoted by Kessler, *Illustrated Bibles*, p. 76; cf. Bede, *Explanatio Apocalypsis* I.v (PL 93, 145).

In the ninth-century Bibles from Tours the significance of the opening of the sealed book by the lamb is emphasized by the parallel scene of Moses unveiled by the evangelists.[63] In the Arenberg manuscript the figure holding the lamb and the book is accompanied by two haloed figures holding a scroll and a book respectively: symbols of the Old and New Testaments. In view of this and the other parallels it seems likely that the open book and lamb held by the Christ figure also represent the Apocalyptic scene of the unveiling of the Old Testament by the New. Christ is portrayed as the one in whom the shadows of the Old Testament are replaced by the reality of the New.

The drawing of Christ standing between two seraphs placed opposite that of Christ holding the lamb (13r) is interpreted by Jane Rosenthal as a representation of the Second Coming.[64] The cross-staff held by Christ is a standard attribute of the risen Christ and reminds the viewer of his death and the salvation which flowed from it; the book in Christ's left hand probably represents the gospels, the word of God, and therefore acts as a metaphor for Christ, the Word. The seraphs derive from the vision of Isaiah: 'In the year of King Uzziah's death I saw the Lord Yahweh seated on a high throne; his train filled the sanctuary; above him stood seraphs, each one with six wings: two to cover its face, two to cover its feet and two for flying' (Isaiah VI.1–2). Three of the drawings in the Utrecht Psalter include representations of six-winged seraphs supporting the mandorla in which God is seated, a reference to the statement in these psalms that Yahweh is enthroned above the cherubs,[65] and the Genesis illustrations to Junius 11 in the Bodleian Library include three drawings of God the Father enthroned between two seraphs.[66] In the San Callisto Bible, the frontispiece to the books of prophets shows a throned figure flanked by the two seraphs of Isaiah's vision and the four tetramorphs from the vision of Ezekiel (Ezekiel I.4–12).[67]

The author of the Apocalypse transformed Ezekiel's tetramorphs into

---

[63] Kessler, *ibid.*, pp. 70–8.    [64] Rosenthal, 'Canon Tables', pp. 263–78.

[65] Psalms XVII.10, LXXIX.1 and XCVIII.1, Utrecht, Universiteitsbibl. 32, 9r, 47r and 57r. Cf. II Samuel VI.2 and II Kings XIX.15.

[66] Oxford, Bodleian Library, Junius 11, pp. 1, 2 and 17 (reprod. Gollancz, *Caedmon Manuscript*).

[67] Rome, San Paolo fuori le Mura, Bible, 117r (reprod. Kessler, *Illustrated Bibles*, pl. 70). The vision of Isaiah is also illustrated in the Vivian Bible, Paris, BN, fonds latin 1, 130v (reprod. Koehler, *Karolingischen Miniaturen* I, pl. I. 89f).

the four animals round God's throne, traditionally interpreted as symbols of the four evangelists and, in art, Isaiah's seraphs followed them, though without any support from the text. The throned figure with lamb and book in the Bernward Gospels, identified above as a representation of the lamb of the Apocalypse taking the scroll from the hand of the One on the throne, is flanked by seraphs[68] and a Boethius manuscript from Fleury, decorated by an English artist working on the Continent, contains an author portrait in which the upper part of the picture is occupied by a figure enthroned between two seraphs.[69] The *alpha* and *omega* to the sides of the seated figure's head and the sealed scroll in his left hand show that this is the One seated on the throne of the Apocalypse (Apoc. V.1) from whom the lamb receives the scroll. The picture was probably intended as a frontispiece to Boethius's *De Trinitate* and a similar figure, accompanied by a lamb and a dove instead of by the seraphs, appears at the top of what may be a historiated letter I on the following page.[70] The ambiguity of the descriptions in the Apocalypse, reflected in the uncertainty of medieval commentators about the identity of the One seated on the throne,[71] resulted in a transfer of motifs which belong, strictly speaking, to God the Father from the Father to the Son. So, the apocalyptic beasts which cluster round the Father's throne become the symbols of the evangelists to form two important Carolingian images: the *Maiestas Agni* and the *Maiestas Domini*. The first, seen in the gospel frontispiece to the Bamberg Bible and in the frontispiece to the St Gauzelin Gospels, shows a lamb with spear, sponge and chalice (symbols of Christ's sacrificial death), accompanied by the evangelist symbols and busts of the four major prophets; the St Gauzelin frontispiece also includes two seraphs.[72] The second image, used as a frontispiece to the gospels in three Carolingian Bibles, shows the

---

[68] Hildesheim, Cathedral Treasury, 18, 174r; see above, p. 132.

[69] Paris, BN, lat. 6401, 158v (reprod. Temple, *Anglo-Saxon Manuscripts*, pl. 94).

[70] 159r (reprod. Temple, *ibid.*, pl. 95). See below, p. 144.

[71] Haymo, *Expositio in Apocalypsin* II.iv and v (PL 117, 1004 and 1013) argues that the one sitting on the throne is sometimes to be interpreted as the Father, sometimes the Son, a point also made by Ambrosius Autpertus, *Expositio in Apocalypsin* III.iv.2b and IV.vii.10 (ed. Weber I, 205–6 and 310–11); both writers also interpret the words *alpha* and *omega* as a reference to Christ: Haymo, *ibid.* I.i (PL 117, 948 and 960) and Ambrosius Autpertus, *ibid.* I.i.8 and 17c (ed. Weber I, 55–6 and 88). See also below, pp. 164–5.

[72] Bamberg, Staatsbibliothek, Bibl. 1, 339v and Nancy, Cathedral, Gospels, 3v (reprod. Kessler, *Illustrated Bibles*, pls. 47 and 64).

enthroned Christ with evangelists, their symbols and figures of the prophets;[73] a similar composition decorates the ivory cover of a manuscript at Sankt Gallen.[74] These compositions symbolize the unity of the gospel accounts and their consistency with Old Testament prophecy and Apocalypse allegory.[75] Elsewhere, seraphs accompany representations of the enthroned and glorified Christ. In the Utrecht illustration to the *Te Deum* the seraphs, mentioned in the verse, 'Tibi cherubim et seraphim incessabili voce proclamant', are shown to the sides of the mandorla of the risen Christ.[76] The jewelled cover of one of the gospelbooks which belonged to Judith of Flanders is decorated with contrasting representations of the Crucifixion and of the risen Christ, enthroned in a mandorla and accompanied by two seraphs.[77] Finally, two seraphs accompany the image of the Virgin and Child in the frame to the opening of St John's Gospel in the Grimbald Gospels (pl. XIII). The parallels between Old and New Testament visions are clearly seen in two Ottonian manuscripts containing glossed copies of the Song of Songs, Daniel and Isaiah.[78] All three texts are in the same hand and it seems likely that originally they belonged together, though the copy of Isaiah is now bound separately. The frontispiece to Isaiah shows a youthful, throned figure, surrounded by flames, who is accompanied by six seraphs, one of whom takes a coal from the altar at the base of the picture. The frontispiece to the Song of Songs shows the baptized arriving in heaven. At the centre of the right-hand page, a figure throned on a globe and holding an orb in his left hand is accompanied by two groups of seraphs and eight other groups of heavenly beings who may represent the other eight orders of angels. Neither figure has any specifically Christological attributes but both are youthful and it seems logical to see in them an assimilation of God the Father and God the Son. Gregory identified the throned figure of Ezekiel I.26 as, 'Mediator

---

73   BL, Additional 10546, 352v, Paris, BN, fonds latin 1, 329v and Rome, San Paolo fuori le Mura, Bible, 259v (reprod. Kessler, *ibid.*, pls. 48–50).

74   Sankt Gallen, Stiftsbibliothek, 53 (reprod. Hubert, Porcher and Volbach, *Carolingian Art*, pl. 241).

75   For discussion, see Kessler, *Illustrated Bibles*, pp. 36–58.

76   Utrecht, Universiteitsbibliotheek, 32, 88r (reprod. van der Horst and Engelbregt, *Utrecht-Psalter*).

77   NY, Pierpont Morgan Library, 708, binding (reprod. Ohlgren, *Textual Illustration*, pl. 12.1).

78   Bamberg, Staatsbibliothek, Bibl. 76, 10v and Bibl. 22, 5r (Mayr-Harting, *Ottonian Book Illumination* II, pp. 31–45, pls. 22 and III).

Dei et hominum, homo Christus Iesus';[79] for Hrabanus Maurus, the figure on the throne was both the Father and the Son.[80] In the same way, the Arenberg drawing of Christ between two seraphs[81] represents Christ, first, as the one who has triumphed over death and, secondly, as the divine being of Isaiah and Ezekiel's prophetic visions.

This assimilation of Christ to the God of the Old Testament is seen very clearly in two pictures in the Boulogne Gospels: the painting of the enthroned Christ, placed between the canon tables and the paintings associated with the beginning of St Matthew's Gospel (pl. IX) and the initial at the beginning of the Gospel of St John.[82] Whereas the representations of Christ's ancestors and the infancy scenes placed before St Matthew's Gospel draw attention to Christ's descent from David and emphasize the reality of his human nature, the drawing at the beginning of St John's Gospel speaks of his divinity: 'Patris Verbum Deus hic est.' The drawing shows the Word made flesh but, more than that, it depicts the Word as *principium finisque*. In the Apocalypse the words, 'alpha et omega, principium et finis' are applied first to the Almighty, 'qui est et qui erat et qui venturus est' (Apoc. I.8), but later in the same chapter they are transferred to the one like a son of man who says, 'It is I, *the First* and *the Last*; I am the Living One, I was dead and now I am to live for ever and ever, and I hold the keys of death and of the underworld' (Apoc. I.17–18). In the final chapter they are used of Christ the judge, who promises, 'Very soon now, I shall be with you again, *bringing the reward to be given to every man according to what he deserves*. I am the Alpha and the Omega, *the First and the Last*, the Beginning and the End' (Apoc. XXII.12–13).[83] The words echo those of Isaiah, 'Ego Dominus, primus et novissimus ego sum' (XLI.4) and 'Ego primus et ego novissimus, et absque me non est Deus' (XLIV.6).[84] The initial to St John's Gospel, then, represents Christ as the image of the Father, of the God who announced to Moses, 'Ego sum qui sum.'[85]

---

[79] Gregory, *Homiliae in Hiezechihelem prophetam* I.viii.20 (ed. Adriaen, p. 112).

[80] Hrabanus, *Commentarii in Ezechielem* II.i (PL 110, 542).

[81] NY, Pierpont Morgan Library, 869, 13r (reprod. Ohlgren, *Textual Illustration*, pl. 6.8).

[82] Boulogne, Bibliothèque municipale, 11, 107v (reprod. Ohlgren, *Textual Illustration*, pl. 5.28).

[83] See below, pp. 164–5.

[84] 'I Yahweh, who am the first and shall be with the last' (Is. XLI.4); 'I am the first and the last; there is no other God besides me' (Is. XLIV.6).

In another passage from Isaiah, the words *primus et novissimus* are linked to God's work as creator: 'I am the first, I am also the last. My hand laid the foundations of earth and my right hand spread out the heavens' (Isaiah XLVIII.12–13). This is the theme of the painting on 10r of the Boulogne manuscript (pl. IX). Below God's rainbow throne is a globe; a second, smaller globe supports his feet. An inscription on this smaller globe reads, 'terra scabellum pedum', a reference to Isaiah's description of the creator: 'Thus says Yahweh: With heaven my throne and earth my footstool, what house could you build me, what place could you make for my rest? All this was made by my hand' (Isaiah LXVI.1–2).[86] This creation theme is further developed by the motifs of sun, moon and stars, placed in the panels to the sides of the mandorla to symbolize day and night. An inscription across these areas reads, 'caelum et terram ego impleo', recalling a verse from Jeremiah, 'Do I not fill heaven and earth? – It is Yahweh who speaks' (Jeremiah XXIII.24).[87] But the picture also refers forward, for the passage in Isaiah forms part of an eschatological discourse which speaks of a new creation: 'Now I create new heavens and a new earth, and the past will not be remembered, and will come no more to men's minds. Be glad and rejoice for ever and ever for what I am creating, because I now create Jerusalem "Joy" and her people "Gladness"' (Isaiah LXV.17–18). Isaiah's prophecy is echoed in the description of the One sitting on the throne in St John's vision who says, 'Now I am making the whole of creation new' (Apoc. XXI.5).

The verses from Isaiah and Jeremiah inscribed on the Boulogne drawing are brought together in a passage in Jerome's commentary on Isaiah.[88] Jerome links the passage from Isaiah LXVI.1, 'With heaven my throne and earth my footstool, what house could you build for me, what place could you make for my rest?', to two episodes in the Acts of the Apostles. In the first, Stephen quotes Isaiah to show that the God who created all things does not live in houses built by human hands (Acts VII.48–50); in the second, Paul, speaking before the Council of the Areopagus (Acts XVII.24–9), explains how God, the creator of all, who does not live in

---

[86] 'Haec dicit Dominus: Caelum sedes mea, terra autem scabellum pedum meorum. Quae est ista domus, quam aedificabitis mihi? Omnia haec manus mea fecit, et facta sunt universa ista dicit Dominus.'

[87] 'Nunquid non caelum et terram ego impleo? dicit Dominus.' See also Jeremiah XXXI.35, XXXIII.20 and XXXIII.25.

[88] Jerome, *In Esaiam* XVIII.lxvi.1 (ed. Adriaen, pp. 769–70).

human shrines, can be known by his creation. Jerome develops this description of a God who exists outside creation and yet can be known by it, in two ways. First, he quotes Jeremiah XXIII.24, 'Do I not fill heaven and earth?', to show that we cannot escape from God, who is everywhere; he makes the same point in his commentary on Jeremiah, where he links the passage to one from the Psalms: 'Where could I go to escape your spirit? Where could I flee from your presence?' (Ps. CXXXVIII.7).[89] Secondly, he returns to an earlier verse from Isaiah: 'Who was it measured the water of the sea in the hollow of his hand and calculated the dimensions of the heavens, gauged the whole earth to the bushel, weighed the mountains in scales, the hills in a balance?' (Isaiah XL.12) to argue that the One who holds the world in his hands cannot be contained within it.

As was noted earlier, Irenaeus was quite explicit in applying the text from Isaiah LXVI to 'the creator of all, who said "heaven is my throne and the earth my footstool"', not to the Word of God.[90] The Blickling homilist, on the other hand, links the passage to Christ. Speaking of the Temptation he says: 'þæt manfulle wuht wolde þæt he hine weorþode se þe stigeþ ofer þa þrym-setl heofona rices, and his fot-sceamul is þis eorþlice rice, þone nænig heonon ne sceawaþ, ac hine ealle halige þær herigaþ and weorþiaþ on his þære hean mihte'.[91] Paschasius Radbertus quotes the verse from Isaiah in connection with the Incarnation, in order to show that the child wrapped in swaddling clothes and lying in the manger and the God who holds the world in his hands are one and the same: 'Qui coelum et terram adimplet, cui coelum thronus est, terra autem scabellum pedum eius, qui palmo coelos tenet, et appendit tribus digitis molem terrae, ac pugillo concludit, hunc Virgo sancta pannis involvit, et in praesepio reclinavit.'[92] Ælfric, like Irenaeus, interprets the passage from Isaiah (and that from Jeremiah) in relation to God the Father. Commenting on the opening words of the *Pater noster*, he says: 'God Fæder is on heofonum, and he is æghwar swa swa he sylf cwæð, Ic gefylle mid me sylfum heofonas and eorðan. And eft þæt halige godspel be him þus cwyð, Heofon is his

---

[89] Jerome, *In Hieremiam* IV.lviii (ed. Reiter, pp. 224–5).     [90] See above, p. 78.

[91] *Blickling Homilies*, no. iii (ed. Morris, p. 31): 'That evil spirit wished him [Christ] to worship him [the devil], he who ascends to the throne of the heavenly kingdom and whose footstool is this earthly realm, whom none can see from here, but all the saints praise and worship him there in his great power.'

[92] Paschasius, *Sermo i, De assumptione* (PL 96, 243).

þrymsetl, and eorðe is his fotsceamul.'[93] But as Augustine points out, the persons of the Trinity cannot be separated from one another: all three are enthroned in heaven, with earth as a footstool and fill the whole world with their presence.[94] So for Byrhtferth it is the Trinity that fills all things: 'Ista Trinitas et individua unitas sua maiestate deitatis omnia penetrat, et penetrando circumdat et circumdando adimplet et adimplendo gubernat et gubernando cuncta creata regit (supera scilicet, media et ima), de cuius laudis preconio dictum est: "Omnia in mensura et in numero et pondere creavit." '[95] This is the God of Psalm LXXIII.16, illustrated in the Bury Psalter by a drawing of a standing figure holding symbols of day and night: 'You are master of day and night, you instituted light and sun, you fixed the boundaries of the world, you created summer and winter.'[96] The picture in the Boulogne Gospels, then, is not simply a representation of Christ as creator of the world. Instead, it shows God himself, the one who both shapes and maintains the world, who is at the same time outside his creation and yet everywhere present and who, at the end of time, will make all things new. Christ is not only the visible form of the Father;[97] he is the visible form of the Godhead.

Ælfric, commenting on the opening chapter of St John's Gospel, stresses the unity of the Godhead:

> On anginne wæs þæt Word: and þæt angin is se Fæder,
> mid þam wæs þæt Word wunigen( . . . );

---

[93] *CH* I.xix (ed. Thorpe, p. 262): 'God the Father is in heaven, and he is everywhere, as he himself said: I fill heaven and earth with myself. And again, the holy gospel says of him: Heaven is his throne and earth his footstool.' See also below, p. 182.

[94] *De Trinitate* II.v.7 and xvii.30 (ed. Mountain, pp. 88 and 120), quoting Jeremiah XXIII.24 and Isaiah LXVI.1.

[95] *Byrhtferth's Enchiridion* (ed. and trans. Baker and Lapidge, pp. 196–7): 'This Trinity and undivided unity permeates all things in the majesty of its divinity, and by permeating, surrounds them, and by surrounding, fills them, and by filling, governs them, and by governing, rules all created things (namely those above, in the middle, and down below); it is said, concerning the distinction of this glory, that "he created all things in measure, and number, and weight".' For the passage from Wisdom XI.21, see above, p. 106, n. 44.

[96] Biblioteca Apostolica Vaticana, Regin. lat. 12, 81r (reprod. Ohlgren, *Textual Illustration*, pl. 3.30). See also Raw, 'Drawing of an Angel'.

[97] Cf. Irenaeus, *Contra haereses* IV.vi.6 (PG 7, 989), 'Invisibile etenim Filii Pater, visibile autem Patris Filius', and an inscription in the Catacomb of Domitilla, quoted by Matthews, *The Clash of Gods*, p. 118, 'Qui Filius diceris et Pater inveneris' ('You are said to be the Son and are found to be the Father').

and þæt Word is anginn, swa swa he eft sæde,
*Ego principium qui et loquor vobis*:
Ic sylf eom anginn, ic ðe to eow sprece.
Be þam awrat Moyses se mæra heretoga,
*In principio fecit Deus celum et terram*:
God geworhte on anginne heofonan and eorðan,
and þæt anginn is his ancenneda Sunu,
þurh þone he gesceop ealle gesceafta
and hi ealle geliffæste þurh þone lyfiendan Gast:
hi þry syndon an anginn and an ælmihtig God.[98]

In a sermon on the text, 'Ego sum alfa et ω, initium et finis dicit dominus Deus, qui est et qui erat et qui venturus est omnipotens', he talks of the one God in three persons who created and redeemed us, in whom we have our beginning and our end.[99] It is not a case, here, of creation by the Father through the Son or of redemption by the Son but of a God who is one and indivisible in his being and actions.[100]

This theme of the unity of the Godhead is clearly expressed in a historiated initial which introduces the blessings for the Sunday after Pentecost in the Benedictional of Æthelwold (pl. X). The painting depicts a crowned figure seated on a rainbow above a globe, a book in his left hand and his right hand raised in blessing. The cruciferous nimbus round the figure's head suggests that the painting represents Christ, but the associated texts require a representation of the Trinity. Robert Deshman, who earlier described the figure as Christ, 'the ruler of the universe',[101] identifies it in his most recent work as 'Christ or the Triune Deity'.[102] In a

---

[98] *Homilies*, no. i (ed. Pope I, 199–200): 'In the beginning was the Word, and that beginning is the Father with whom the Word was dwelling; and that Word is the beginning, as he said again, *Ego principium qui et loquor vobis*: I who speak to you am myself the beginning. Moses, the famous leader, wrote about him, *In principio fecit Deus celum et terram*: In the beginning God made heaven and earth, and that beginning is his only-begotten Son, through whom he created all that is made, and gave life to them all through the living Spirit: these three are one beginning and one almighty God.' See also above, pp. 45–6, and below, p. 142.

[99] Ælfric, *LS* I.xvi (ed. Skeat I, 336).

[100] See also Ælfric, *Homilies*, no. xxi (ed. Pope II, 677), above, pp. 33, 41 and 84, and below, p. 167.

[101] '*Christus rex*', pp. 368 and 399, and '*Benedictus monarcha*', pp. 217–18.

[102] Deshman, *Benedictional*, pp. 92–108.

lengthy and complex discussion, he relates the image to the visions of God in Ezekiel I.27–8 and the Apocalypse IV.2–3, to the theme of Christ as judge and to the ruler theology of tenth-century England. There is a further dimension to the picture, however.

The most striking feature of the painting is the jewelled diadem on the head of the throned figure. Anglo-Saxon artists frequently represented Christ as a crowned figure. He is depicted wearing a diadem in the drawing of Christ as judge in the manuscript of homilies discussed earlier (pl. VIII); the frontispiece to the Trinity Gospels shows him wearing a fleur-de-lis crown,[103] and several late Anglo-Saxon manuscript pictures and carvings of the Crucifixion include a crowned figure.[104] The theme of Christ's kingship is well known and there are many allusions to it in the decoration of Æthelwold's Benedictional: the figure of Christ in the painting of the Second Coming is inscribed, 'Rex regum'; the Magi (here represented as kings) offer crowns to the infant Christ; in the baptism scene, angels bring crowns and sceptres.[105] The term 'king of kings' is not confined to Christ, however: it belongs primarily to the Godhead.[106] When appropriated to Christ, the words 'Rex regum' draw attention to his role as the one who makes visible the God whom no-one has seen. Similarly, the Adoration of the Magi and the Baptism are manifestations of the God who is both One and Three. The *Laterculus Malalianus* states that the three gifts of the Magi signified that a single undivided Godhead is adored in Christ and that, at Christ's baptism, God revealed 'unam constans indivisa deitas adque magestas' ('a single, constant, undivided deity and majesty').[107]

The word *monarchia* was used by early theologians to refer to the single origin of the three divine persons.[108] The etymology of the word was certainly known to the Anglo-Saxons for it occurs in Isidore's *Etymologiae*:

---

[103] Cambridge, Trinity College B. 10. 4, 16v (reprod. Ohlgren, *Textual Illustration*, pl. 7.16).

[104] See the Crucifixion scenes discussed in Raw, *Crucifixion Iconography*, pp. 129–46.

[105] BL, Additional 49598, 9v, 24v and 25r (reprod. Deshman, *Benedictional*, pls. 10, 18 and 19).

[106] See above, pp. 117–18.

[107] *Laterculus Malalianus*, 15 and 18 (ed. Stevenson, pp. 140 and 146).

[108] Torrance, *Trinitarian Faith*, pp. 312–13, 321–2 and 329–30. I am grateful to Aidan Nichols for discussing this point with me.

Monarchae sunt, qui singularem possident principatum, qualis fuit Alexander apud Graecos, et Iulius apud Romanos. Hinc et monarchia dicitur. *Monas* quippe singularitas Graeco nomine, *arche* principatus est.[109]

Ælfric speaks of the three persons of the Trinity as 'an anginn', a single principle,[110] and the jewelled diadem on the head of the figure in the Benedictional draws attention to this *mon-arche* in a kind of visual pun on the opening words of the blessing:

Omnipotens Trinitas unus et verus Deus, Pater et Filius et Spiritus Sanctus, det vobis eum desiderare fideliter, agnoscere veraciter, diligere sinceriter. Amen.
Aequalitatem atque incommutabilitatem suae essentiae ita vestris mentibus infigat, ut ab eo numquam vos quibuscumque fantasiis oberrare permittat. Amen.
Sicque vos in sua fide et caritate perseverare concedat ut per ea postmodum ad sui manifestationem visionemque interminabilem introducat. Amen.[111]

The vision for which the speaker hopes is of the Godhead, the divine nature, not the separate persons of the Trinity. The distinction is appropriate, for in eternity the missionary roles of the Son and the Holy Spirit will no longer matter. In representing the Godhead by an image of Christ the artist is conveying a profound theological point. The revelation of the gospels is not concerned with facts about the divine; God *is* the revelation.

[109] Isidore, *Etymologiae* IX.iii.23 (ed. Lindsay): 'They are monarchs who possess a single rule, as Alexander among the Greeks and Julius among the Romans. From this comes the word monarchy. *Monas* in Greek means singleness and *arche* means rule.' Cf. Ælfric's remark, *LS*, Praef. (ed. Skeat, pp. 2–4), a reference I owe to Malcolm Godden.

[110] *Homilies*, no. i (ed. Pope I, 200); see above, p. 140 and below, p. 167.

[111] Additional 49598, 70r–v (ptd *Benedictional of Æthelwold*, ed. Warner and Wilson, p. 26).

# 7

# Symbols of the divine

The varied images through which the risen Christ was depicted served to convey the many different facets of his being: his divine nature, his descent from David, his roles as king and judge. Each, in turn, drew attention to some part of a truth impossible to grasp in its entirety. The changing symbols of the Trinity, on the other hand, were expressions of human inadequacy in the face of a mystery.

The artists of the Codex Amiatinus, written at Wearmouth or Jarrow at some date before 716, retained the early Christian symbols of the lamb and the dove for the second and third persons of the Trinity but replaced the *dextera Dei* by an equally symbolic human bust.[1] Variants on these symbols are still found in the late Anglo-Saxon period. In the early eleventh-century Bury Psalter the motifs of the lamb and dove are combined with a representation of a throned figure to accompany a group of prayers addressed to God the Father, God the Son and God the Holy Spirit.[2] The cruciferous nimbus which surrounds the head of the throned figure might suggest that it represents God the Son; but this cannot be the case, for the figure is labelled 'Maiestas Dei Patris'. The combination of inscription and nimbus indicates that what we have here is a sign: just as the dove and lamb are signs which stand for the second and third persons of the Trinity, so a representation of Christ, the image of God, can stand as a sign of God the Father who, being without form, cannot be represented directly.

The combination of throned figure, lamb and dove is found in two

---

[1] Florence, Biblioteca Medicea-Laurenziana, Amiatinus 1, vii, vi and 8 (reprod. Alexander, *Insular Manuscripts*, fig. 27 and pls. 24–5). See also above, p. 80.

[2] Biblioteca Apostolica Vaticana, Regin. lat. 12, 168v–169r (reprod. Ohlgren, *Textual Illustration*, pls. 3.48–9).

other late Anglo-Saxon manuscripts. A historiated initial in a tenth-century Boethius manuscript in Paris shows Boethius worshipping the Trinity.[3] At the top is a throned figure, his head framed by a cruciferous nimbus and the *alpha* and *omega*, a sealed scroll in his left hand; below him is a roundel framing a lamb with a cross-staff and below that a second roundel framing a dove. The upper figure represents the one whom St John sees seated on a throne and holding a scroll sealed with seven seals (Apoc. IV.2–3 and V.1–10). This figure, seen only as light, is neither Father nor Son but God himself, described as follows in the first chapter of the Apocalypse: 'I am the Alpha and the Omega says the Lord God, who is, who was, and who is to come, the Almighty' (Apoc. I.8).[4]

The drawing in the Tiberius Psalter (pl. XIa), Winchester work of the 1060s,[5] is similar to that in the Boethius manuscript though the three main figures have been arranged differently. The drawing shows a throned figure wearing a jewelled fillet, his head surrounded by a cruciferous nimbus; his left hand holds an open book and an unrolled scroll; to the sides of his head are the *alpha* and *omega*. The figure is accompanied by representations of the dove of the Holy Spirit and of the *Agnus Dei*, holding a cross-staff and book, and shown as a horned ram. The drawing is placed next to Psalm CIX, 'Yahweh's oracle to you, my Lord, Sit at my right hand and I will make your enemies a footstool for you', the text illustrated in the Utrecht Psalter and the Harley 603 copy of it by a drawing of the risen Christ seated at the right hand of his Father.[6] In the Tiberius drawing the passage from the psalm, quoted in all three synoptic gospels,[7] is linked to the scene of the lamb standing at the right of God's throne in the Apocalypse (Apoc. V.6–7). As in the Boethius manuscript, the throned figure is the one who is both Son and Father, who was dead and is alive, who was and who is and who is to come;[8] to his right is the risen Christ under the form of the apocalyptic lamb who has opened the sealed scroll.

A variant on these scenes of the lamb at the right hand of God is found

---

[3]  Paris, BN, lat. 6401, 159r (reprod. Temple, *Anglo-Saxon Manuscripts*, pl. 95).

[4]  See also Apoc. I.4 and IV.8, and above, p. 134.

[5]  This psalter has recently been redated on the basis of its Easter tables to 'sometime after Easter 1063': Heslop, 'A Dated "Late Anglo-Saxon" Illuminated Psalter', p. 171.

[6]  Utrecht, Universiteitsbibliothek, 32, 64v (reprod. van der Horst and Engelbregt), and BL, Harley 603, 56v (reprod. Ohlgren, *Textual Illustration*, pl. 2.72).

[7]  Matt. XXII.44, Mark XII.36 and Luke XX.43.      [8]  See above, p. 134.

in the Bury Psalter, next to Psalm LXXVIII (pl. XIb). The psalm speaks of those who 'have left the corpses of your servants to the birds of the air for food, and the flesh of your devout to the beasts of the earth', who 'have shed blood like water throughout Jerusalem' (Ps. LXXVIII.2–3). The artist of the psalter has interpreted these verses as prophetic references to the massacre of the innocents, depicted in the margins of 87v, and the death of the deacon, Stephen, shown partly on 87v and partly on 88r. The interpretation does not come from psalter commentaries and it seems likely that the source is a responsory for the Feast of the Holy Innocents:

Effuderunt sanguinem sanctorum velut aquam in circuitu Jerusalem, et non erat qui sepeliret.
V.A. Vindica, Domine, sanguinem sanctorum tuorum qui effusus est. R. In circuitu, *or* Et non.
V.B. Posuerunt mortalia servorum tuorum, Domine, escas volatilibus coeli, carnes sanctorum bestiis terrae. R. Et non.[9]

The responsory does not feature in the liturgy for the Feast of Stephen, but both feasts occur close to each other and, if New Testament scenes in the Psalter were based on a liturgical cycle as seems likely from other evidence, this might account for the link.[10] The account of Stephen's martyrdom in the Acts of the Apostles tells how he looked up to heaven and saw Christ standing at the right hand of God: 'I can see heaven thrown open, he said, and the Son of Man standing at the right hand of God' (Acts VII.56). In the initial for the Feast of St Stephen in the Drogo Sacramentary, produced at Metz between 850 and 855, God's right hand is depicted literally as the *dextera Dei*; to the right is a standing figure of Christ, holding a cross-staff and book.[11] In the Benedictional of Æthelwold Stephen is shown looking up towards a figure of Christ standing in a mandorla held by two angels; there is no attempt to represent God the Father.[12] The artist of the Bury Psalter, by contrast, does not merely show Christ at the Father's right; he interprets Stephen's vision as one of the Trinity.[13] In the centre of the scene is God the Father, holding a book and raising his right hand in

---

9 *Corpus antiphonalium*, ed. Hesbert I, 52–3 (no. 22b), II, 84–5 (no. 22b), IV, 160. The two versicles are alternatives.

10 See Harris, 'Marginal Drawings', pp. 232–46 for discussion of this point.

11 Paris, BN, lat. 9428, 27r (reprod. Koehler and Mütherich, *Drogo-Sakramentar*).

12 Additional 49598, 17v (reprod. Deshman, *Benedictional*, pl. 14).

13 Cf. ps.-Augustine, *Sermo ccxvi*, 1 (PL 39, 2147), which says that Stephen saw the Trinity while still in the body.

blessing; to his left is a dove, representing the Holy Spirit and, to his right, a standing figure of Christ, carrying shield and sword.

For medieval commentators, Stephen's vision, in which Christ appeared as Son of man rather than Son of God, was seen as a condemnation of the Jews: Christ's appearance in the form in which he had lived on earth confounds the unbelief of the Jews by demonstrating that his human nature is now endowed with the glory he always possessed as God.[14] Ælfric explains that Christ appeared in human form so that 'seo heofenlice soðfæstnyss' might be revealed 'be ðam cydde gecyðnysse'.[15] In the biblical account of Stephen's death, his vision is related to an earlier passage in which he is transfigured: just as Moses was transfigured after his encounter with God on Sinai, so Stephen's face reflects God's glory.[16] There is a difference, however. For Moses, God was essentially one; for the Christian, God was both three and one. In gazing on God, therefore, Stephen contemplates and reflects the Trinity and this is what the artist of the Bury Psalter shows. A second point which concerned medieval commentators was that Stephen saw Christ standing at God's right rather than seated, as in the often-quoted verse from Psalm CIX. Ælfric says:

Se eadiga Stephanus geseah Crist standan, forðan þe he wæs his gefylsta on ðam gastlicum gefeohte his martyrdomes. Witodlice we andettað on urum credan, þæt Drihten sitt æt his Fæder swiðran. Setl gedafenað deman, and steall fylstendum oððe feohtendum. Nu andet ure geleafa Cristes setl, forðan ðe he is se soða dema lybbendra and deadra; and se eadiga cyðere Stephanus hine geseah standende, forðan ðe he wæs his gefylsta, swa swa we ær sædon.[17]

---

[14] E.g. Bede, *Expositio Actuum Apostolorum*, vii.56 (ed. Laistner, p. 38): 'ut hoc testimonio Iudaeorum confunderetur infidelitas' ('in order that the infidelity of the Jews should be confounded by this testimony').

[15] *CH* I.iii (ed. Thorpe, p. 48): 'so that the heavenly truth might be revealed through the testimony which was proclaimed'.

[16] Exodus XXXIV.29–35, Acts VI.15, II Cor. III.7–18. See also Ælfric, *CH* I.iii (ed. Thorpe, p. 46). For the image of man as a mirror, see above, pp. 85 and 92.

[17] Ælfric, *CH* I.iii (ed. Thorpe, p. 48): 'The blessed Stephen saw Christ standing because he was his helper in the spiritual battle of his martyrdom. Truly, we confess in our creed that the Lord sits at his Father's right. Sitting is fitting for a judge and standing for a helper or fighter. Now our faith confesses Christ as sitting, because he is the true judge of the living and the dead, and the blessed martyr Stephen saw him standing because he was his helper as we said before.' Cf. Bede, *Expositio Actuum Apostolorum*, vii.56 (ed. Laistner, p. 38), *Homeliae* II.7 and II.10 (ed. Hurst, pp. 227–8 and 249) and Gregory, *Homiliae in evangelia* II.xxix.7 (PL 76, 1217).

The drawing in the Bury Psalter, which shows Christ armed with shield and sword, picks up these references to fighting and spiritual warfare.

Pictures in which Christ is symbolized by the lamb and the Holy Spirit by the dove emphasize the missionary roles of the second and third persons of the Trinity rather than their relationship to one another or their identity of nature:[18] they say nothing about the central mystery of the Trinity. A different attempt at such portrayal is seen in the Grimbald Gospels, Canterbury work of about AD 1020 (pls. XII and XIII).[19] The opening of St John's Gospel in this manuscript is marked by a particularly elaborate series of scenes. The border of the left-hand page, surrounding the figure of St John, shows the three persons of the Trinity enthroned side by side and surrounded by angels; to the sides are figures of saints, kings and priests, while at the bottom of the page angels hold a group of souls up towards God. The right-hand page shows an enthroned Virgin and Child accompanied by two seraphs; to the sides are groups of saints and kings. The three nearly identical throned figures signify the three persons within a single nature: the Trinity in Unity theme.[20] There is one puzzle, however. One would expect God the Father to occupy the central position; here, the cruciferous nimbus of the central figure suggests that this is Christ. Yet this need not be the case if, as was suggested above, the Father is symbolized by the image of the Son, in whom image and archetype are one.[21]

Jennifer O'Reilly interprets the borders of these pages as illustrations of the themes of the opening chapter of St John's Gospel, namely the presence of the Word with God in the beginning and the entry of that same Word into human history at the Nativity. She contrasts the Word with God (shown above the figure of St John on the left-hand page), with the Word made flesh (on the opposite page) and sees the figures of saints and angels who surround these images as a sign that 'Christ's humanity

[18] On the missions or sending of the Son and the Spirit, see Augustine, *De Trinitate* II (ed. Mountain, pp. 80–126).

[19] For a colour reproduction, see *Golden Age*, pl. xvi, and for discussion: Raw, *Crucifixion Iconography*, pp. 36 and 39; O'Reilly, 'St John', pp. 179–80; Gameson, 'Manuscript Art at Christ Church', pp. 216–17.

[20] Deshman, *Benedictional*, p. 98, suggests that the figures in the Grimbald Gospels should be seen as an expansion of the Trinitarian image in the Benedictional. See also above, pp. 141–2.

[21] I owe this point to Aidan Nichols OP.

shares in the glory of his eternal divinity'.[22] Richard Gameson, on the other hand, emphasizes the relationship established in these borders between the opening passage of St John's Gospel and the Apocalypse:

As well as exploring the nature of the Trinity, through text and image these two pages offer a synthetic vision of Christian cosmic history: the mystery of the Word in the beginning, before the world; God's entry into the world through the Incarnation; the continuance of Christianity in the world through the work of apostles, ecclesiastics and kings; and finally, beyond the world, the heavenly Jerusalem with the twenty-four elders, and the Last Judgement.[23]

Like the decoration to the canon tables in the Pembroke, Trinity and Harley Gospels, the two pages in the Grimbald Gospels offer a vision of the next world, with its companies of saints and angels and, above all, the presence of the Trinity and of Mary.[24]

Two of the most important late Anglo-Saxon pictures of the Trinity – those in the Ælfwine Prayerbook and the Arenberg Gospels – resemble the Grimbald Gospels in including a figure of Mary (pls. XVb and XIVb). Both scenes derive from the illustrations to the Utrecht Psalter, produced at Hautvillers, near Rheims, in the second quarter of the ninth century.[25] In addition to the representations of historical events associated with the Canticle of Habakkuk (85v), the *Benedictus* (88v) and the Apostles' Creed (90r), the Psalter includes three representations of the Trinity: at the *Te Deum* (88r), the *Gloria* (89v) and the Apostles' Creed (90r). The drawing preceding the Athanasian Creed (90v), on the other hand, makes no attempt to depict the complex Trinitarian definitions of the text and instead shows the church council at which the Creed was supposedly composed.[26]

The *Te Deum* and the *Gloria* are hymns of praise to God and the illustrations to both texts in the Utrecht Psalter show the authors of the texts, together with groups of the faithful, gazing upwards to a symbolic

---

[22] O'Reilly, 'St John', p. 179.

[23] Gameson, 'Manuscript Art at Christ Church', p. 217. Cf. the discussion of the miniature to St John's Gospel in the Bernward Gospels, which links Christ's birth to the apocalyptic scene of the opening of the book by the lamb, above, pp. 131–2.

[24] See above, pp. 127–8.

[25] Utrecht, Universiteitsbibliothek, 32 (reprod. van der Horst and Engelbregt).

[26] Cf. the drawings in a ninth-century collection of canon law, Vercelli, Biblioteca Capitolare, clxv (reprod. Hubert, Porcher and Volbach, *Europe in the Dark Ages*, pls. 157–8).

image of the Godhead. The focus of their worship in the illustration to the
*Te Deum* (88r) is the risen Christ, seated in a globe-mandorla and crowned
with a wreath by the hand of God;[27] a dove, representing the Holy Spirit,
perches on the book held by Christ and beneath his feet lies the figure of
death, defeated by Christ's death; to the sides of the mandorla are two
seraphs. The opening section of the text praises God as Lord and Father, a
definition later expanded to include his 'true and only Son, who is to be
adored, [and] the Holy Spirit sent to be our Advocate'.[28] Much of the
hymn, however, focuses on Christ's incarnation and death, his enthronement at his Father's side and his future return as judge:

Tu rex gloriae, Christe, tu Patris sempiternus es Filius. Tu ad liberandum
suscepturus hominem, non horruisti Virginis uterum. Tu devicto mortis aculeo,
aperuisti credentibus regna caelorum. Tu ad dexteram Dei sedes, in gloria Patris.
Judex crederis esse venturus.[29]

The illustration makes no attempt to show these narrative elements: there
is no reference to Mary or to the Incarnation, nor is Christ seated at the
right hand of the Father, as he is described in the text. The theme of the
drawing is the worship offered by the Church, the saints and angels to
Christ, who has defeated death, received the victor's crown from his
Father, and is now revealed as God. As St Paul says:

After that will come the end, when he hands over the kingdom to God the
Father, having done away with every sovereignty, authority and power. For he
must be king *until he has put all his enemies under his feet* and the last of the enemies
to be destroyed is death ... And when everything is subjected to him, then the
Son himself will be subject in his turn to the One who subjected all things to
him, so that God may be all in all (I Cor. XV.24–8).[30]

---

[27] Cf. Heb. II.9.

[28] 'aeternum Patrem ... Patrem immensae maiestatis, venerandum tuum verum et
unicum Filium, Sanctum quoque Paraclitum Spiritum'.

[29] 'You, Christ, are the king of glory, eternal Son of the Father. When you took our nature
to save mankind you did not shrink from birth in the Virgin's womb. You overcame
the power of death, opening the kingdom of heaven to all who believe in you.
Enthroned at God's right hand in the glory of the Father, you will come in judgement
according to your promise.'

[30] Cf. Ephes. I.20–3: 'This you can tell from the strength of his power at work in Christ,
when he used it to raise him from the dead and to make him sit at his right hand, in
heaven, far above every Sovereignty, Authority, Power or Domination, or any other
name that can be named, not only in this age but also in the age to come. *He has put all*

The illustration to the *Gloria* (89v), like that to the *Te Deum*, focuses on a youthful figure seated in a globe-mandorla; to his left is a lamb and, to his right, a representation of Mary holding the Christ child, while the dove of the Holy Spirit perches on her head. A rather similar motif forms the focal point of the illustration to the Apostles' Creed (90r), though here the lamb is missing. The central figure in both drawings must represent God the Father, addressed in the opening section of the *Gloria* as 'Domine Deus, Rex caelestis, Deus Pater omnipotens'. The lamb is a symbol of Christ, described in the text of the *Gloria* as 'Agnus Dei, Filius Patris, qui tollis peccata mundi'.[31] The figure of Mary, overshadowed by the dove of the Spirit and holding her child, recalls the conception and birth of Christ. But whereas in the illustration to the *Gloria* Mary simply stands at God's right, in the illustration to the Apostles' Creed she places her child on a throne.

The Apostles' Creed sets out the articles of faith to which candidates for baptism gave their assent.[32] The Utrecht illustration includes representations of many of the Creed's individual clauses: Christ's death on the cross, the dead rising from their graves, the Harrowing of Hell, the three women at the tomb and the Ascension. What is missing from this sequence is any reference to Christ's birth, to his place at the right hand of God and his return as judge. The group of figures at the top of the drawing links these events in one complex scene. The detail of the throne relates Christ's birth to his glorification. In the Acts of the Apostles the opening verse of Psalm CIX is linked to other Messianic prophecies from the psalms to argue that Christ has been constituted Lord by his resurrection:

Brothers, no one can deny that the patriarch David himself is dead and buried: his tomb is still with us. But since he was a prophet, and knew that God *had sworn him* an oath *to make one of his descendants succeed him on the throne*, what he foresaw and spoke about was the resurrection of the Christ; he is the one who was *not abandoned to Hades*, and whose body did not *experience corruption*. God raised this man Jesus to life, and all of us are witnesses to that. Now raised to the heights by God's right hand, he has received from the Father the Holy Spirit, who was

things under his feet, and made him, as the ruler of everything, the head of the Church; which is his body, the fullness of him who fills the whole creation.' The reference is to Ps. VIII.6–8: 'Yet you have made him little less than a god, you have crowned him with glory and splendour, made him lord over the work of your hands, set all things under his feet.' See also Bede, *Homeliae* II.8 (ed. Hurst, pp. 234–5).

[31] Cf. John I.29.      [32] Kelly, *Creeds*, pp. 368–97.

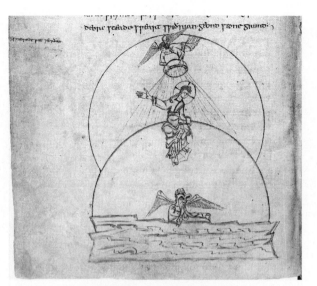

Ia    Oxford, Bodleian Library, Junius 11, p. 6, Creation

Ib    London, British Library, Cotton Tiberius C. vi
(Tiberius Psalter), 7v, Creation

II   London, British Library, Cotton Tiberius C. vi (Tiberius Psalter), 18v,
enthroned figure of Christ

III    London, British Library, Additional 49598 (Benedictional of Æthelwold),
9v, the Second Coming

IV   Oxford, Bodleian Library, Auct. F. 4. 32 (Dunstan Classbook), 1r,
St Dunstan with Christ

V   London, British Library, Cotton Vespasian A. viii (New Minster Charter), 2v,
Edgar offering his charter to Christ

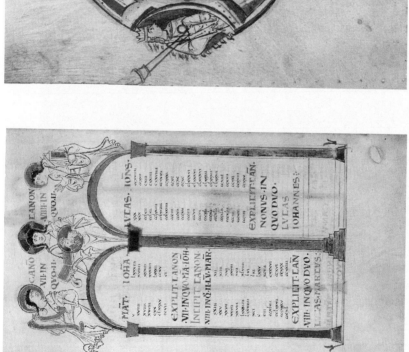

VIa   New York, Pierpont Morgan Library, 869 (Arenberg
      Gospels), 12v, Christ holding the *Agnus Dei*

VIb   Cambridge, University Library, Ii. 3. 12, 62v, detail,
      Mary holding the *Agnus Dei*

VIIb  London, British Library, Cotton Galba A. xviii
(Athelstan Psalter), 21r, Christ showing his wounds

VIIa  London, British Library, Cotton Galba A. xviii
(Athelstan Psalter), 2v, Christ with symbols of the passion

VIII   Cambridge, Trinity College B. 15. 34, 1r, Christ as judge

IX    Boulogne, Bibliothèque municipale, 11 (Boulogne Gospels), 10r,
God the creator

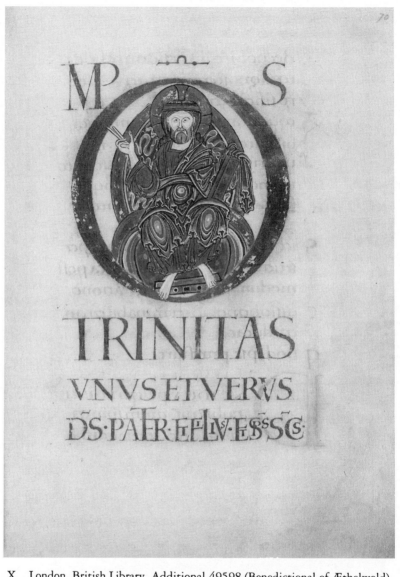

X    London, British Library, Additional 49598 (Benedictional of Æthelwold),
70r, Christ as image of the Trinity

XIa   London, British Library, Cotton Tiberius C. vi (Tiberius Psalter),
126v, Trinity

XIb   Vatican City, Biblioteca Apostolica Vaticana, Regin. lat. 12
(Bury Psalter), 88r, detail, Trinity

XII   London, British Library, Additional 34890 (Grimbald Gospels),
114v, Trinity

XIII    London, British Library, Additional 34890 (Grimbald Gospels), 115r,
Virgin and Child

XIVb  New York, Pierpont Morgan Library, 869
(Arenberg Gospels), 11v, Trinity with Mary

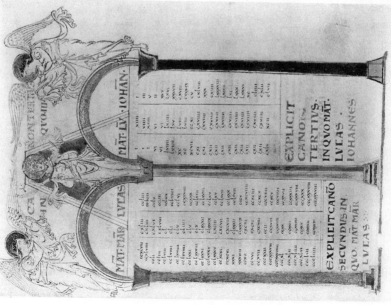

XIVa  New York, Pierpont Morgan Library, 869
(Arenberg Gospels), 11r, Virgin and Child

XVb   London, British Library, Cotton Titus D. xxvii
(Ælfwine Prayerbook), 75v, Trinity with Mary

XVa   London, British Library, Harley 603 (Harley Psalter),
1r, Trinity

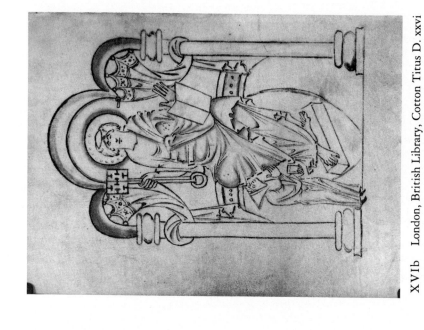

XVIb London, British Library, Cotton Titus D. xxvi
(Ælfwine Prayerbook), 19v, Ælfwine with St Peter

XVIa London, British Library, Cotton Titus D. xxvii
(Ælfwine Prayerbook), 65v, Crucifixion

promised, and what you see and hear is the outpouring of that Spirit. For David himself never went up to heaven; and yet these words are his: *The Lord said to my Lord: Sit at my right hand until I make your enemies a footstool for you.*

(Acts II.29–35)[33]

In this passage, Christ's seat at his Father's right is presented as the fulfilment of God's promise to David that his son – interpreted as the Messiah – would succeed to his throne:

> Yahweh swore to David
> and will remain true to his word,
> 'I promise that your own son
> shall succeed you on the throne'. (Ps. CXXXI.11)[34]

These words were echoed by Gabriel at the Annunciation:

You are to conceive and bear a son, and you must name him Jesus. He will be great and will be called Son of the Most High. The Lord God will give him the throne of his ancestor David; he will rule over the House of Jacob for ever and his reign will have no end. (Luke I.31–3)

By showing Mary placing her child on the heavenly throne, the artist of the Utrecht drawing has put a gloss on the words of the Creed, and has shown Christ taking his seat at the right hand of God the Father at the time of his birth, not at the Ascension. At the same time, he has drawn attention to Mary's presence in heaven and to the reason for it, a point made in an antiphon for the Feast of the Assumption: 'O Maria semper virgo, cuius fructus uteri positus est in solio David, intercede pro populo qui petit a te suffragium, alleluia.'[35] The figure of Mary holding the Christ child and with the dove of the Holy Spirit above her head is not a picture of the birth of Christ but a symbol, and the child she holds, both here and in the illustration to the *Gloria*, is an emblem, comparable to St Peter's keys or the lamb held by John the Baptist.

---

[33] Cf. Rom. VIII.34, Heb. X.12 and I Pet. III.22. The quotations are from Psalms CXXXI.11, XV.10 and CIX.1. See also Ælfric, *CH* I.xxii (ed. Thorpe, p. 314).

[34] The verse is quoted by Paschasius Radbertus in a sermon on the Assumption, *Sermo i, De assumptione* (PL 96, 240); for the attribution to Paschasius, see *De partu*, ed. Matter and Ripberger, p. 10, n. 8. See also Ælfric, *CH* I.xiii (ed. Thorpe, p. 198) and *Laterculus Malalianus*, 14 (ed. Stevenson, p. 140).

[35] *Corpus antiphonalium*, ed. Hesbert III, 370: 'O Mary, ever virgin, the fruit of whose womb is set on the throne of David, intercede for the people who seek help from you, alleluia.'

It seems likely that the inclusion of Mary in these scenes, and her position to the right of God the Father, derives from a verse in Psalm XLIV, 'Adstitit regina a dextris tuis in vestitu deaurato, circumdata varietate.'[36] Psalm XLIV was regularly used as one of the psalms for the second nocturn of the Feast of the Assumption[37] and the ninth-century *Officia per ferias* includes the psalm in the office for Saturday under the heading, 'Psalmus in honore S. Mariae'.[38] A responsory based on the same psalm is a regular feature of the night office for the Feast of the Assumption in early antiphoners:

Ornatam in monilibus filiam Jerusalem Dominus concupivit, et videntes eam filiae Sion beatissimam praedicaverunt dicentes: Unguentum effusum nomen tuum.
*V.A.* Astitit regina a dextris tuis in vestitu deaurato, circumdata varietate. *R.* Et videntes.
*V.B.* Omnis gloria eius filiae regum ab intus, in fimbriis aureis circumamicta varietate. *R.* Et videntes.[39]

Augustine interpreted Psalm XLIV as a celebration of the marriage of Christ and the Church: 'Sponsa ecclesia est, sponsus Christus'; the queen stands at the right hand of Christ rather than the left because that is where the saved will stand at the judgement.[40] The two who are joined together in marriage, however, are not Christ and the Church but the two natures

---

[36] Ps. XLIV.10: 'The queen has taken her place at your right hand, in a garment of cloth of gold, swathed in a many-coloured robe' (trans. Bettenson, *City of God*, p. 747). The first writer to interpret Psalm XLIV with reference to Mary was Jerome, *Epist.* cvii.7 (PL 22, 874); see Graef, *Mary*, p. 93.

[37] *Corpus antiphonalium*, ed. Hesbert I, 284–5 (no. 106b) and II, 532 (no. 106c).

[38] *Officia per ferias* (PL 101, 586).

[39] *Corpus antiphonalium*, ed. Hesbert I, 284–5 (no. 106b), II, 532–3 (no. 106c) and IV, 334: 'The Lord has desired the daughter of Jerusalem, decorated with necklaces, and seeing her the daughters of Sion called her most blessed, saying: Your name is an oil poured out (Song of Songs I.3). *Versicle A.* The queen has taken her place at your right hand, in a garment of cloth of gold, swathed in a many-coloured robe. *R.* And seeing. *Versicle B.* The king's daughter is all glorious within, swathed in a many-coloured robe with golden fringes. *R.* And seeing'. See also the Old English Martyrology under 15 August, quoted by Clayton, *Cult of the Virgin*, p. 214, and Bernard of Clairvaux, *In laudibus Virginis matris*, *Hom.* ii, 2 (ed. Leclercq and Rochais, p. 22).

[40] *Enarrationes in Psalmos*, Ps. XLIV, 3 and 24 (ed. Dekkers and Fraipont I, 495 and 512). See also Augustine, *De civitate Dei* XVII.xvi (ed. Dombart and Kalb, pp. 580–1), where the queen represents not only the Church but the city of Sion and the heavenly Jerusalem.

of Christ, 'verbum et caro', while the wedding bed is the womb of the Virgin Mary.[41] Paschasius Radbertus followed Augustine in identifying the queen of Psalm XLIV as the Church[42] but he also applied the words of the psalm to Mary, particularly in relation to her assumption into heaven. In the *Epistula ad Paulam et Eustochium* he speaks of Mary being raised to the right hand of God the Father, where Christ had preceded her,[43] and in a later passage he alludes to the following responsory for the Feast of the Assumption:

Veni, electa mea, et ponam in te thronum meum, quia concupivit Rex speciem tuam.
V. Specie tua et pulchritudine tua, intende, prospere procede et regna. R. Quia.[44]

Paschasius's clearest statements about Mary's position in heaven are found in three sermons on the Assumption. Today, he says, Mary has entered into the marriage of the bridegroom and the bride; Christ placed her beside him on his throne and she now sees the son she mourned, as he hung on the cross, seated at the right hand of his Father; she has been raised to the throne at God's right, as the psalm says, 'Adstitit regina a dextris tuis in vestitu deaurato, circumdata varietate.'[45] In these passages Paschasius makes explicit what is implicit in his other Marian writings: that Mary has entered into the marriage of Christ and his Church and now reigns at Christ's side;[46] that her throne was prepared in heaven even before time began;[47] that she is the true temple and tabernacle, the ark

---

[41] *Enarrationes in Psalmos*, Ps. XLIV.1–3 (ed. Dekkers and Fraipont I, 493–5). There is, of course, still an allusion to the Church, which is, metaphorically, the body of Christ.

[42] *Expositio* III.xliv.10 and 14 (ed. Paulus, pp. 77 and 93).

[43] *Epistula* vii. 39 (ed. Matter and Ripberger, p. 125).

[44] *Ibid.*, xiv. 91 (ed. Matter and Ripberger, p. 151): 'Come my chosen one, and I will place my throne in you, for the king has desired your beauty. In your majesty and beauty advance, proceed in prosperity and reign' (Ps. XLIV.5). Paschasius quotes the responsory again in his *Sermo iii, De assumptione* (PL 96, 255). The responsory was used for the Feasts of the Annunciation and the Assumption, and for the Common of Virgins, see *Corpus antiphonalium*, ed. Hesbert IV, 448; verse 5 of the psalm, which referred originally to the king of the psalm, has here been transferred to Mary. Verse 12 is quoted in several prayers in honour of Mary; see Barré, *Prières*, pp. 79, 114, 121 and 123.

[45] *Sermo i, De assumptione* (PL 96, 241, 243 and 246). See also *Sermo ii* and *iii* (PL 96, 251 and 255) and Ælfric, *CH* I.xxx (ed. Thorpe, p. 442).

[46] *Sermo i, De assumptione* (PL 96, 241) and above, p. 152.

[47] *Sermo ii, De assumptione* (PL 96, 251).

containing the manna and the rod of Aaron, which flowered when God's Wisdom took flesh in her womb.[48]

Paschasius wrote about Mary's privileged status many times; his praise of her, however, is always dependent on his Christology. He stresses that Mary did not enter heaven as of right; her position at God's side results from her role as the one who was overshadowed by the Holy Spirit and who bore one who was both God and man.[49] In his *De partu virginis*, he talks at length about Christ's two natures.[50] He stresses that Christ was not merely son of God by adoption[51] and, in an allusion to the Nestorian controversy, sets out the orthodox position: that the Church worships one Christ, God and man, one person with two natures.[52] It was this God-man who lay in the tomb and rose from the dead, who is no longer hanging on the cross but seated at the right hand of God, reigning over all.[53] For Paschasius, Christ reveals the true nature of the Trinity: before his birth we knew only that God was One; he was a hidden God; we knew nothing of his Son and so did not rightly know the Father.[54] In the *Epistula ad Paulam et Eustochium* these themes are set out at greater length. Christ is the Word of God, present with him in the beginning;[55] in Christ, the disciples saw and touched God himself.[56] Christ is a single person, uniting the divine and the human and Mary is therefore rightly called *Dei genetrix* and *Theotokos*.[57] Christ had two births, from his Father before time and from Mary in time,[58] but we should not talk of two Sons, as though Christ was something other than the Son of God.[59] Christ, the Word, never left the Father when he became man for, as St John said, 'No one has gone up to heaven except

---

[48] *Sermo i, De assumptione* and *iii* (PL 96, 241, 246, 248 and 255).

[49] *Epistula* vii. 40 (ed. Matter and Ripberger, p. 126).

[50] *De partu virginis* I (ed. Matter and Ripberger, pp. 49–50).

[51] *Ibid.* I (ed. Matter and Ripberger, p. 51).

[52] *Ibid.* II (ed. Matter and Ripberger, p. 83).

[53] *Ibid.* II (ed. Matter and Ripberger, pp. 88–9).

[54] *Ibid.* II (ed. Matter and Ripberger, p. 85); see also *Expositio* II.xliv.1 (ed. Paulus, p. 31).

[55] *Epistula* iii. 18 (ed. Matter and Ripberger, p. 117).

[56] *Ibid.* xii. 76 (ed. Matter and Ripberger, p. 143); see also *Expositio* II.xliv.1 (ed. Paulus, p. 31).

[57] *Epistula* v. 31 and ix. 54–5 (ed. Matter and Ripberger, pp. 123 and 132–3).

[58] *Ibid.* ix. 54 (ed. Matter and Ripberger, p. 132).

[59] *Ibid.* x. 65 (ed. Matter and Ripberger, p. 139).

the one who came down from heaven, the Son of Man who is in heaven' (John III.13).[60]

In his commentary on Psalm XLIV, written for the nuns of Soissons to encourage devotion to Mary,[61] Paschasius again sets out the orthodox belief about the Incarnation in meticulous detail. The verse, 'Eructavit cor meum verbum bonum' is explained as an allusion to Christ, the Word spoken by God.[62] In God the whole Christ, both God and man, is adored; he is not divided in person or confused in substance, nor is he an adopted son; Mary therefore is correctly called 'mater Dei et vera Dei genetrix'.[63] Christ has handed over the kingdom to his Father and has taken his place at God's right, together with the queen of the psalm.[64] This emphasis on the inseparability of Christ's divine and human natures and on its relationship to Mary's privileged position in heaven throws new light on the drawings in the Utrecht manuscript.[65] The inclusion of Mary in the illustrations to the *Gloria* and the Apostles' Creed proclaims her presence in heaven at the right hand of God; that she is shown overshadowed by the dove of the Spirit and holding her child corresponds to Paschasius's insistence that her assumption into heaven resulted from her position as the mother of one who was both God and man. That Christ is shown trampling death under foot in the illustration to the *Te Deum* corresponds to Paschasius's statement that Christ triumphed over his enemies on the cross, and then took his seat on his Father's throne, a king for ever.[66] Paschasius's reference to the praise offered by the choirs of prophets, apostles and martyrs to Christ, who is seated at the right hand of God, recalls the Psalter's illustrations to the *Te Deum* and *Gloria*.[67] His

---

[60] *Ibid.* v. 30 and xii. 73 (ed. Matter and Ripberger, pp. 122 and 141–2).

[61] *Expositio* III.xliv.18 (ed. Paulus, p. 98); cf. also *Epistula* iv. 20 (ed. Matter and Ripberger, p. 118) where Mary is described as 'exemplum perfectionis virginibus', and xvi.107 (*ibid.*, p. 158) where the nuns are exhorted to reform God's image in themselves by impressing the image of Mary, the form of virginity, on themselves.

[62] 'My heart is stirred by a noble theme' (Ps. XLIV.2), *Expositio* II.xliv.2 (ed. Paulus, pp. 32–3). This verse was used at an earlier period to counter Arian arguments that Christ was not co-eternal with God the Father; see Kelly, *Christian Doctrines*, p. 234.

[63] *Expositio* II.xliv.3 and 8 and III.xliv.12 (ed. Paulus, pp. 36, 64–5 and 83).

[64] *Ibid.* III.xliv.10 (ed. Paulus, pp. 74 and 78); cf. I Cor. XV.25–6.

[65] Paschasius's writings show that these ideas were current in the second quarter of the ninth century; they did not necessarily influence the artists of the Utrecht Psalter directly.

[66] *Expositio* I.xliv.1 (ed. Paulus, p. 16).    [67] *Ibid.* I.xliv.1 (ed. Paulus, p. 23).

comments on the verse, 'Sedes tua, Deus, in saeculum saeculi, virga directionis virga regni tui' (Ps. XLIV.7), are particularly important for the understanding of the Utrecht drawings. Christ's throne, Paschasius says, existed before time began and it will last to the end of time;[68] this is the throne referred to in God's promise to David, 'De fructu ventris tui ponam super sedem tuam' (Ps. CXXXI.11) and in Gabriel's promise to Mary, 'Hic erit magnus et Filius Altissimi vocabitur, et dabit illi Dominus Deus sedem David patris eius, et regnabit in domo Iacob in aeternum, et regni eius non erit finis' (Luke I.32–3).[69] Christ's enthronement is therefore linked to his birth from Mary, not, as is more usual, to his ascension; it confirms his position as the Messiah, the Son of God but also, through his mother, the descendant of David.[70]

The drawing of the Trinity with Mary in the Ælfwine Prayerbook (pl. XVb) shows God the Father and God the Son seated side by side on an arc; to their right stands Mary holding the Christ child in her arms and with the dove of the Holy Spirit above her head. The devil lies bound in the jaws of hell below the feet of the central figure, and to the sides of hell's jaws are seated figures of Arius and Judas. Kantorowicz showed many years ago that the upper part of this drawing combines motifs from two scenes in the Utrecht Psalter: the illustration to the *Gloria* and that to Psalm CIX, illustrating the text, 'Dixit Dominus Domino meo: Sede a dextris meis, donec ponam inimicos tuos scabellum pedum tuorum.'[71] He followed de Wald in identifying the two seated figures of the Utrecht illustration to Psalm CIX as Christ's divine and human natures: Christ, *Filius Dei*, seated on the globe as ruler of the universe and Christ, *Filius David*, seated on a throne.[72] This separation of Christ's divine and human natures is fundamental to Kantorowicz's interpretation of the Ælfwine drawing and of the Utrecht illustrations to the *Gloria* and Apostles' Creed

[68] *Ibid.* II.xliv.7 and 8 (ed. Paulus, pp. 62 and 66).

[69] *Ibid.* II.xliv.7 (ed. Paulus, p. 61).

[70] Cf. Rom. I.3–4, 'This news is about the Son of God who, according to the human nature he took, was a descendant of David; it is about Jesus Christ our Lord who, in the order of the spirit, the spirit of holiness that was in him, was proclaimed Son of God in all his power through his resurrection from the dead.'

[71] 'Yahweh's oracle to you, my Lord, Sit at my right hand and I will make your enemies a footstool for you', Utrecht, Universiteitsbibliothek, 32, 89v and 64v (reprod. van der Horst and Engelbregt). For discussion of the scene, see Kantorowicz, 'Quinity', Kidd, 'Quinity' and Raw, 'What do we Mean by the Source of a Picture?', pp. 292–7.

[72] de Wald, *Utrecht Psalter*, p. 50; Kantorowicz, 'Quinity', pp. 104–5.

to which it is related. Kantorowicz saw the apocalyptic motifs of the lamb and the cushioned throne in the Utrecht illustrations to the *Gloria* and the Apostles' Creed as symbols of Christ's divine nature, and the child in Mary's arms as a symbol of his humanity.[73] He retained this identification of the figure of Mary holding her child in his interpretation of the Ælfwine drawing but argued that the two seated figures, who are not distinguished from each other as they are in the Utrecht manuscript, represent *Christus Deus* at the right hand of God the Father. According to Kantorowicz, then, the Ælfwine picture shows 'the throned *Christus Deus* and the infant *Jesus homo*', the two figures together forming one person.[74] Kantorowicz was well aware that such an interpretation was heretical, but he explained the presence of what he saw as Nestorian elements in the Ælfwine drawing and its antecedents in the Utrecht Psalter as an over-reaction to Arianism.[75] It is true, of course, that Psalm CIX was quoted against the Arians by patristic writers and that a figure of Arius is placed beneath Mary's feet in the Ælfwine drawing, but it is highly unlikely that the artist would have split Christ's person in this way. Jerome points out in his commentary on Psalm CIX that one should not create two persons out of the two sons (Son of God and son of David)[76] and Augustine states the consequences of separating Christ's two natures very clearly in his *Liber de praedestinatione sanctorum*:

Praedestinatus est ergo Jesus, ut qui futurus erat secundum carnem filius David, esset tamen in virtute Filius Dei secundum Spiritum sanctificationis; quia natus est de Spiritu sancto et virgine Maria. Ipsa est illa ineffabiliter facta hominis a Deo Verbo susceptio singularis, ut Filius Dei et filius hominis simul, filius hominis propter susceptum hominem, et Filius Dei propter suscipientem unigenitum Deum veraciter et proprie diceretur: ne non trinitas, sed quaternitas crederetur.[77]

---

[73] Kantorowicz, 'Quinity', pp. 109–10.

[74] *Ibid.*, p. 110. See also Raw, 'What do we Mean by the Source of a Picture?', p. 295.

[75] Kantorowicz, 'Quinity', pp. 111–13.

[76] Jerome, *Breviarium in Psalmos*, cix (PL 26, 1163). See also Acts of Nicaea II, 260A and 261D (trans. Sahas, pp. 90 and 92), and above, p. 55.

[77] *Liber de praedestinatione sanctorum*, xv.31 (PL 44, 982–3, and trans. Modern Roman Breviary, Friday of Week 13): 'And so Jesus was predestined, so that he who was to be the son of David according to the flesh should nevertheless be the Son of God in power according to the Spirit of holiness; for he was born of the Holy Spirit and of the Virgin Mary. Thus in a unique and inexpressible way a man was assumed by God the Word and so could truly and properly be called at once Son of God and son of man: son of

Paschasius Radbertus states specifically that Christ is a single person who is not to be divided into two sons: the point is important for his argument that Mary is rightly called *mater Dei et vera Dei genetrix*.[78] Ælfric was familiar with at least two works by Paschasius[79] and both Bede and Ælfric knew of the condemnation of Nestorius for appearing to claim that there were two persons in Christ.[80] Ælfric stresses the identity of the son of man and the Son of God in a comment on the passage, 'No one has gone up to heaven except the one who came down from heaven' (John III.13):

He cwæð þis unleaslice, for ðære soðan annysse his hades. He is on twam gecyndum an Crist, soð man, and soð God, and se mannes sunu is Godes sunu, and se Godes sunu is mannes sunu, anes mannes swa we ær cwædon, Marian þæs mædenes.[81]

It is inconceivable that an artist working at Winchester during the early eleventh century would have chosen to represent Christ's two natures in a way which might be thought to imply that the Son of God and the son of man were two separate persons.

Whereas Kantorowicz discussed the drawing in the Ælfwine manuscript largely in relation to its artistic sources and to patristic commentaries on Psalm CIX, Judith Kidd has attempted to relate it to the thought of the early eleventh century. She retains Kantorowicz's identification of the central, seated, figure and of the child in Mary's arms as representations of Christ's divine and human natures,[82] but her main interest is in the grouping of Mary, Arius and Judas, something which

---

man because of the man assumed, Son of God because of the only-begotten God who assumed. Otherwise we should believe not in the Trinity but in a quaternity.' See above, p. 55.

[78] *Expositio* III.xliv.12 (ed. Paulus, p. 83); see above, p. 155.

[79] *Epistula* and *De corpore et sanguine*. Æthelwold invited monks from Corbie to Abingdon to teach his monks the chant (see above, p. 96) and it is likely that this provided a route for Paschasius's writings and ideas.

[80] Bede, *HE* IV.xvii (ed. Colgrave and Mynors, p. 386) and Ælfric, 'First Latin Letter to Wulfstan', 57 (ed. Fehr, p. 42). It seems likely that the condemnation misrepresented Nestorius's position; see Kelly, *Christian Doctrines*, pp. 310–17.

[81] *CH* II.xxiv (ed. Godden, p. 224): 'He said this without lying, because of the real unity of his person. He is one Christ in two natures, true man and true God, and the son of man is God's Son, and the Son of God is the son of man: of one man, as we said before, that is, of the Virgin Mary.' Ælfric is expanding the comments of Bede, *Homeliae* II.18 (ed. Hurst, pp. 314–15). Cf. also Paschasius, above, pp. 154–5.

[82] Kidd, 'Quinity', pp. 21, 22 and 27.

cannot be explained with reference to the Utrecht Psalter, and which she links to anti-Jewish sentiment in the early eleventh century and to the outbreaks of heresy in France and Italy during the 1020s.[83] In support of her argument she quotes a responsory, known at Winchester, in which Mary is said to have destroyed all heresies:

Gaude Maria Virgo: cunctas haereses sola interemisti, quae Gabrielis archangeli dictis credidisti, dum virgo Deum et hominem genuisti, et post partum virgo inviolata permansisti.

V. Gabrielem archangelum credimus divinitus te esse affatum; uterum tuum de Spiritu Sancto credimus impraegnatum; erubescat Judaeus infelix, qui dicit Christum ex Joseph semine esse natum. R. Dum virgo.[84]

The text dates from long before the eleventh century, however: it appears in the Antiphonary of Compiègne, which dates from the last quarter of the ninth century, and, according to legend, was composed in Rome between about 610 and 615.[85] Moreover, the responsory does not mention either Arius or Judas, though it does refer to the Jews, and Jews and Arians were frequently linked.[86]

The Ælfwine drawing is better interpreted in relation to Paschasius's teaching on Mary, outlined above. The upper part of the drawing is a celebration of Christ, the Son of God and son of David, and of his mother. The central figure is the risen Christ, who is shown seated at his Father's right, as he is described in the *Gloria* and the Creed. The figures of Father and Son are similar because Christ is the true image of the Father, identical to him in substance.[87] The bound devil, who forms Christ's footstool, offers a reminder of Christ's defeat of the devil; he recalls Christ's prophecy of his death (John XII.31–2) and the common belief that Christ had bound Satan during his descent into hell.[88] The figure of Mary is an image

---

[83] *Ibid.*, pp. 27–30. On Ælfric's attitude to the Jews and eleventh-century heresies, see above, pp. 25–6.

[84] *Corpus antiphonalium*, ed. Hesbert IV, 191, trans. Kidd, *ibid.*, pp. 23–4: 'Rejoice, Virgin Mary, you alone have destroyed all heresies and believed what the archangel Gabriel spoke; while a Virgin you brought forth God and man, and after the birth you remained a chaste virgin. We believe that the archangel Gabriel addressed you by divine inspiration. We believe that your womb was impregnated by the Holy Spirit. Let the unhappy Jew blush with shame, who says that Christ was born from the seed of Joseph.'

[85] Brou, 'Marie Destructrice', pp. 322–3.    [86] See above, p. 25.

[87] Cf. Col. I.15 and II Cor. IV.4.

[88] Raw, 'What do we Mean by the Source of a Picture?', pp. 293–4.

of the Assumption. She stands at the right hand of God, like the queen of Psalm XLIV. She is shown crowned, as queen of the world, reigning with Christ in heaven.[89] She has been raised to the right hand of God, where Christ had preceded her.[90] She is the first of those redeemed by Christ to enter heaven and, therefore, a pledge to others of their eventual resurrection. She represents the human race and is their advocate with God.[91] The child in her arms and the dove above her head show that her assumption into heaven springs from her role as *Dei genetrix*.

The lower part of the picture shows those who are excluded from the circle of heaven: the devil, Arius and Judas. The first two are condemned for failing to recognize that Christ was both God and man. Arius claimed that the *Logos* was created by God as an intermediary between the Godhead and the rest of creation and that Christ was therefore not the Son of God in any real sense.[92] It followed from this that Mary herself could not be referred to as Mother of God; Arius is therefore appropriately placed beneath Mary in the Ælfwine drawing. Satan's power was destroyed because he laid claim to Christ as though he was a man, subject to death; he, too, denied Christ's divine nature.[93] Judith Kidd links Judas with the Jew of the responsory, 'Gaude Maria', 'qui dicit Christum ex Joseph semine esse natum', and therefore sees him as similar to Arius.[94] For the Anglo-Saxons, however, Judas was a symbol of treachery and of despair.[95] The author of the Blickling homily for Quadragesima reminds unjust judges that Judas was in hell because he sold Christ for a bribe;[96] Ælfric saw Judas as a thief and a betrayer,[97]

---

[89] Paschasius, *Epistula* iv. 23 (ed. Matter and Ripberger, p. 119); Ælfric, *CH* I.xxx (ed. Thorpe, pp. 442 and 446).

[90] Paschasius, *Epistula* vii. 38 (ed. Matter and Ripberger, p. 125).

[91] Ælfric, *CH* I.xxx (ed. Thorpe, pp. 452–4).

[92] Kelly, *Christian Doctrines*, pp. 226–31.

[93] *Gospel of Nicodemus* (trans. Allen and Calder, *Sources*, pp. 179–80); Raw, *Crucifixion Iconography*, p. 170, and 'What do we Mean by the Source of a Picture?', p. 296.

[94] Kidd, 'Quinity', p. 30: 'who says that Christ was born from the seed of Joseph'. It is (just) possible that Judas was thought to have denied Christ's divinity, for the condemnation of Nestorius at the Council of Ephesus was addressed to 'Nestorio novo Judae'; see Mansi, *Sacrorum conciliorum collectio* V, 559, and Kelly, *Christian Doctrines*, p. 327.

[95] Ælfric, *CH* II.xiv (ed. Godden, pp. 142–3).

[96] *Blickling Homilies*, nos. v and vi (ed. Morris, pp. 63 and 69).

[97] *CH* I.xxvii (ed. Thorpe, p. 398).

though also as one whose actions led to the overthrow of the devil when Christ descended into hell.[98]

A parallel to part of the upper section of the Ælfwine drawing appears on the handle of the Godwine ivory seal, dated to the first half of the eleventh century.[99] This carving, which offers a modification of the scene from the Utrecht Psalter illustration to Psalm CIX, shows two seated figures who represent the risen and glorified Christ at the right hand of God the Father. Christ holds a book or scroll, while his Father holds a sceptre in his right hand; beneath their feet is a prostrate figure, representing either death or the devil, and between their heads is a dove, symbolizing the Holy Spirit. The presence of the dove between the two figures and, as it were, joining them, makes it clear that this is a representation of the Trinity. A later variant on the Ælfwine figures of Mary and Christ fills the initial to a twelfth-century copy of Boethius's *De musica* from Christ Church, Canterbury (pl. VIb). The scene shows a throned, haloed figure, holding a book and a torch in his left hand and blessing with his right; to his right is a standing female figure holding a disk decorated with a lamb; between their heads is the *dextera Dei*. The seated figure represents the risen Christ: like the Christ of the Utrecht illustration to Psalm CIX, he is seated above a prostrate figure which symbolizes his defeat of either death or the devil; to his sides are torch-bearing symbols of the sun and moon, signs of his divine status, and he himself carries a torch to indicate that he is 'God from God, light from light'.[100] The female figure at Christ's right places one foot on the head of the figure below Christ's feet, recalling God's words to the serpent in the Garden of Eden, 'I will make you enemies of each other: you and the woman, your offspring and her offspring. It will crush your head and you will strike his heel' (Genesis III.15). This passage was commonly interpreted as a reference to a future conflict between Satan and the

---

[98] *CH* I.i (ed. Thorpe, p. 26); Raw, 'What do we Mean by the Source of a Picture?', p. 296.

[99] Reprod. Beckwith, *Ivory Carvings*, pl. 78.

[100] Christ is described as 'sol iustitiae' in Malachi IV.2. See also the Advent antiphon, 'O oriens', together with its development in the Old English *Christ I*, 104–29; and Bede, *Homeliae* I.3 (ed. Hurst, p. 19) on the relationship between Malachi IV.2, the Incarnation, and the Trinitarian image of the sun, its light and heat, discussed above, p. 35.

Church[101] and Schiller, therefore, identifies the woman in the Boethius initial as Ecclesia, holding a symbol of the eucharist and trampling the devil under foot.[102] But the passage was also interpreted with reference to Mary:

*Inimicitias ponam inter te et mulierem* de Virgine, de qua Dominus natus est, intellexerunt ... illud quod subiunctum est, *Ipsa conteret caput tuum, et tu insidiaberis calcaneo eius*: hoc de fructu ventris Mariae, qui est Christus, intelligitur, id est, Tu eum supplantabis, ut moriatur: ille autem victor resurget, et caput tuum conteret, quod est mors. Sicut et David dixerat ex persona Patris ad Filium: *Super aspidem et basiliscum ambulabis, et conculcabis leonem et draconem.*[103]

The same point is made in an Anglo-Saxon ivory of the Virgin and Child, where a serpent is placed beneath Mary's feet.[104] In view of this interpretation, and the relationship between the Boethius initial and the drawing in the Ælfwine Prayerbook, it seems likely that the female figure represents Mary rather than Ecclesia. The emphasis is different, however, for here she holds a lamb, a symbol usually associated with John the Baptist. In the case of St John, the lamb is an emblem, recalling his description of Christ as the lamb of God who takes away the sin of the world (John I.29). In the Boethius initial Mary is depicted, not as *Theotokos*, but as the one who offers the world the lamb who was to be sacrificed. The image recalls a passage in a homily of Melito of Sardis where Christ is described as, 'the silent lamb, the slain lamb, who was born of Mary the fair ewe'.[105] There is no evidence that the artist could have known this work, but a prayer in the Arundel Psalter, a Winchester manuscript of about 1060, addresses Mary as the one 'que genuisti agnum purgantem crimina mundi',[106] and there is a similar reference in one of

---

[101] E.g. Bede, *Libri quatuor in principium Genesis* I.iii.15 (ed. Jones, p. 66). See also above, p. 116.

[102] Schiller, *Ikonographie* IV.1, 95–6. Whereas the Greek text of Genesis had a masculine pronoun ('he will crush'), the Latin text read, 'she will crush'.

[103] Ps.-Bede, *Quaestiones super Genesim* (PL 93, 282): '*I will place enmity between you and the woman* refers to the Virgin from whom Christ was born ... that which follows, *She will crush your head and you will bruise his heel*, refers to the fruit of Mary's womb, which is Christ; that is, You will trip him up in order that he may die; but he will rise victorious, and crush your head, which is death. As David said in the person of the Father to the Son: *You will walk on the asp and basilisk, and crush the lion and dragon.*'

[104] Oxford, Ashmolean Museum (reprod. Beckwith, *Ivory Carvings*, pl. 36).

[105] *Homily on the Pasch*, trans. Modern Roman Breviary, Holy Thursday.

[106] BL, Arundel 60, 145r-147v (ptd Barré, *Prières*, pp. 140–2, at 140).

162

the Advent antiphons: 'Emitte Agnum, Domine, dominatorem terrae, de petra deserti ad montem filiae Sion.'[107]

The drawing of the Trinity in the Arenberg Gospels (pl. XIVb) is close to the illustration to the *Gloria* in the Utrecht Psalter, though there are some important differences: Mary holds a book instead of the Christ Child and the central, throned figure holds a globe in his right hand. This picture has to be considered in relation to the preceding drawing of the Virgin and Child (pl. XIVa). According to Jane Rosenthal the two pictures represent Christ's descent to earth and his return to heaven.[108] The figures of the Virgin and Child represent Christ's human nature and its source in Mary: the palm branch held by Mary is a sign that Christ's victory over death took place through the human nature he received from her, and the purple background to the figures is a reminder of Christ's death on the cross.[109] The second scene shows the risen Christ, who has returned to his throne in heaven in the flesh which he received from Mary. To his right is his mother. She no longer holds her child, whose body has been taken up into heaven; instead, she holds the gospels, a symbol of the embodiment of the Word. To Christ's left is a horned ram, recalling the ram sacrificed by Abraham in place of his son Isaac, and symbolizing Christ's human nature.[110]

Rosenthal's interpretation of these two drawings has to be seen in relation to her interpretation of the Utrecht illustration to the *Gloria*, on which

---

[107] *Corpus antiphonalium*, ed. Hesbert I, 18–19 (no. 9), and III, 201.

[108] Rosenthal, 'Canon Tables', p. 200; Ælfric, *CH* II.xxiv (ed. Godden, p. 224); see also Augustine, *In Iohannis evangelium*, xii.8–10 (ed. Willems, pp. 125–6).

[109] Rosenthal, 'Canon Tables', pp. 200–18. The purple background occurs in only two scenes, those of the Virgin and Child (11r) and the Crucifixion (9v).

[110] The representation of the *Agnus Dei* by a ram instead of a lamb is not unique: a sketch on a flyleaf of BL, Additional 47967 (reprod. Temple, *Anglo-Saxon Manuscripts*, pl. 28) shows a horned ram, labelled 'Agnus Dei', and the illustration to Ps. CIX in BL, Cotton Tiberius C. vi, 126v (pl. XIa), also shows a ram instead of a lamb. Ælfric, commenting on the Old Testament sacrifices, says that Christ was symbolized by a ram as a sign of his authority, *CH* II.xii (ed. Godden, p. 120); cf. *Book of Enoch*, LXXXIX.45–6 (trans. Charles, *Apocrypha* II, 254) where the Messiah is symbolized by the ram who leads the flock. The identification of the ram sacrificed by Abraham with Christ's human nature is simply a mnemonic: the ram, like the lamb, is a symbol of the undivided person of Christ; see Ambrosius Autpertus, *Expositio in Apocalypsin* IV.vii.10 and III.v.7 (ed. Weber, pp. 310–11 and 263–4), Bede, *Homeliae* I.14 (ed. Hurst, p. 100), and Raw, 'Verbal Icons', pp. 134–5.

they are based.[111] Unlike de Wald and Kantorowicz, who interpreted the Utrecht scene as a representation of the Trinity, Rosenthal sees the central figure in the Utrecht drawing as *Christus Deus*; to his right is an image of the Incarnation and to his left, the sacrificial lamb. The scene, then, shows three manifestations of Christ: his eternal existence as the *Logos*; his existence as incarnate child in Mary's arms and, finally, his resurrection in the body in which he suffered (symbolized here by the lamb).

The first problem with Rosenthal's interpretation of the Arenberg drawings concerns the meaning of the image of the Virgin and Child. As she notes, the figures are surrounded by a capital *A*, which she considers is a reference to the beginning of Christ's earthly life.[112] This would be a very unusual meaning for the symbol. In the Apocalypse, the words *alpha* and *omega*, *initium* and *finis* are applied to both God the Father and God the Son.[113] Bede interprets Apocalypse I.8 as a reference to God the Father, '*initium* quem nullus praecedit; *finis*, cui nullus in regno succedit',[114] and the words *primus* and *novissimus* later in the same chapter (Apoc. I.17) as a reference to Christ: '*Primus*, quia omnia per ipsum facta sunt. *Novissimus*, quia in ipso restaurantur omnia.'[115] When the words *alpha* and *omega* apply to Christ, rather than to the Father, they are regularly interpreted as a reference to his two natures, the *alpha* being taken as a proof of Christ's presence with the Father from before time. Bede, for example, commenting on ch. XII of the Apocalypse, says: 'In *A* Verbi divinitatem, et in *Ω* susceptam humanitatem designat.'[116] Haymo says:

*Primus*, ante quem nullus; *et novissimus*, post quem nullus. *Principium*, a quo omnis creatura sumpsit initium; *et finis*, quia in eo omne redigitur. *Alpha* pertinet ad verbi dignitatem, *omega* ad susceptam in fine temporum humanitatem. Ipse est

---

[111] Rosenthal, 'Canon Tables', pp. 219–30.

[112] *Ibid.*, pp. 206–7.      [113] See above, p. 136.

[114] Bede, *Explanatio Apocalypsis* I.i (PL 93, 135): 'The beginning, whom none preceded; the end, to whose kingdom none shall succeed.' Cf. Primasius, *Commentaria super Apocalypsim* I (PL 68, 812).

[115] Bede, *Explanatio Apocalypsis* I.i (PL 93, 137): 'The first, because all things were made by him. The last, because in him all things were restored.' Cf. Primasius, *Commentaria super Apocalypsim* I (PL 68, 802–3), and Ambrosius Autpertus, *Expositio in Apocalypsin* I.i.8 (ed. Weber, p. 55).

[116] Bede, *Explanatio Apocalypsis* III.xxii (PL 93, 205).

ergo *alpha*, id est *principium* manens cum Patre. Ipse et *omega*, id est, *finis*, natus temporaliter ex matre.[117]

Byrhtferth, in his treatise on number symbolism, says: 'Primus numerus proprie pertinet ad eum qui dicit: "Ego principium qui et loquor vobis." Et item idem de se: "Ego sum alpha et o" – alpha Deus ante secula, Deus et homo in fine seculorum Ω.'[118] The frame round the figures of the Virgin and Child in the Arenberg manuscript, therefore, draws attention to Christ's eternal birth from the Father, not to his birth in time: it is a reminder that Mary was mother of the one who was God. The palm branch, interpreted by Rosenthal as an allusion to Christ's death, more probably refers to the belief, based on Simeon's words to Mary at the time of the presentation in the Temple (Luke II.35), that Mary herself was a martyr or, as Paschasius and Ælfric maintained, more than a martyr.[119]

The omission of the Child from Mary's arms in the second of the Arenberg drawings (pl. XIVb) avoids any possibility of misinterpreting the figure as a symbol of the Nativity. As was the case in the illustrations to the Utrecht Psalter, Mary has taken her place in heaven and the dove above her head indicates that this took place because she had been overshadowed by the Holy Spirit.[120] The book which she holds may be the gospels, as Rosenthal states, in which case it symbolizes the word or Word of God,[121] and asserts that Mary was not merely the mother of Christ's human nature, but the mother of the Word made flesh. Another possibility is that the motif of the book refers to Mary's role as the source

---

[117] Haymo, *Expositio in Apocalypsin* VII.xxii (PL 117, 1217): 'The first, before whom was no one; and the last, after whom was no one. The beginning, from whom every creature took its beginning; and the end, because in him everything was completed. *Alpha* belongs to the dignity of the Word, *omega* to the humanity assumed at the end of time. He is therefore *alpha*, that is, the beginning, residing with the Father. He is also *omega*, that is, the end, born in time from his mother.'

[118] *Byrhtferth's Enchiridion* (ed. and trans. Baker and Lapidge, pp. 196–7): 'The first number pertains specially to him who says, "I am the beginning, who also speak unto you." And again, likewise concerning himself, "I am Alpha and Omega" – Alpha or God before all ages, Omega or God and man at the end of the ages.'

[119] Paschasius, *Epistula* xiv. 90 (ed. Matter and Ripberger, p. 151); Ælfric, *CH* I.ix and xxx (ed. Thorpe, pp. 146 and 444). Mary also holds a palm branch in the painting in the Grimbald Gospels (pl. XIII) and in the frontispiece to the New Minster Charter (pl. V). See also Clayton, *Cult of the Virgin*, pp. 221–2, and Raw, *Crucifixion Iconography*, p. 157.

[120] See above, pp. 151 and 154–5.     [121] Rosenthal, 'Canon Tables', p. 238.

of wisdom: St John saw Christ as both the Word and wisdom of God and the description of wisdom in the Book of Proverbs (VIII.22–35) was used as the epistle for the Feast of Mary's Nativity from at least the tenth century.[122] The interpretation of the other figures is more problematic.

In some ways, Rosenthal's identification of the seated figure in the Arenberg drawing as the ascended Christ is plausible.[123] Carolingian artists frequently portrayed Christ seated on the arc of heaven and holding a small disk, symbolizing the world, in his right hand.[124] Ottonian artists introduced a more imperial symbolism and depicted Christ holding an orb similar to that seen in portraits of Charles the Bald or Otto III,[125] and, as Robert Deshman has shown, the artists of the Benedictional of Æthelwold introduced imperial symbols into their pictures of the Adoration of the Magi and the Baptism of Christ.[126] The decoration of the canon-tables in the gospels at Trinity College, Cambridge, includes pictures of angels holding orbs[127] and the Christ child himself holds an orb in the drawing of the Trinity at the beginning of the Harley Psalter (pl. XVa).

The expression 'The King of kings and Lord of lords' was not confined to Christ, however, for it goes back to the Old Testament: 'Yahweh your God is God of gods and Lord of lords' (Deut. X.17).[128] In Psalm XCIV it is the God of the Old Testament, described as *rex magnus*, who holds the world in his hand,[129] while in the Utrecht Psalter the illustration to Psalm

---

[122] Raw, *Crucifixion Iconography*, p. 106; Capelle, 'Epitres sapientiales', p. 320.

[123] Rosenthal, 'Canon Tables', pp. 234–6.

[124] E.g. the Vivian and San Callisto Bibles; see Kessler, *Illustrated Bibles*, pp. 41–2 and 56 and pls. 49 and 50. Note, however, that the disk in the Vivian Bible is inscribed with the XP and that some scholars believe it represents the eucharistic host.

[125] E.g. Bamberg, Staatsbibl., Bibl. 22, 5r, and Munich, Bayerische Staatsbibl., Clm. 4454, 20r, or the Basle altar-frontal (reprod. Mayr-Harting, *Ottonian Book Illumination* II, pls. III and 21 and I, pl. 34). For the portraits of Charles and Otto, see Paris, BN, lat. 1152, 3v (reprod. Hubert, Porcher and Volbach, *Carolingian Art*, pl. 135), Munich, Bayerische Staatsbibl. Clm. 4453, 24r, and Bamberg, Staatsbibl., Bibl. 140, 59v (reprod. Mayr-Harting, *Ottonian Book Illumination* I, pl. XXI, and II, pl. 2).

[126] Deshman, *'Christus rex'*, and *Benedictional*, pp. 26–7, 45–50 and 192–214.

[127] Cambridge, Trinity College B. 10. 4, 11r and 13r (reprod. Ohlgren, *Textual Illustration*, pls. 7.5 and 7.9). The angel Gabriel is depicted holding a disk inscribed with a cross, interpreted by O'Reilly as an orb, on the Anglo-Saxon portable altar in the Musée de Cluny, Paris; see Okasha and O'Reilly, 'Anglo-Saxon Portable Altar', p. 48 and pl. 15.

[128] See above, pp. 117 and 141.

[129] Psalm XCIV.3–4: 'Quoniam Deus magnus Dominus et rex magnus super omnes deos.

XLVII.3 includes a drawing of the Almighty standing in the doorway of a palace, holding an orb in his right hand.[130] A prayer in the Bury Psalter addresses God the Father as 'Rex regum et Dominus dominantium' and, in the carving of the Trinity on the handle of the Godwine seal, it is God the Father who holds a sceptre, not God the Son.[131] Moreover, a painting of God the Father sending Gabriel to Mary, dating from the early twelfth century, shows the Father crowned and holding an orb in his left hand.[132] There is no reason, therefore, why the seated figure in the Arenberg drawing should not represent God the Father, an interpretation which seems far more likely in view of the frequency with which a throned figure accompanied by symbols of a lamb and a dove is used as a formula for the Trinity in late Anglo-Saxon manuscripts. There is another possibility, however. It was argued earlier that the historiated initial for the Sunday after Pentecost in the Benedictional of Æthelwold was a symbolic representation of the Godhead, not a portrait of Christ.[133] The divine activity in relation to created beings is indivisible[134] and when Ælfric talks in the *Hexameron* of God holding the world in his hand he is thinking of him as the single principle (*an anginn*) of creation, not as the Father who creates by means of the Son.[135] It may be, therefore, that the historiated initial in the Paris Boethius, the drawing at Psalm CIX in the Tiberius Psalter (pl. XIa)[136] and the scene in the Arenberg Gospels are attempts to indicate simultaneously the unity of the Godhead (the throned figure), and the signs through which it manifests itself (the dove of the baptism story and the metaphorical lamb).[137]

Quia in manu eius sunt omnes fines terrae'; cf. Is. XL.12, 'Quis mensus est pugillo aquas et caelos palmo ponderavit? quis appendit tribus digitis molem terrae et libravit in pondere montes et colles in statera?' See above, p. 138.

[130] Utrecht, Universiteitsbibliothek, 32, 27v (reprod. van der Horst and Engelbregt) and BL, Harley 603, 27v (reprod. Ohlgren, *Textual Illustration*, pl. 2.47).

[131] Prayer no. xviii (ed. Wilmart, 'Prayers of the Bury Psalter', pp. 211–12); on the other hand, prayer no. ix (Wilmart, p. 204) addresses Christ as 'Rex regum'.

[132] BL, Lansdowne, 383, 12v (reprod. Kauffmann, *Romanesque Manuscripts*, pl. 131); see Henderson, 'Idiosyncrasy', p. 243.

[133] See above, pp. 140–2.

[134] Ælfric, *CH* I.xiii (ed. Thorpe, p. 196) and *CH* II.xxii (ed. Godden, p. 211).

[135] *Exameron anglice* (ed. Crawford, p. 47) and *CH* I.i (ed. Thorpe, pp. 8–10); see also *Exameron anglice* (Crawford, pp. 34, 39, 40 and 58–9). See also above, pp. 33, n. 21 and 142.

[136] See above, p. 144.

[137] I owe this idea to Paul Parvis OP. Ælfric points out several times that the Holy Spirit

There can be no such confusion over the picture of the Trinity at the beginning of the Harley Psalter, which shows God the Father seated on a throne within a mandorla, his face pressed to that of his Son, who is curled on his lap, holding the globe of the world in his hand; uniting the two is the dove of the Holy Spirit (pl. XVa).[138] The scene forms a variant on those representations of the Virgin and Child where the dove of the Holy Spirit is seen above Mary's head to indicate her overshadowing by the Spirit at the Incarnation: it represents the eternal birth of Christ (as opposed to his temporal birth) and is an imaginative representation of the way in which the persons of the Trinity are related to one another in love. Whereas representations of Christ's birth from Mary are frequent, the Harley Psalter drawing shows, uniquely, the related theme of Christ's birth from his Father before time. It is the only one of the Anglo-Saxon pictures of the Trinity to focus on the inner relations of the Trinity as opposed to its actions in relation to the world and to suggest the kind of contemplation of the Godhead envisaged in the devotional works discussed above in ch. 1.[139]

---

is invisible and that the dove at the Baptism and the fire at Pentecost were merely signs (*hiw* or *getacnung*): *CH* I.xxii (ed. Thorpe, pp. 320 and 322) and *CH* II.iii and xii (ed. Godden, pp. 24 and 116). Similarly, terms such as lamb or rock are merely symbols of Christ, having nothing to do with his substance: *CH* I.vi (Thorpe, p. 98) and *CH* II.xii and xv (Godden, pp. 116 and 152–3). See also above, p. 80.

[138] Henderson, 'Idiosyncrasy', p. 243, links the drawing to two verses from St John: 'the Father is greater than I', and, 'the only Son, who is nearest to the Father's heart' (John XIV.28 and I.18).

[139] See above, pp. 15–18.

# 8

# Art, prayer and the vision of God

The pictures discussed in ch. 7 are a form of exegesis; they explain and comment on the doctrine of the Trinity. They do more than this, however. Like the representations of Christ discussed in ch. 6, they reveal something beyond themselves and invite a response from those who view them. This is particularly clear in the case of the groups of figures depicted in the decorative frames to the opening of St John's Gospel in the Grimbald Gospels (pls. XII and XIII), which invite the viewer to share in the worship of heaven, or the frontispiece to the Harley Psalter (pl. XVa), which prompts those studying it to meditate on the love which binds together the members of the Trinity.

Contemplation of the Trinity, a sharing in the worship of heaven and in the divine life, constituted the focus of the religious life of prayer. The most basic form of prayer, suited to all Christians, was recitation of the *Pater noster*.[1] Even laymen, however, were expected to go beyond this. The author of a sermon in the Vercelli Book, intended for preaching during Lent, lists six activities which he considers particularly important during this season: confession, repentance, vigils, fasting, prayer and almsgiving.[2] Prayer, he says, springs from reading: 'swa swa Isidorius cwæð: Mid þam gebedum ge beoð geclænsode and mid þam rædingum ge bioð intimbrede.'[3] After listing various examples of efficacious prayer from the Old Testament, the author continues: 'þonne we us gebiddaþ, þonne sprecaþ we wið God, and þonne we rædaþ, þonne spricþ God wið us'.[4] Prayer,

---

[1] See above, p. 29.　　[2] *Vercelli Homilies*, no. iii (ed. Scragg, pp. 73–83).

[3] *Ibid.*, p. 81: 'As Isidore said, You are cleansed through prayers and built up by reading'; Smaragdus, *Diadema monachorum*, iii (PL 102, 597).

[4] *Ibid.*, p. 82: 'When we pray, we speak to God, and when we read, then God speaks to

169

then, is a two-way process: it is not enough simply to speak to God; our thoughts and hopes need to be nourished by what God says to us.

For monks, prayer was dominated by the recitation of the psalter which filled much of the Office. Private prayer, too, was frequently based on recitation of the psalms. Alcuin recommended the private recitation of the psalms and drew up a series of suggestions about psalms suitable for various needs.[5] Two more complex works, linking psalms, prayers and canticles, are not by Alcuin, though printed under his name. The *Abbreviatio furtivae orationis*, an Italian production of about 850, was designed for monastic use; the *Officia per ferias*, which groups psalms, canticles and prayers under the days of the week, was produced in France during the first half of the ninth century and seems to have been intended for lay people.[6] Similar arrangements of psalms, antiphons and prayers are found in several English manuscripts.[7] Ælfric stressed the value of the psalter as a form of prayer in a sermon for the First Sunday in Advent where he says, 'Þonne ge eow to gereorde gaderiað, hæbbe eower gehwilc halwende lare on muðe, and sealmboc on handa',[8] and the role of the psalter in private prayer is seen, too, in the addition to psalter manuscripts of collections of prayers.[9]

Evidence for more meditative prayer is hard to come by. When the word *meditatio* is used, it refers to the repetition and memorization of a text rather than the visualization of a gospel event and reflection on it.[10] When St Benedict talks of private prayer he says simply, 'Sed et si aliter vult sibi forte secretius orare, simpliciter intret et oret, non in clamosa voce, sed in

us.' Cf. Isidore, *Sententiae*, viii.2 (PL 83, 679) and Smaragdus, *Diadema monachorum*, iii (PL 102, 597).

[5] See Alcuin's letter to Charlemagne, 'Beatus igitur David' (PL 101, 509–10), and *De psalmorum usu* (PL 101, 465–8).

[6] *Abbreviatio furtivae orationis* and *Officia per ferias* (PL 101, 468–92 and 509–612).

[7] E.g. BL, Cotton Tiberius A. iii, 58r–59v and 114v–115v, Cotton Titus D. xxvii, 66r–70r, and *Portiforium Wulstani* (ed. Hughes II, 24).

[8] *CH* I.xxxix (ed. Thorpe, p. 604): 'When you meet for speech, have healing teaching in your mouth and psalter in your hand.' Possibly echoing Ephesians V.19, 'Sing the words and tunes of the psalms and hymns when you are together', since Ælfric is talking of watching and St Paul has told his readers to wake from sleep so that Christ will shine on them (Ephes. V.14).

[9] E.g. the prayers at the end of the Bury Psalter, ptd Wilmart, 'The Prayers of the Bury Psalter', pp. 201–16.

[10] Leclercq, 'Vocabulaire monastique', p. 134.

lacrimis et intentione cordis.'[11] The authors of the *Regularis concordia* envisage private prayer before and after the Office.[12] Much of this prayer consists of the recitation of psalms and set prayers, though there are some hints of more meditative prayer. In one place, the younger monks are said to occupy themselves with spiritual reading, while the older ones are intent on prayer.[13] Elsewhere, in the section on reading, the monks are exhorted to meditate on God and the state of their souls; the context suggests that this meditation was linked to reading.[14] The Old English expansions of Psalm L, or of the *Pater noster*, *Gloria* and Creed, may be examples of the way in which the thoughtful recitation of well-known texts could form a basis for more extended meditation.[15] Two poems in Old English, *A Summons to Prayer* and *A Prayer*, suggest something freer.[16] Both poems look forward to the time when the speakers will praise God face to face in heaven. *A Summons to Prayer* is addressed to the three persons of the Trinity, to Mary and to all the saints; God the Father is described as the one who rules the world, seated on his throne; God the Son is the source of peace, the saviour of the world, creator of the universe; the Holy Spirit is the one who was sent from his throne above to announce to Mary that she would bear the king of kings. The poet of *A Prayer* considers the state of his soul, the wretched state of those tempted by the devil and the blessedness of those who obey God. He then turns to God, who is light and life, ruler of all; no one, he says, can praise God or understand his greatness; it is amazing that God himself can grasp his power.[17] The poem ends with a confession of belief in God, the three in one, and a plea for help in doing God's will. The best examples of more extended meditation are the poems known as *Christ I* and *The Dream of the Rood*.[18] The first, based on the Magnificat antiphons for the period before Christmas, brings together the longing of the patriarchs and prophets for the Messiah and the longing of the Church for the coming of Christ, the sin and darkness

---

[11] *Benedicti regula*, lii (ed. Hanslik, p. 122).

[12] *Regularis concordia*, i.15, i.19, i.25, i.27 and ii.29 (ed. Symons, pp. 12, 14, 22, 24 and 26).

[13] *Ibid.*, i.25 (ed. Symons, p. 22).     [14] *Ibid.*, vi.56 (ed. Symons, p. 55).

[15] See above, p. 30, and *Psalm 50* (ASPR VI, 88–94).

[16] ASPR VI, 69–70 and 94–6. Discussed Raw, *Art and Background*, pp. 123–7.

[17] See above, pp. 83–4.

[18] ASPR III, 3–15 and II, 61–5. Discussed Raw, *Art and Background*, pp. 39–40 and 127–32, and 'Biblical Literature', pp. 233–5 and 239–41, and above, p. 100.

which surrounds the human race and the light brought into the world by Christ, the role of Mary and the wonder of a God who became man to save the world. The second, which tells the story of Christ's death from the point of view of the cross, is more eschatological: the cross is seen, not as an instrument of execution from the past, but as the messenger which will lead those honouring it into the presence of God.

The contemplation of the Trinity envisaged in the poems *A Summons to Prayer* and *A Prayer*, and the Vercelli homily's emphasis on listening to God as well as speaking to him, means that prayer requires awareness of God's presence. Contemplative prayer, unlike vocal prayer, involves receptiveness, a silent standing before God. It is here that art becomes important. In contemplating a picture or a statue one becomes open to what it says: the picture speaks, as though it were a text. Just as the statues of saints such as those of the four virgins of Ely were placed near their tombs to give visual expression to the presence of the saint in the relics, so statues and pictures of Christ reminded those looking at them of his presence:[19] the image, as it were, combines with what it signifies. Sometimes this process is simply an imaginative act: the statue is treated 'as if' it were alive. So Leofric of Mercia's wife, Godgifu, placed one of her necklaces round the neck of a statue of the Virgin[20] and Cnut's standard-bearer hung his sword on the crucifix at Waltham.[21] In many cases, however, the records claim that statues actually behaved as though alive. When Harold prayed before the crucifix at Waltham before the Battle of Hastings, the crucifix bowed its head towards him in sorrow at his coming death.[22] At Winchester, the crucifix in the refectory spoke to King Edgar, warning him against allowing the secular canons back into the Old Minster.[23]

The same process can be seen in manuscript art. In many pictures the figures are either unframed or refuse to be confined within the frame. The choirs of confessors, virgins and apostles depicted on the opening pages of the Benedictional of Æthelwold spill over on to the pillars and frames to

---

[19] On the role of images in Anglo-Saxon churches, see Raw, *Crucifixion Iconography*, pp. 16–25.

[20] L-B 1131 (quoting William of Malmesbury, *De gestis pontificum Anglorum*).

[21] L-B 4470 (quoting *De inventione sacrae crucis Walthamensis*).

[22] L-B 4478 and 4480 (quoting *Vita Haroldi regis* and *De inventione sanctae crucis Walthamensis*).

[23] L-B 4676 and 4677 (quoting *Liber monasterii de Hyda* and Osbern's *Vita S. Dunstani*).

make contact with the world outside the picture.[24] The figures of God the Father and God the Son in the Sherborne Pontifical, though enclosed by a frame, place their feet on it and seem to emerge from it.[25] The absence of frame or mandorla in the drawing of the risen Christ in a gathering added to a manuscript of the *Cura pastoralis* conveys the impression that this is not an image but an actual presence.[26] Two of the drawings of Christ above the canon tables in the Arenberg Gospels are similarly unframed and perhaps intended to symbolize Christ's universal presence.[27] Where Christ is shown enclosed in a mandorla to indicate the divine light which shines from him, he again refuses to remain confined. In the painting of the Second Coming in the Benedictional of Æthelwold (pl. III), Christ strides out from the area of light into the clouds, while the angels who accompany him, carrying the instruments of his passion, move out from the picture itself. The painting of the appearance to Thomas again shows Christ moving out from the area of the divine into the world of the disciples while they, in turn, move from the picture space towards the observer.[28] The same is true of the Christ of the Trinity Gospels[29] and even of the painting of Christ as image of the Trinity in the Benedictional of Æthelwold (pl. X). Some drawings and paintings do make a distinction between human and divine space. A painting intended as a frontispiece to Boethius's *De Trinitate* shows God enthroned between seraphs in the upper compartment of the picture, while Boethius writes at his desk in the compartment below.[30] In the drawing of Christ as judge which forms the frontispiece to a copy of Ælfric's homilies, the figure of Christ remains firmly within its mandorla (pl. VIII). Other pictures, however, mingle divine and human space. The artist of the Bury Psalter showed God leaning out from heaven to make contact with the psalmist.[31] In the

---

24  BL, Additional 49598, 1r–4r (reprod. Deshman, *Benedictional*, pls. 1–7).

25  Paris, BN, lat. 943, 5v–6r (reprod. Temple, *Anglo-Saxon Manuscripts*, pls. 135–6).

26  Oxford, St John's College 28, 2r (reprod. Temple, *Anglo-Saxon Manuscripts*, pl. 42).

27  NY, Pierpont Morgan Library 869, 12v and 13r (reprod. Ohlgren, *Textual Illustration*, pls. 6.7–8).

28  BL, Additional 49598, 56v (reprod. Deshman, *Benedictional*, pl. 24).

29  Cambridge, Trinity College B. 10. 4, 16v (reprod. Ohlgren, *Textual Illustration*, pl. 7.16).

30  Paris, BN, lat. 6401, 158v (reprod. Temple, *Anglo-Saxon Manuscripts*, pl. 94).

31  Biblioteca Apostolica Vaticana, Regin. lat. 12, 36r (reprod. Ohlgren, *Textual Illustration*, pl. 3.13).

drawing of Dunstan at the feet of Christ the presumed owner of the manuscript enters Christ's space (pl. IV). In other manuscripts, the living are depicted within the same space as the saints in heaven, yet separated from the divine light. A drawing in a manuscript of Gregory's Homilies on Ezekiel, illustrated by an English artist working at Fleury, shows Christ enthroned in a mandorla, an open book in his left hand and his right hand raised in blessing; to the sides are figures of SS Benedict and Gregory the Great, the former holding a book and crozier and pointing to a kneeling monk, who looks up at the saint, raising his hands in a plea for help; in turn, the saint directs his gaze on Christ.[32] The choice of Gregory and Benedict as intermediaries between monk and Christ is particularly appropriate. Both saints were contemplatives. The life of Benedict which occupies the second book of Gregory's Dialogues includes an important account of Benedict's vision of divine light filling the whole world,[33] while Gregory's commentary on Ezekiel contains some of the pope's most developed teaching on contemplation.[34]

The frontispiece to Edgar's Charter to New Minster (pl. V), and the related drawing in the New Minster *Liber vitae*,[35] portray a similar relationship between the heavenly and the earthly. The first shows the king, flanked by SS Mary and Peter, offering a book to Christ; the second shows Cnut and Emma placing a cross on the altar of the monastic church; above them, Christ is enthroned between SS Mary and Peter. In both pictures, Christ is framed in a mandorla and separated from the other figures; the relationship between king and Christ is therefore similar in the two scenes. The relationship between king and saints, however, is different. In the earlier picture, Edgar stands on the same level as Mary and Peter, apparently on equal terms; in the later scene Winchester's patron saints are placed in the upper part of the picture, close to Christ though not in the same space, and the link between heaven and earth is made by the two angels who fly down to place crown and veil on the heads of the king and queen. In these scenes, there is no sense of an immediate and direct presence of Christ; instead, the living, whether monks or kings, rely on the saints as intermediaries and advocates.

In these different ways, artists made clear how God reveals himself to

---

[32] Orleans, Bibliothèque municipale, 175, 149r (reprod. Temple, *Anglo-Saxon Manuscripts*, pl. 144).

[33] *Dialogues* II.xxxv (ed. Hecht, pp. 169–74).     [34] See also above, pp. 135–6.

[35] BL, Stowe 944, 6r (reprod. Temple, *Anglo-Saxon Manuscripts*, pl. 244).

humans, and allows them to enter his presence. The drawings in the Ælfwine Prayerbook (pls. XVb; XVIa and XVIb) extend these glimpses of what prayer means into a complete programme for prayer. The manuscript, written between 1023 and 1032 for Ælfwine, dean and later abbot of New Minster, Winchester, is unusual in two respects: first, its small size (130 × 95 mm.) and, secondly, its illustrations. Most Anglo-Saxon prayerbooks are considerably larger than the Ælfwine manuscript and may, perhaps, have been intended for public use.[36] The eighth- to ninth-century Harley prayerbook, for example, measures 225 × 155 mm., the slightly later Royal prayerbook, 233 × 170 mm., and the ninth-century Book of Nunnaminster, 215 × 160 mm.;[37] the Book of Cerne is comparable at 230 × 184 mm..[38] Moreover, the prayers in these manuscripts are not illustrated: the evangelist portraits in the Book of Cerne are associated with the extracts from the gospels, not with the prayers; the Royal and Harley Prayerbooks, the Book of Nunnaminster, the Galba prayerbook, the collections of prayers in the Arundel and Eadwig Psalters[39] and the prayers added to the Vespasian Psalter[40] contain no illustrations. Some early continental prayerbooks do contain pictures, but they are very different from those in the Ælfwine manuscript. The prayerbook of Charles the Bald contains a frontispiece which shows the king kneeling before a crucifix.[41] A prayerbook which belonged to Arnulph, archbishop of Milan from 998 to 1018, includes representations of standing figures of the saints to whom the prayers in the manuscript are addressed.[42] The pictures in two twelfth-century copies of the prayers and devotions of Anselm of Canterbury, thought to derive from an illustrated copy of the text produced in England in the late eleventh century, depict people praying in front of Christ or a saint or episodes from the lives of the

---

[36] One exception is BL, Cotton Galba A. xiv, which measures 138 × 103 mm.: Ker, *Catalogue*, pp. 198–201 (no. 157) and Muir, *Pre-Conquest Prayer-book*.

[37] BL, Harley 7653, Royal 2. A. XX and Harley 2965: *Making of England*, pp. 208–11 (nos. 162, 163 and 164).

[38] CUL, Ll. 1. 10: *Making of England*, p. 211 (no. 165).

[39] BL, Arundel 60 and 155.      [40] BL, Cotton Vespasian A. i (155r–160v).

[41] Munich, Schatzkammer der Residenz; see Koehler and Mütherich, *Karolingischen Miniaturen* V, pl. 1b, and Deshman, 'The Exalted Servant'.

[42] BL, Egerton 3763, described in Turner, 'The Prayer-Book of Archbishop Arnulph II of Milan', pp. 360–92; the pictures are described in Warner, *Descriptive Catalogue*, pp. 130–5 (item 48), and reprod. in Johnston (no title), *Proceedings of the Society of Antiquaries* 24, 159–70.

saints to whom the prayers are addressed.[43] The drawings in the Ælfwine manuscript, on the other hand, are theological pictures and present a programme for meditation which is independent of the prayers they accompany.

The Ælfwine manuscript contains three drawings. A picture of the Crucifixion (pl. XVIa) is placed before a group of prayers in honour of the cross; a drawing of the Trinity with the Virgin and Child (pl. XVb) precedes prayers in honour of the Trinity, Mary and various saints; a drawing of St Peter accompanied by a monk (pl. XVIb) precedes the chapters and collects for the common of apostles, martyrs and confessors and for the Sundays from Pentecost to Christmas.[44] The pictures of the Crucifixion and of the Trinity are not inappropriate to the texts they precede. They are not textual illustrations, however, and their function was not to allow the person reading the prayers in the manuscript to visualize their content. Nor are they representations of gospel events: they could not have provided a focus for the imaginative reliving of gospel events common in late medieval private prayer such as that of Margery Kemp. Instead, they remind those looking at them of the relationship between those praying and those to whom they pray, of the nature and purpose of the monastic life and of the role of the visual arts in that life.

The closest parallel to the Ælfwine manuscript in both size and decoration is the manuscript known as the Athelstan Psalter.[45] The manuscript consists of a ninth-century continental psalter to which a calendar and computistical material (3r–20v) were added in England during the second quarter of the tenth century, together with five paintings.[46] Two of these paintings, representing Christ among choirs of saints, are associated with the calendar and computistical material at the beginning of the book (pls. VIIa–b); paintings of the Nativity and the Ascension, together with a painting now lost, but probably depicting the

---

[43] Pächt, 'Illustrations of St Anselm's Prayers and Meditations'.

[44] Titus D. xxvii, 66r–73v and 76r–93v, Titus D. xxvi, 20r–37v (ptd Günzel, pp. 123–42 and 158–69). The drawings are on a series of bifolia which do not form part of the regular quires on which the texts were written.

[45] BL, Cotton Galba A. xviii. The manuscript measures 128 × 88 mm.

[46] The paintings are on added leaves, 2v, 21r and 120v; one painting, probably depicting the Crucifixion, has been lost before Ps. LI and another, originally before Ps. I, is now Oxford, Bodleian Library, Rawlinson B. 484, 85r. Further additions, of prayers and Greek texts (178r–199v and 199v–200v), were made in the second quarter of the tenth century.

Crucifixion, marked the three main divisions of the psalter at Psalms I, LI and CI. These scenes juxtapose the crucial events in Christ's life: the coming to earth of the second person of the Trinity, his saving death and his return to heaven, with its promise of his return as judge. They show the significance of Christ's earthly life rather than the life itself.[47]

The paintings in the Athelstan Psalter, like the drawings in the Ælfwine Prayerbook, offer a sequence of themes for meditation which is largely independent of the text. There are two major differences between the sequences, however: first, the Athelstan pictures lack the personal element seen in the Ælfwine manuscript and, secondly, they do not develop the theology of redemption in so coherent and rich a way.

The drawings in the Ælfwine manuscript show three stages in the process of redemption. The first drawing, of the Crucifixion (pl. XVIa), shows God taking flesh to save mankind; the second drawing reverses the process and shows the incarnate Son returning to his Father, taking with him the human nature he assumed (pl. XVb); the third drawing, of St Peter, shows the divinization of man, brought about by Christ's death and resurrection (pl. XVIb). In the drawing of the Crucifixion a crowned figure of Christ stands with open eyes in front of the cross; above the arms of the cross are symbols of the sun and moon, represented as classical, torch-bearing figures, and beneath it stand Mary and John; Mary is represented as an orant, while John is shown writing in a book.[48] When Mary appears in Anglo-Saxon pictures of the Crucifixion, she represents the source of Christ's human nature.[49] It is for this reason that the inscriptions on Anglo-Saxon Crucifixion pictures describe her as *Sancta Maria* or *Maria virgo*, whereas Byzantine artists normally identified her as *meter theou*, 'mother of God'.[50] The choice of words is deliberate, for Mary's title of *Theotokos* was known to Bede[51]

---

[47] See above, p. 124.

[48] For discussion of this iconography, see Raw, *Crucifixion Iconography*, pp. 129–46 and 'What do we Mean by the Source of a Picture?', pp. 286–92.

[49] Bede, *Homeliae* I.14 (ed. Hurst, p. 97). Cf. Augustine, *In Iohannis evangelium* VIII.9 and CXIX.1 (ed. Willems, pp. 87–8 and 658) and *Sermo ccxviii*, x.10 (PL 38, 1086). For discussion, see Raw, *Crucifixion Iconography*, pp. 103–5 and above, pp. 48–9.

[50] BL, Cotton Titus D. xxvii, 65v (pl. XVIa), Arundel 60, 12v, and CUL, Ff. 1. 23, 88r (reprod. Raw, *Crucifixion Iconography*, pls. IX and X). See Kartsonis, *Anastasis*, pp. 107–9, for discussion of Byzantine representations of Mary after 787; pre-iconoclastic pictures of Mary refer to her as *hagia Maria*.

[51] Bede, *In Lucam* I.i.35 (ed. Hurst, p. 34). See above, p. 8, n. 6.

and she is regularly addressed as 'Sancta Dei genitrix' in the litanies of the period.[52]

By depicting Mary under the cross, artists emphasized that Christ was truly man; at the same time, they took care to remind those studying their pictures that he was also God. In practically all Anglo-Saxon representations of the Crucifixion, the *dextera Dei* is shown above Christ's head. In addition, artists included reminders of Christ's divine status: images of the sun and moon to show his rule over the natural world; angels, who symbolize the presence of heavenly beings at his death; a serpent beneath his feet as a sign that the prophecy of Genesis III.15 had been fulfilled; crowns or sceptres to indicate his kingship.[53] The artist of the Ælfwine manuscript went further, however, and placed an inscription across the top of his drawing in which Christ was identified unambiguously as God:

> Hec crux consignet Ælfwinum corpore mente
> In qua suspendens traxit Deus omnia secum.[54]

The second line of the inscription derives ultimately from Christ's words to his disciples shortly before his death. In St John's Gospel (XII.28) Christ calls on God to glorify his name and a voice comes from heaven saying, 'I have glorified it and I will glorify it again.' Christ continues: 'Now sentence is being passed on this world; now the prince of this world is to be overthrown. And when I am lifted up from the earth, I shall draw all men to myself' (John XII.31–2). The statement recalls Christ's words to Nicodemus earlier in the Gospel: 'No one has gone up to heaven except the one who came down from heaven, the Son of Man who is in heaven; and the Son of Man must be lifted up as Moses lifted up the serpent in the desert, so that everyone who believes may have eternal life in him' (John III.13–15). The immediate source of the inscription, however, is the elaborate *Kyrie* sung at Tenebrae on the last three days of Holy Week. The chant is mentioned in the *Regularis concordia*, but this gives only parts of

---

[52] Lapidge, *Anglo-Saxon Litanies*, pp. 93, 115, 122, 125, 128, 138, 142, 148, 155, 157, 174, 178, 182, 193, 214, 235, 240, 244, 250, 265, 270, 276, 283, 296 and 300.

[53] For examples, see Raw, *Crucifixion Iconography*, pls. I–IVa, VII–XIIb and XVI.

[54] 'This cross, hanging on which God drew all things to himself, is a seal placed on Ælfwine's body and mind.'

the text.[55] A fuller version is included among the prayers to be said in front of a crucifix in the Ælfwine manuscript:

Qui passurus advenisti propter nos,
Domine, miserere nobis.
Christus Dominus factus est oboediens usque ad mortem,
  mortem autem crucis.
Qui prophetice promisisti, ero mors tua, O mors,
Domine, miserere nobis.
Qui expansis in cruce manibus, traxisti omnia ad te secula,
Domine, miserere nobis.
Vita in ligno moritur, infernus et mors despoliatur,
Domine, miserere nobis.
Christus Dominus factus est oboediens, usque ad mortem,
  mortem autem crucis.[56]

In this chant, the one who comes to suffer on the cross and the one who prophesies in the Old Testament are brought together and become one Lord. This is not some human figure or Christ's human nature, separated from his divinity: it is God himself.

The Ælfwine inscription's reference to Christ as God is echoed in a prayer later in the manuscript:

Deus qui voluisti pro redemptione mundi a Iudeis reprobari, a Iuda osculo tradi, vinculis alligari, et agnus innocens ad victimam duci, atque conspectibus Pilati offerri, a falsis quoque testibus accusari, flagellis et obprobriis vexari, et conspui, spinis coronari, colaphis cedi, cruce elevari, atque inter latrones deputari, clavorum quoque aculeis perforari, lancea vulnerari, felle et aceto potari; tu per sanctissimas has poenas tuas ab inferni poenis me libera, et per sanctam crucem tuam salva et custodi, et illuc perduc me miserum peccatorem, quo perduxisti tecum crucifixum latronem, tibi cum Deo Patre et Spiritu Sancto honor, virtus, et gloria, nunc et in omnia secula. Amen.[57]

55  *Regularis concordia*, iv.37 (ed. Symons, p. 36); *Corpus antiphonalium*, ed. Hesbert I, 170–1 (no. 72c) and II, 306–7 and 320 (nos. 72c and 74c).
56  Titus D. xxvii, 67v–68r (ptd Günzel, p. 124). The manuscript reads 'O mors' in line 5, not Günzel's 'Mosis'. The closest parallel to the text is that in the Hartker Antiphoner for Holy Saturday, *Corpus antiphonalium*, ed. Hesbert II, 320 (no. 74c). For discussion of the inscription, see Raw, *Crucifixion Iconography*, pp. 173–4.
57  BL, Cotton Titus D. xxvii, 71v–72r (ptd Günzel, p. 126): 'Oh God who wished, for the redemption of the world, to be rejected by the Jews, betrayed by the kiss of Judas, bound in chains, led to slaughter like an innocent lamb, brought before the sight of Pilate, accused also by false witnesses, injured by scourges and insults, spat on, crowned

A similar point is made in the extracts from the Old English poem, *The Dream of the Rood* carved on the eighth-century Ruthwell Cross, which talk of almighty God ascending the gallows of the cross; the corresponding passage in the Vercelli text of the poem (line 39) speaks of Christ as the young hero who was God, emphasizing his dual nature rather than his divinity.

The second drawing, of the Trinity with Mary (pl. XVb), shows Christ seated at the right hand of the Father. The risen Christ, like the suffering Christ, is both God and man. The picture, then, asserts the permanence of Christ's human nature, now assumed into heaven.[58] At the same time it takes up other themes from the drawing of the Crucifixion earlier in the manuscript. The passage from St John's Gospel which lies behind the inscription to the Crucifixion scene links Christ's being lifted up on the cross to the defeat of the devil (John XII.31–2); the drawing of the Trinity shows the devil chained beneath Christ's feet. Mary, who represents the source of Christ's human nature in the Crucifixion scene, is shown overshadowed by the dove of the Holy Spirit to indicate her position as mother of God. In addition, she has been assumed into heaven to stand next to her son, offering a pledge to others that they, too, can some day enter heaven. Augustine interprets Christ's words to Nicodemus (quoted above) as a promise of future redemption for those who have been joined to Christ through his incarnation:

Dictum est propter unitatem, quia caput nostrum est, et nos corpus eius. Hoc ergo nemo nisi ipse, quia et nos ipse secundum id quod ipse filius hominis propter nos, et nos Dei filii propter ipsum ... Descendit itaque de caelo per misericordiam, nec ascendit nisi ipse, cum et nos in ipso per gratiam. Ac per hoc non nisi Christus descendit, nec nisi Christus ascendit; non quod capitis dignitas confundatur in corpore, sed quod corporis unitas non separetur a capite.[59]

with thorns, struck, raised on the cross, assigned a place between thieves, pierced by the points of the nails, wounded by the spear, given gall and vinegar to drink; free me from the punishments of hell through your most holy sufferings, and save and keep me through your holy cross, and lead me, a wretched sinner, where you led with you the crucified thief; to you, with God the Father and the Holy Spirit, be honour, power and glory, now and for ever. Amen.'

[58] See above, p. 50.

[59] Augustine, *De ascensione Domini*, 2 (PLS 2, 495, trans. modern Roman Breviary for the feast of the Ascension): 'He said this because of the unity between us and himself, for he is our head and we are his body. The words "no one but he" are true, since we are Christ, in the sense that he is the Son of man because of us, and we are the children of

This unity of body and head is symbolized in the drawing by the presence of Mary, the first of Christ's human brothers and sisters to join him in heaven.

These two themes, of Christ as both God and man and of the implications of this for the salvation of the human race, are developed in the third drawing in the manuscript, that of a monk standing next to an enthroned figure of St Peter (pl. XVIb). Representations of the owner or the author of a book at the feet of Christ or a saint are a commonplace in late Anglo-Saxon art.[60] Peter was one of the patrons of New Minster and the simplest explanation of the drawing is that it was intended to show Ælfwine offering his book to St Peter, just as Edgar is shown offering his charter to Christ in the frontispiece to the New Minster Charter (pl. V). Presentation pictures, however, usually place more emphasis on the book than this picture does.[61] A prayer to St Peter earlier in the Ælfwine manuscript addresses him as custodian of the keys of the kingdom of heaven (*custos clavium regni celorum*), rock of the Church (*petra ecclesiae*) and shepherd of Christ's sheep (*pastor ovium Christi*); the prayer ends with a plea that Peter, the doorkeeper and shepherd (*ianitor et pastor*), will intercede for the speaker so that after the end of his life he may be found worthy of the reward of eternal happiness.[62] The keys held by Peter in the Ælfwine drawing draw attention to his role as *ianitor* and remind the viewer of a recurring theme in the prayers in the manuscript: the desire for protection at the hour of death. Ælfric points out that no one can enter heaven unless Peter opens the door to him[63] and Peter's power as

God because of him ... He came down from heaven, then, in mercy; and it is he alone who has ascended, since we are in him through grace. This is why no one has descended but Christ, and no one but Christ has ascended: not that the dignity of the head is fused with the body but that the body in its unity is not separated from its head.'

60   The best-known is the drawing of St Dunstan at the feet of Christ (pl. IV). Other examples are the painting of Judith of Flanders at the foot of the cross (NY, Pierpont Morgan Library, 709, 1v), the drawing of a monk at the feet of St Benedict (Orleans, Bibliothèque municipale, 175, 149r) and the painting of Boethius with the Trinity (Paris, BN, lat. 6401, 159r); see Temple, *Anglo-Saxon Manuscripts*, pls. 289, 144 and 95.

61   E.g. the pictures of Hrabanus Maurus offering his book to Pope Gregory, Cambridge, Trinity College B. 16. 3, 1v, and the monks of Canterbury presenting a book to St Benedict, BL, Arundel 155, 133r (reprod. Temple, *Anglo-Saxon Manuscripts*, pls. 48 and 213).

62   Titus D. xxvii, 88r–v (ptd Günzel, p. 138).

63   *CH* I.xxvi (ed. Thorpe, p. 370). See above, p. 28.

doorkeeper of heaven plays a major part in one of the drawings in the New Minster *Liber vitae*, where he is shown welcoming the redeemed into heaven and defending a soul from the devil.[64] The Peter of the Ælfwine drawing is very different from the Peter of the *Liber vitae*, however. The saint who protects the soul in the drawing in the *Liber vitae* is a standing figure, a helper; the Peter of the Prayerbook is seated, to indicate his role as judge.[65]

It is not inappropriate to represent Peter as a judge, for Christ had promised his apostles that they would sit in judgement: 'When all is made new and the Son of Man sits on his throne of glory, you will yourselves sit on twelve thrones to judge the twelve tribes of Israel' (Matt. XIX.28). The drawing goes far beyond this text, however, for it shows Peter seated on the arc of the firmament and on a globe, not on the more usual cushioned bench. The arc indicates that Peter is throned in heaven; it is a common motif in late Anglo-Saxon representations of Christ and appears occasionally in representations of Mary.[66] The globe-throne, on the other hand, is an attribute of God. The source of the motif is a passage from Isaiah, quoted by Ælfric in his exposition of the Lord's Prayer: 'Thus says Yahweh: With heaven my throne and earth my footstool, what house could you build me, what place could you make for my rest?'[67] The globe-throne is a common motif in Carolingian art, though it does not seem to be combined with the arc as it is in the drawing of Peter.[68] English artists, however, sometimes combined the two motifs. The painting of God enthroned between two seraphs in a Boethius manuscript from Fleury

---

[64] BL, Stowe 944, 7r (reprod. Temple, *Anglo-Saxon Manuscripts*, pl. 248).

[65] Cf. Ælfric, *CH* I.iii (ed. Thorpe, p. 48), discussed above, p. 146.

[66] E.g. BL, Cotton Vespasian A. viii, 2v (pl. V), NY, Pierpont Morgan Library, 869, 11v (pl. XIVb), Boulogne, Bibliothèque municipale, 11, 10r (pl. X), Stowe 944, 6r, Paris, BN, lat. 6401, 158v, and Orleans, Bibliothèque municipale, 175, 149r (reprod. Temple, *Anglo-Saxon Manuscripts*, pls. 244, 94 and 144). Mary is shown throned on the arc of heaven on an ivory of the Virgin and Child, (reprod. Beckwith, *Ivory Carvings*, pl. 75).

[67] Isaiah LXVI.1 and Acts VII.49; see above, pp. 137–9.

[68] See the gospel frontispieces of the Tours Bibles and the Trier Apocalypse, Cod. 31, 15v (reprod. Kessler, *Illustrated Bibles*, pls. 48–50 and 55), the Utrecht Psalter *passim*, and a picture of St John from a Tours gospelbook (Stuttgart, Württembergische Landesbibliothek, H. B. II, 40, 146v, reprod. Hubert, Porcher and Volbach, *Carolingian Art*, pl. 116).

includes both arc and globe,[69] as do the frontispiece to Edgar's Charter to New Minster (pl. V) and the painting of God the creator in the Boulogne Gospels (pl. IX). The artist of the Ælfwine prayerbook must have seen the painting in the New Minster Charter, since it was almost certainly displayed on the altar of the church, and he could well have based his representation of Peter on the figure of Christ in that manuscript. Peter, then, is shown as in some sense divine; by contemplating Christ he has become like him.[70]

This developing theme of redemption is presented very differently in the three pictures, however. In the drawing of the Trinity the figures are remote, isolated, an object of contemplation; in the drawing of the Crucifixion the figures reach out to those who look at them; in the final scene, of Ælfwine with St Peter, the boundaries of time and space are completely broken.

The drawing of the Trinity with Mary shows the object of religious desire and the reward of faith. The picture does not represent an actual scene; it is a diagram of the spiritual world, a way of making abstract theological ideas visible. It displays the central truths of Christian belief in which, as the Athanasian Creed states, man must believe if he wishes to be saved:[71] Christ's divine nature, the perfect image of the Father; the truth of the Incarnation; the glorification of Christ's human nature which has been raised to God's throne; Christ's triumph over the devil; the entry of the human race into heaven in the person of Mary and her role in salvation; the fate of those who do not believe in Christ as Son of God. But the picture does not simply present a series of propositions to be believed: it is concerned with relationship to a person and the effect this relationship has on the viewer. This relationship is at the same time close and remote: the scene is a heavenly one and its relationship to the viewer is one of contemplation; the figures, therefore, stay within their frame, in a world apart. Yet, at the same time, they offer a promise for the future, a sign of hope.

The eternal life promised by Christ is not merely a matter of reaching heaven, but involves a sharing in the divine life: 'In making these gifts, he has given us the guarantee of something very great and wonderful to

---

[69] Paris, BN, lat. 6401, 158v (reprod. Temple, *Anglo-Saxon Manuscripts*, pl. 94).

[70] This assimilation of Peter to Christ is hinted at by Ælfric, *CH* II.xxiv (ed. Godden, p. 226) and Bede, *Homeliae* I.20 (ed. Hurst, p. 144).

[71] See above, p. 32.

come; through them you will be able to share the divine nature' (II Peter I.4). St Paul puts the point very clearly in a passage which links the raising of Christ to the right hand of God, depicted in the Ælfwine drawing, to the theme of Christ as the second Adam (1 Cor. XV.20–8). After describing Christ's triumph over his enemies, his handing over the kingdom to his Father and the time when God will be all in all, he goes on to talk of the Resurrection:

The first man, being from the earth, is earthly by nature; the second man is from heaven. As this earthly man was, so are we on earth; and as the heavenly man is, so are we in heaven. And we, who have been modelled on the earthly man, will be modelled on the heavenly man. (I Cor. XV.47–9)

The theme of the restoration of the divine image was well-known.[72] What is more important is that it was understood to come about through contemplation of the divine. Bede, for example, commenting on the text, 'On that day you will understand that I am in my Father and you in me and I in you' (John XIV.20), explains that after their resurrection the righteous will 'begin to know more perfectly all the things that are to be known, to the extent that they endlessly look, from closer by, at the very font of knowledge.'[73] This promise, he says, is made to all: our reward will be to contemplate Christ's glory for ever and, since Father, Son and Spirit are one, this vision will encompass all three members of the Trinity.[74]

The picture of the Trinity, then, is central to the meditative programme of the Ælfwine manuscript because it shows the object of religious contemplation, in this world and in heaven. The picture of the Crucifixion shows the precondition for that contemplation, namely the redemption brought by Christ's death. It does not simply recall the gospel event, however, nor does it suggest the kind of meditation which involves a reliving of that event. Whereas some Crucifixion pictures demand a response of grief at the death of Christ, here the open eyes of the figure on the cross invite a relationship between living persons. This sense of relationship is increased by the way in which the two supporting figures are portrayed. Mary is shown as an orant, a symbolic pose intended to indicate her faith in her Son and her prayer for the Church; she reassures

---

[72] See above, p. 43.
[73] Bede, *Homeliae* II.17 (ed. Hurst, p. 304, trans. Martin and Hurst, *Homilies* II, 168).
[74] Bede, *Homeliae* II.17 (ed. Hurst, p. 305).

those praying before the picture that they have an advocate. John writes in a book, a detail derived from the closing words of his gospel: 'This disciple is the one who vouches for these things and has written them down, and we know that his testimony is true' (John XXI.24).[75] He testifies that what is contemplated is true: that Christ truly died, that Christ was in truth both God and man, that faith in Christ's redemptive death is not vain.

In the picture of the Crucifixion, figures from the gospel story are depicted as accessible to those in this world. From their place in an eternal present, freed from the constraints of history, they speak to those still in the world. The drawing of a monk with St Peter carries this relationship between the one who contemplates and the person behind the image he contemplates one stage further. In it the two worlds unite and the monk, while still in this world, is able, through the medium of the picture, to enter the eternal world in which Peter now lives. The picture shows (by proxy as it were) the reward which the contemplative can experience already in this life.

In studying the picture of the Trinity, the owner of the manuscript was already sharing, symbolically, in the contemplation of the Godhead in heaven. The pictures of the Crucifixion and of St Peter give a more personal, individual tone to this theme. The inscription above the arms of the cross in the drawing of the Crucifixion links it specifically to the owner of the manuscript:

> Hec crux consignet Ælfwinum corpore mente
> In qua suspendens traxit Deus omnia secum.

These lines identify the cross on which Christ died with the cross with which Ælfwine was marked at baptism. St Paul refers several times to the seal with which God has marked believers, a seal referred to again in the Apocalypse:

Then I saw another angel rising where the sun rises, carrying the seal of the living God; he called in a powerful voice to the four angels whose duty was to devastate

---

[75] The text echoes John's comment on Christ's death, 'This is the evidence of one who saw it – trustworthy evidence, and he knows he speaks the truth – and he gives it so that you may believe as well' (John XIX.35), though here John is described as speaking, not writing.

land and sea, Wait before you do any damage on land or at sea or to the trees, until we have put the *seal on the foreheads* of the servants of our God.

(Apoc. VII.2–3)[76]

Ambrose, talking of the baptismal ceremonies of the Easter Vigil says: 'Signavit te Deus Pater, confirmavit te Christus dominus; et dedit pignus Spiritus in cordibus tuis.'[77] In contemplating Christ's death, therefore, Ælfwine remembers that the cross is the sign of his own salvation, that he is already sealed with the sign of life.[78] It is this sealing which allows him, in the second drawing, to contemplate the Trinity, mentally sharing in the worship of heaven. At this point he is still in this world. In the final picture, however, he escapes the constraints of time to stand, at least in imagination, at the feet of St Peter who, as Christ's deputy, will judge whether he is fit to enter heaven.

The three drawings in the prayerbook therefore show the stages in God's redemption of man and those by which Ælfwine comes to share that redemption. The starting point is Christ's death on the cross, the death of one who was God. From that death comes the glorification of human nature when Christ returns to heaven. In Mary and Peter the divine life is extended to mankind. Ælfwine comes to share this process through baptism and through contemplation of the Trinity. When he was signed with the cross at his baptism, and went down into the tomb with Christ,[79] he was entering into the redemptive process through which the divine image was restored to the human race; when he stands before Peter in the last drawing in his prayerbook he attains the final stage in his journey.

[76] Cf. Ezekiel IX.4, 'Go all through the city, all through Jerusalem, and mark a cross on the foreheads of all who deplore and disapprove of all the filth practised in it.'

[77] Ambrose, *De mysteriis*, vii.42 (PL 16, 403), quoted O'Carragáin, 'Liturgical Interpretation', pp. 25–6: 'God the Father has marked you with his seal, Christ the Lord has confirmed you and the Spirit has given you a pledge within your hearts.'

[78] 'Remember it is God himself who assures us all, and you, of our standing in Christ, and has anointed us, marking us with his seal and giving us the pledge, the Spirit, that we carry in our hearts' (II Cor. I.22); 'you have been stamped with the seal of the Holy Spirit' (Ephes. I.13); 'the Holy Spirit of God who has marked you with his seal for you to be set free when the day comes' (Ephes. IV.30).

[79] On the symbolism of baptism, see Raw, 'Why does the River Jordan Stand Still?', pp. 35–7.

# Bibliography

Acts of Nicaea II. *See* Sahas

Adémar of Chabannes. *Historiarum libri tres*, ed. G. Waitz, MGH Scriptores in folio 4 (1841), 106–48 (item xvii)

Adriaen, M. *See* Cassiodorus, Gregory the Great *and* Jerome

Adso of Montier-en-Der. *Adso Dervensis. De ortu et tempore Antichristi*, ed. D. Verhelst, CCCMed 45 (Turnhout, 1976)

Advent Lyrics. *The Advent Lyrics of the Exeter Book*, ed. J. J. Campbell (Princeton, NJ, 1959)

*See also* Burlin

Ælfric. *Ælfric's Catholic Homilies, the Second Series*, ed. M. Godden, EETS ss 5 (London, 1979)

*Ælfric's Lives of Saints*, ed. W. W. Skeat, EETS os 76, 82, 94 and 114 (London, 1881–1900, repr. in 2 vols., 1966)

*Angelsächsische Homilien und Heiligenleben*, ed. B. Assmann, Bibliothek der angelsächsischen Prosa 3 (Kassel, 1889), reissued with introduction by P. Clemoes (Darmstadt, 1964)

*Die Hirtenbriefe Ælfrics in altenglischer und lateinischer Fassung*, ed. B. Fehr, Bibliothek der angelsächsischen Prosa 9 (Hamburg, 1914), reissued with supplement by P. Clemoes (Darmstadt, 1966)

*Epistula ad monachos Egneshamnenses directa*, ed. H. Nocent, CCM 7.3 (1984), 149–85

*Exameron Anglice, or The Old English Hexameron*, ed. S. J. Crawford, Bibliothek der angelsächsischen Prosa 10 (Hamburg, 1921, repr. 1968)

*Homilies of Ælfric: a Supplementary Collection*, ed. J. C. Pope, 2 vols., EETS os 259–60 (London, 1967–8)

*The Homilies of the Anglo-Saxon Church*, ed. B. Thorpe, 2 vols. (London, 1844–6)

*The Old English Version of the Heptateuch, Ælfric's Treatise on the Old and New Testament and his Preface to Genesis*, ed. S. J. Crawford, EETS os 160 (London, 1922, repr. with additions by N. R. Ker, 1969)

187

*See also under* Hexateuch for a facsimile of BL, Cotton Claudius B. iv

Ælfwine. *Ælfwine's Prayerbook (London, British Library, Cotton Titus D. xxvi + xxvii)*, ed. B. Günzel, HBS 108 (London, 1993)

Æthelwold, Benedictional. *See* Benedictional

Æthelwold, Life by Wulfstan. *See* Wulfstan of Winchester

Agobard. *Liber adversus Felicem Urgellensem*: PL 104, 29–70

Alcuin. *Adversus Felicis haeresin*: PL 101, 85–120

    *Beatus igitur David*: PL 101, 509–10

    *Contra Felicem Urgellitanum Episcopum*: PL 101, 119–230

    *De animae ratione*: PL 101, 639–47

    *De fide sanctae et individuae Trinitatis*: PL 101, 9–58

    *De psalmorum usu*: PL 101, 465–8

    *Libellus de processione Spiritus Sancti*: PL 101, 63–82

    *Liber sacramentorum*: PL 101, 445–66

    *Quaestiones xxviii de Trinitate*: PL 101, 57–64

Ps.-Alcuin. *Abbreviatio furtivae orationis*: PL 101, 468–92

    *Officia per ferias*: PL 101, 509–612

Alexander, J. J. G., 'The Benedictional of St Æthelwold and Anglo-Saxon Illumination of the Reform Period', in *Tenth-Century Studies. Essays in Commemoration of the Millennium of the Council of Winchester and Regularis Concordia*, ed. D. Parsons (London, 1975), pp. 169–83

    *Insular Manuscripts, 6th to the 9th Century*, A Survey of Manuscripts Illuminated in the British Isles 1 (London, 1978)

Alfred. *König Alfreds des Grossen Bearbeitung der Soliloquien des Augustinus*, ed. W. Endter, Bibliothek der angelsächsischen Prosa 11 (Hamburg, 1922, repr. 1964)

    *King Alfred's Version of St Augustine's Soliloquies*, ed. T. A. Carnicelli (Cambridge, MA, 1969)

Allen, M. J. B., and D. G. Calder, *Sources and Analogues of Old English Poetry. The Major Latin Texts in Translation* (Cambridge, 1976)

Amalarius. *Amalarii episcopi opera liturgica omnia*, ed. J. M. Hanssens, 3 vols., Studi e testi 138–40 (Vatican City, 1948–50)

Ambrose. *De mysteriis*: PL 16, 389–410

    *De officiis*: PL 16, 23–184

Ambrosius Autpertus. *Expositio in Apocalypsin*, ed. R. Weber, CCCMed 27 and 27A (Turnhout, 1975)

    *De adsumptione Sanctae Mariae*, ed. R. Weber, CCCMed 27B (Turnhout, 1979), 1027–36

Anastos, M. V., 'The Ethical Theory of Images Formulated by the Iconoclasts in 754 and 815', *Dumbarton Oaks Papers* 8 (1954), 151–60

Anderson, D. *See* John of Damascus

Andrieu, M., 'L'*Ordo Romanus antiquus* et le *Liber de divinis officiis* du Pseudo-Alcuin', *Revue des sciences religieuses* 5 (1925), 642–50

Anselm, archbishop of Canterbury. *Monologion*, in *S. Anselmi Cantuariensis archiepiscopi opera omnia*, ed. F. S. Schmitt, 6 vols. (Edinburgh, 1946–61) I, 5–87

    *Orationes sive meditationes*, ed. F. S. Schmitt, *ibid.* III, 3–91, and trans. B. Ward, *The Prayers and Meditations of St Anselm* (Harmondsworth, 1973)

    *Proslogion*, ed. F. S. Schmitt, *ibid.* I, 93–122

Anselm of Lucca. *See* Wilmart

Antiphons. *Corpus antiphonalium officii*, ed. R.-J. Hesbert, 6 vols., Rerum ecclesiasticarum documenta, Series maior, Fontes 7–12 (Rome, 1963–79)

Assmann, B. *See* Ælfric

Athanasian Creed. *Quicumque*, in Augustine, *De Trinitate*, ed. W. J. Mountain, CCSL 50A (Turnhout, 1968), 566–7

Auerbach, E., 'Figura' in *Scenes from the Drama of European Literature* (New York, 1959), pp. 11–76

Augustine of Hippo. *Confessionum Libri XIII*, ed. L. Verheijen, CCSL 27 (Turnhout, 1981) and trans. R. S. Pine-Coffin, *Saint Augustine, Confessions* (Harmondsworth, 1961)

    *De Civitate Dei*, ed. B. Dombart and A. Kalb, CCSL 47–8 (Turnhout, 1955) and trans. H. Bettenson, *St Augustine: Concerning the City of God against the Pagans* (London, 1984)

    *De diversis quaestionibus*, ed. A. Mutzenbecher, CCSL 44A (Turnhout, 1975), 2–249

    *De doctrina christiana*, ed. J. Martin, CCSL 32 (Turnhout, 1962), 1–167 and trans. D. W. Robertson, *Saint Augustine, On Christian Doctrine* (New York, 1958)

    *De fide rerum invisibilium*, ed. M. P. J. van den Hout, CCSL 46 (Turnhout, 1969), 1–19

    *De Genesi ad litteram*, ed. J. Zycha, CSEL 28 (Vienna, 1894), 1–435

    *De praedestinatione sanctorum*: PL 44, 959–92

    *De Trinitate Libri XV*, ed. W. J. Mountain, 2 vols., CCSL 50 and 50A (Turnhout, 1968) and trans. E. Hill, *The Trinity* (Brooklyn, New York, 1991)

    *Enarrationes in Psalmos*, ed. E. Dekkers and J. Fraipont, 3 vols., CCSL 38, 39 and 40 (Turnhout, 1956)

    *Epistolae*: PL 33

    *In Iohannis evangelium tractatus cxxiv*, ed. R. Willems, CCSL 36 (Turnhout, 1954)

    *Liber de videndo Deo seu Epistula 147*, ed. M. Schmaus, Florilegium Patristicum 23 (1930)

    *Quaestiones evangeliorum*, ed. A. Mutzenbecher, CCSL 44B (Turnhout, 1980), 1–118

*Sermo Mai 98, De ascensione Domini*: PLS 2, 494–7

*Sermones*: PL 38 and 39

*Soliloquiorum Libri duo*: PL 32, 869–904

Ps.-Augustine, *Sermones*: PL 39, 1735–2354

Backhouse, J., 'The Making of the Harley Psalter', *British Library Journal* 10 (1984), 97–113

*See also* Golden Age *and* Making of England

Bätschmann, O., 'Text and Image: Some General Problems', *Word and Image* 4.1 (1988), 11–20

Baker, P. S. *See* Byrhtferth

Bakka, E., 'The Alfred Jewel and Sight', *AntJ* 46 (1966), 277–82

Balthasar, H. U. von, *The Glory of the Lord: A Theological Aesthetics. I: Seeing the Form*, trans. E. Leiva-Merikakis (Edinburgh, 1982)

Banks, R. A., 'Some Anglo-Saxon Prayers from British Museum MS Cotton Galba A. xiv', *N&Q* 210 (1965), 207–13

Barasch, M., *Icon. Studies in the History of an Idea* (New York, 1992)

Barb, A. A., '*Mensa sacra*: the Round Table and the Holy Grail', *JWCI* 19 (1956), 40–67

Barbet, J. *See* John Scotus

Barré, H., *Prières anciennes de l'occident à la Mère du Sauveur des origines à Saint Anselme* (Paris, 1963)

Bastgen, H. See *Libri Carolini*

Beckwith, J., *Ivory Carvings in Early Medieval England* (London, 1972)

Bede. *De tabernaculo*, ed. D. Hurst, CCSL 119A (Turnhout, 1969), 3–139 and trans. A. G. Holder, *Bede: On the Tabernacle*, Translated Texts for Historians 18 (Liverpool, 1994)

*De templo*, ed. D. Hurst, CCSL 119A (Turnhout, 1969), 143–234

*Explanatio Apocalypsis*: PL 93, 129–206

*Expositio Actuum Apostolorum*, ed. M. L. W. Laistner, CCSL 121 (Turnhout, 1983), 3–99

*Historia abbatum*: *Venerabilis Baedae opera historica*, ed. C. Plummer, 2 vols. (Oxford, 1896) I, 364–87 and trans. J. F. Webb and D. H. Farmer, *The Age of Bede*, rev. ed. (London, 1988), pp. 185–208

*Historia ecclesiastica gentis Anglorum*: *Bede's Ecclesiastical History of the English People*, ed. and trans. B. Colgrave and R. A. B. Mynors (Oxford, 1969)

*Homeliae evangelii*, ed. D. Hurst, CCSL 122 (Turnhout, 1955), 1–378 and trans. L. T. Martin and D. Hurst, *Bede the Venerable. Homilies on the Gospels*, 2 vols., Cistercian Studies Series 110–11 (Kalamazoo, MI, 1991)

*In canticum Abacuc*, ed. J. E. Hudson, CCSL 119B (Turnhout, 1983), 381–409

*In Lucae evangelium expositio*, ed. D. Hurst, CCSL 120 (Turnhout, 1960), 5–425

*In Marci evangelium expositio*, ed. D. Hurst, CCSL 120 (Turnhout, 1960), 431–648

*Libri quatuor in principium Genesis*, ed. C. W. Jones, CCSL 118A (Turnhout, 1967)

Ps.-Bede, *De sex dierum creatione*: PL 93, 207–34

*Quaestiones super Genesim*: PL 93, 233–64

*Quaestiones super Numeros*: PL 93, 395–410

Benedict of Aniane, *Forma fidei*: 'Les *Munimenta fidei* de Saint Benoit d'Aniane', ed. J. Leclercq, *Studia Anselmiana* 20 [*Analecta monastica* 1] (1948), 21–74

Benedictine Office. *The Benedictine Office: An Old English Text*, ed. J. M. Ure (Edinburgh, 1957)

Benedictine Rule. *Benedicti regula*, ed. R. Hanslik, CSEL 75 (Vienna, 1960)

Benedictional. *The Benedictional of Archbishop Robert*, ed. H. A. Wilson, HBS 24 (London, 1903)

*The Benedictional of Saint Æthelwold Bishop of Winchester 963–984*, ed. G. F. Warner and H. A. Wilson, Roxburghe Club (Oxford, 1910)

Bernard of Clairvaux. *In laudibus Virginis matris, homilia ii*: *Sancti Bernardi Opera* IV, ed. J. Leclercq and H. Rochais (Rome, 1966), pp. 21–35

Bestul, T. H., 'St Anselm and the Continuity of Anglo-Saxon Devotional Traditions', *Annuale mediaevale* 18 (1977), 20–41

'Continental Sources of Anglo-Saxon Devotional Writing', in *Sources of Anglo-Saxon Culture*, ed. P. E. Szarmach (Kalamazoo, MI, 1986), pp. 103–26

Bestul, T. H., ed., *A Durham Book of Devotions*, Toronto Medieval Latin Texts 18 (Toronto, 1987)

Bethurum, D. *See* Wulfstan of Worcester

Bettenson, H. *See* Augustine of Hippo

Beumann, H. *See* Gospels of Otto III

Biddle, M., ed., *Winchester in the Early Middle Ages: An Edition and Discussion of the Winton Domesday*, Winchester Studies 1 (Oxford, 1976)

Bieler, L. *See* Boethius

Birch, W. de G. *See* Book of Nunnaminster *and* New Minster

Bischoff, B. and M. Lapidge, ed., *Biblical Commentaries from the Canterbury School of Theodore and Hadrian*, CSASE 10 (Cambridge, 1994)

Blickling Homilies. *The Blickling Homilies*, ed. R. Morris, EETS os 58, 63 and 73 (London, 1874–80, repr. as one vol., 1967)

Blumenkranz, B., '*Altercatio Aecclesie contra Synagogam*. Texte inédit du Xe siècle', *Revue du Moyen Age Latin* 10 (1954), 5–159

Boethius, *Philosophiae consolatio*, ed. L. Bieler, CCSL 94 (Turnhout, 1984)

Book of Cerne. *The Prayer Book of Aedeluald the Bishop Commonly Called The Book of Cerne*, ed. A. B. Kuypers (Cambridge, 1902)

Book of Nunnaminster. *An Ancient Manuscript of the Eighth or Ninth Century*

*Formerly Belonging to St Mary's Abbey, or Nunnaminster, Winchester*, ed. W. de G. Birch, Hampshire Record Society (London, 1889)

Bovini, G., *Ravenna Mosaics*, trans. G. Scaglia (Oxford, 1978)

Braun, R. *See* Quodvultdeus

Brooks, N., *The Early History of the Church of Canterbury. Christ Church from 597 to 1066* (Leicester, 1984)

Brou, L., 'Marie "Destructrice de toutes les hérésies" et la belle légende du répons *Gaude Maria Virgo*', *EL* 62 (1948), 321–53

Brubaker, L., 'Perception and Conception: Art, Theory and Culture in 9th-Century Byzantium', *Word and Image* 5.1 (1989), 19–32

Bruce-Mitford, R. L. S., 'Iconography of the Fuller Brooch', in D. M. Wilson, *Anglo-Saxon Ornamental Metalwork 700–1100*, Catalogue of Antiquities of the Later Saxon Period I (London, 1964), 91–8

  *Aspects of Anglo-Saxon Archaeology. Sutton Hoo and other Discoveries* (London, 1974)

Bruyne, D. de, *Préfaces de la Bible Latine* (Namur, 1920)

Budny, M., 'St Dunstan's Classbook and its Frontispiece: Dunstan's Portrait and Autograph', in *St Dunstan: his Life, Times and Cult*, ed. N. Ramsay, M. Sparks and T. Tatton-Brown (Woodbridge, 1992), pp. 103–42

Burlin, R. B., *The Old English Advent: a Typological Commentary*, Yale Studies in English 168 (New Haven, CT, 1968)

Burrows, D. R. *See* Keefer

Byrhtferth. *Byrhtferth's Enchiridion*, ed. P. S. Baker and M. Lapidge, EETS ss 15 (London, 1995)

Caesarius of Arles. *Sancti Caesarii Arelatensis sermones*, ed. G. Morin, 2 vols., CCSL 103–4 (Turnhout, 1953)

Calder, D. G. *See* Allen

Callahan, D., 'Adémar of Chabannes, Apocalypticism and the Peace Council of Limoges of 1031', *RB* 101 (1991), 32–49

  'The Problem of the "Filioque" and the Letter from the Pilgrim Monks of the Mount of Olives to Pope Leo III and Charlemagne', *RB* 102 (1992), 75–134

Camille, M., 'Seeing and Reading: some Visual Implications of Medieval Literacy and Illiteracy', *Art History* 8 (1985), 26–49

Campbell, J. J. *See* Advent Lyrics

Capelle, B., 'Les épîtres sapientiales des fêtes de la Vierge', in his *Travaux liturgiques de doctrine et d'histoire* III (Louvain, 1967), 316–22

Cappuyns, M. *See* John Scotus

Carnicelli, T. A. *See* Alfred

Carruthers, M. J., *The Book of Memory: a Study of Memory in Medieval Culture* (Cambridge, 1990)

Cassidy, B., ed., *The Ruthwell Cross: Papers from the Colloquium Sponsored by the Index of Christian Art, Princeton University, 8 December 1989*, Index of Christian Art Occasional Papers 1 (Princeton, NJ, 1992)

*Iconography at the Crossroads: Papers from the Colloquium Sponsored by the Index of Christian Art, Princeton University, 23–24 March 1990*, Index of Christian Art Occasional Papers 2 (Princeton, NJ, 1993)

Cassiodorus. *Expositio psalmorum*, ed. M. Adriaen, CCSL 97–8 (Turnhout, 1958)

Cavadini, J., 'The Sources and Theology of Alcuin's *De fide sanctae et individuae Trinitatis*', *Traditio* 46 (1991), 123–46

Cerne. *See* Book of Cerne

Charles, R. H., *The Apocrypha and Pseudepigrapha of the Old Testament in English* II (Oxford, 1913)

Chazelle, C., 'Matter, Spirit and Image in the *Libri Carolini*', *Recherches Augustiniennes* 21 (1986), 163–84

'Figure, Character and the Glorified Body in the Carolingian Eucharistic Controversy', *Traditio* 47 (1992), 1–36

Chenu, M.-D., *Nature, Man and Society in the Twelfth Century. Essays on New Theological Perspectives in the Latin West*, trans. J. Taylor and L. K. Little (Chicago, 1968)

*Christ and Satan, an Old English Poem*, ed. M. D. Clubb (New Haven, CT, 1925)

Clayton, M., 'Feasts of the Virgin in the Liturgy of the Anglo-Saxon Church', *ASE* 13 (1984), 209–33

'Ælfric and *Cogitis me*', *N&Q* 231 (1986), 148–9

*The Cult of the Virgin Mary in Anglo-Saxon England*, CSASE 2 (Cambridge, 1990)

Clemoes, P., 'The Chronology of Ælfric's Works', in *The Anglo-Saxons. Studies in Some Aspects of their History and Culture, Presented to Bruce Dickins*, ed. P. Clemoes (London, 1959), pp. 212–47

'Ælfric', in *Continuations and Beginnings. Studies in Old English Literature*, ed. E. G. Stanley (London, 1966), pp. 176–209

'Language in Context: *Her* in the 890 *Anglo-Saxon Chronicle*', *Leeds Studies in English* ns 16 (1985), 27–36

'King and Creation at the Crucifixion: the Contribution of Native Tradition to *The Dream of the Rood* 50–6a', in *Heroes and Heroines in Medieval English Literature: a Festschrift Presented to André Crépin on the Occasion of his Sixty-Fifth Birthday*, ed. L. Carruthers (Cambridge, 1994), pp. 31–43

*See also* Ælfric, Hexateuch *and* Lapidge and Gneuss

Clemoes, P. and K. Hughes, ed., *England before the Conquest. Studies in Primary Sources Presented to Dorothy Whitelock* (Cambridge, 1971)

Clubb, M. D. *See Christ and Satan*

Codex Egberti. *Codex Egberti der Stadtbibliothek Trier*, ed. H. Schiel, 2 vols. (Basle, 1960)

Colgrave, B. *See* Bede

Corrigan, K., *Visual Polemics in the Ninth-Century Byzantine Psalters* (Cambridge, 1992)

Crawford, S. J. *See* Ælfric

Cross, J. E., 'Ælfric and the Mediaeval Homiliary – Objection and Contribution', *Scripta Minora Regiae Societatis Humaniorum Litterarum Lundensis, 1961–2* (1963), item 4, 3–34

'The "Coeternal Beam" in the OE Advent Poem (Christ I) ll. 104–129', *Neophilologus* 48 (1964), 72–81

D'Alverny, M.-T., 'Le symbolisme de la sagesse et le Christ de Saint Dunstan', *Bodleian Library Record* 5 (1954–6), 232–44

Dekkers, E. *See* Augustine of Hippo

Deshman, R., 'Anglo-Saxon Art after Alfred', *Art Bulletin* 56 (1974), 176–200

'*Christus rex et magi reges*: Kingship and Christology in Ottonian and Anglo-Saxon Art', *Frühmittelalterliche Studien* 10 (1976), 367–405

'The Exalted Servant: the Ruler Theology of the Prayerbook of Charles the Bald', *Viator* 11 (1980), 385–417

'The Imagery of the Living Ecclesia and the English Monastic Reform', in *Sources of Anglo-Saxon Culture*, ed. P. E. Szarmach, Studies in Medieval Culture 20 (Kalamazoo, MI, 1986), 261–82

'*Benedictus monarcha et monachus*. Early Medieval Ruler Theology and the Anglo-Saxon Reform', *Frühmittelalterliche Studien* 22 (1988), 204–40

*The Benedictional of Æthelwold*, Studies in Manuscript Illumination 9 (Princeton, NJ, 1995)

de Wald, E. T. *See* Utrecht Psalter

Dewick, E. S. *See* Leofric Collectar

Ps.-Dionysius. *Pseudo-Dionysius: the Complete Works*, trans. C. Luibheid (London, 1987)

Dix, G., *The Shape of the Liturgy* (London, 1945)

Dobbie, E. van K. *See* The Anglo-Saxon Poetic Records

Dodwell, C. R., *Anglo-Saxon Art: a New Perspective* (Manchester, 1982)

*The Pictorial Arts of the West 800–1200* (New Haven, CT, 1993)

*See also* Hexateuch

Dombart, B. *See* Augustine of Hippo

Dressler, F. *See* Gospels of Otto III

Drogo Sacramentary. *Drogo-Sakramentar. MS lat. 9428, Bibliothèque Nationale, Paris. Vollständige Faksimile-Ausgabe im Originalformat*, ed. W. Koehler and F. Mütherich (Graz, 1974)

Duchesne, L., *Le Liber pontificalis, texte, introduction et commentaire* I (Paris, 1886)

Dufrenne, S., *Les illustrations du Psautier d'Utrecht: sources et apport carolingien* (Paris, 1979)

# Bibliography

Duggan, L., 'Was Art Really the Book of the Illiterate?', *Word and Image* 5.3 (1989), 227–51

Dungal. *Liber adversus Claudium Taurinensem*: PL 105, 457–530

Dunstan. *Memorials of Saint Dunstan, Archbishop of Canterbury*, ed. W. Stubbs, RS 63 (London, 1874)

   *Saint Dunstan's Classbook from Glastonbury: Codex Biblioth. Bodleianae Oxon. Auct. F. 4. 32*, ed. R. W. Hunt, Umbrae Codicum Occidentalium 4 (Amsterdam, 1961)

Edith of Wilton. *See* Goscelin

Elbern, V. H., 'Der eucharistische Kelch im frühen Mittelalter', *Zeitschrift des deutschen Vereins für Kunstwissenschaft* 17 (1963), 1–76 and 117–88

Elsen, A. E., *Purposes of Art: an Introduction to the History and Appreciation of Art*, 3rd ed. (New York, 1972)

Endter, W. *See* Alfred

Engelbregt, J. H. A. *See* Utrecht Psalter

*Epistula ad Paulam et Eustochium*. *See* Paschasius Radbertus

Evans, G. R., 'Mens devota: the Literary Community of the Devotional Works of John of Fécamp and St Anselm', *MÆ* 43 (1974), 105–15

Farmer, D. H. *See* Bede

Fehr, B., 'Uber einige Quellen zu Ælfrics *Homiliae Catholicae*', *Archiv* 130 (1913), 378–81

   *See also* Ælfric

Finberg, H. P. R., *The Early Charters of Wessex* (Leicester, 1964)

Förster, M., 'Uber die Quellen von Ælfrics exegetischen *Homiliae Catholicae*', *Anglia* 16 (1894), 1–6

   *See also* Vercelli Homilies

Fraipont, J. *See* Augustine of Hippo

France, J. *See* Ralph Glaber

Freedberg, D., *The Power of Images. Studies in the History and Theory of Response* (Chicago, 1989)

Freeman, A., 'Theodulf of Orléans and the *Libri Carolini*', *Speculum* 32 (1957), 663–705

   'Further Studies in the *Libri Carolini*', *Speculum* 40 (1965), 203–89

   'Carolingian Orthodoxy and the Fate of the *Libri Carolini*', *Viator* 16 (1985), 65–108

Frere, W. H. *See* Leofric Collectar

Gaehde, J. E., 'The Turonian Sources of the Bible of San Paolo fuori le Mura in Rome', *Frühmittelalterliche Studien* 5 (1971), 359–400

   'Carolingian Interpretations of an Early Christian Picture Cycle to the Octateuch in the Bible of San Paolo fuori le Mura in Rome', *Frühmittelalterliche Studien* 8 (1974), 351–84

## Bibliography

'The Pictorial Sources of the Illustrations to the Books of Kings, Proverbs, Judith and Maccabees in the Carolingian Bible of San Paolo fuori le Mura in Rome', *Frühmittelalterliche Studien* 9 (1975), 359–89

*See also* Mütherich

Gameson, R., 'English Manuscript Art in the Mid-Eleventh Century: The Decorative Tradition', *AntJ* 71 (1991), 64–122

'Manuscript Art at Christ Church, Canterbury, in the Generation after St Dunstan', in *St Dunstan: his Life, Times and Cult*, ed. N. Ramsay, M. Sparks and T. Tatton-Brown (Woodbridge, 1992), pp. 187–220

'Ælfric and the Perception of Script and Picture in Anglo-Saxon England', *Anglo-Saxon Studies in Archaeology and History* 5 (1992), 85–101

*The Role of Art in the Late Anglo-Saxon Church* (Oxford, 1995)

Ganz, D., *Corbie in the Carolingian Renaissance* (Sigmaringen, 1990)

Gatch, M. McC., 'Eschatology in the Anonymous Old English Homilies', *Traditio* 21 (1965), 117–65

*Preaching and Theology in Anglo-Saxon England: Ælfric and Wulfstan* (Toronto, 1977)

'King Alfred's Version of Augustine's *Soliloquia*: some Suggestions on its Rationale and Unity', in *Studies in Earlier Old English Prose*, ed. P. E. Szarmach (New York, 1986), pp. 17–45

Gem, R. D. H., 'The Anglo-Saxon Cathedral Church at Canterbury: a Further Contribution', *ArchJ* 127 (1970), 196–201

'Towards an Iconography of Anglo-Saxon Architecture', *JWCI* 46 (1983), 1–18

'Reconstructions of St Augustine's Abbey, Canterbury, in the Anglo-Saxon Period', in *St Dunstan: his Life, Times and Cult*, ed. N. Ramsay, M. Sparks and T. Tatton-Brown (Woodbridge, 1992), pp. 57–73

Gem, R. D. H. and P. Tudor-Craig, 'A "Winchester School" Wall-Painting at Nether Wallop, Hampshire', *ASE* 9 (1981), 115–36

Gero, S., 'Byzantine Iconoclasm and the Failure of a Medieval Reformation', in *The Image and the Word*, ed. J. Gutmann (Missoula, MT, 1977), pp. 49–62

Gilbert Crispin. *Disputatio Judaei cum Christiano de fide Christiana*: PL 159, 1005–36

Gneuss, H., 'Dunstan und Hrabanus Maurus. Zur Hs. Bodleian Auctarium F. 4. 32', *Anglia* 96 (1978), 136–48

'A Preliminary List of Manuscripts Written or Owned in England up to 1100', *ASE* 9 (1981), 1–60

*See also* Lapidge

Godden, M. R., 'The Development of Ælfric's Second Series of *Catholic Homilies*', *ES* 54 (1973), 209–16

'Anglo-Saxons on the Mind', in *Learning and Literature in Anglo-Saxon England*, ed. M. Lapidge and H. Gneuss (Cambridge, 1985), pp. 271–98

# Bibliography

'Biblical Literature: the Old Testament', in *The Cambridge Companion to Old English Literature*, ed. M. Godden and M. Lapidge (Cambridge, 1991), pp. 206–26

*See also* Ælfric

Godden, M. R. and M. Lapidge, ed., *The Cambridge Companion to Old English Literature* (Cambridge, 1991)

Godescalc. *Œuvres théologiques et grammaticales de Godescalc d'Orbais*, ed. D. C. Lambot, Spicilegium sacrum Lovaniense, Etudes et documents, 20 (Louvain, 1945)

Golden Age. *The Golden Age of Anglo-Saxon Art 966–1066*, ed. J. Backhouse, D. H. Turner and L. Webster (London, 1984)

Gollancz, I., ed., *The Cædmon Manuscript of Anglo-Saxon Biblical Poetry, Junius XI in the Bodleian Library* (Oxford, 1927)

Goscelin. *De Sancta Editha virgine et abbatissa*: A. Wilmart, 'La légende de Ste Edith en prose et vers par le moine Goscelin', *AB* 56 (1938), 5–101 and 265–307

Gospels of Otto III. *Das Evangeliar Ottos III, Clm 4453 der Bayerischen Staatsbibliothek München*, ed. F. Dressler, F. Mütherich and H. Beumann, 2 vols. (Frankfurt, 1978)

Gougaud, L., 'Muta praedicatio', *RB* 42 (1930), 168–71

Gouillard, J., *La vie religieuse à Byzance*, Variorum Reprints (London, 1981)

'Contemplation et imagerie sacrée dans le christianisme byzantin', *ibid.* item ii, from *Annuaire de la Ve Section de l'Ecole Pratique des Hautes Etudes* 86 (Paris, 1977–8), 29–50

'Aux origines de l'iconoclasme: le témoignage de Grégoire II', *ibid.* item iv, from *Travaux et mémoires* 3 (1968), 243–307, Centre de recherche d'histoire et de civilisation byzantines (Paris)

Grabar, A., *Ampoules de Terre Sainte (Monza-Bobbio)* (Paris, 1958)

*Byzantium from the Death of Theodosius to the Rise of Islam*, trans. S. Gilbert and J. Emmons (London, 1966)

*The Beginnings of Christian Art 200–395*, trans. S. Gilbert and J. Emmons (London, 1967)

*Christian Iconography: a Study of its Origins*, trans. T. Grabar (London, 1969)

Graef, H., *Mary: a History of Doctrine and Devotion*, 2 vols. (London, 1963–5)

Grégoire, R., *Les homéliaires du moyen âge: inventaire et analyse des manuscrits*, Rerum ecclesiasticarum documenta, Series Maior, Fontes 6 (Rome, 1966)

Gregory the Great. *Homiliae .xl. in evangelia*: PL 76, 1075–1312, trans. D. Hurst, *Gregory the Great. Forty Gospel Homilies*, Cistercian Studies Series 123 (Kalamazoo, MI, 1990)

*Homiliae in Hiezechihelem prophetam*, ed. M. Adriaen, CCSL 142 (Turnhout, 1971)

Letter to Secundinus (*Ep.* IX.148): *S. Gregorii Magni Registrum Epistolarum*, ed. D. Norberg, CCSL 140–140A (Turnhout, 1982), 698–704 and Appendix X, pp. 1104–11

Letters to Serenus of Marseilles (*Ep.* IX.209 and XI.10): *ibid.*, pp. 768 and 873–6

*Moralia in Iob*, ed. M. Adriaen, 3 vols., CCSL 143–143B (Turnhout, 1979–85) *See also* Wærferth of Worcester

Gregory of Nyssa. *De hominis opificio*: PG 44, 123–256

Grodecki, L., F. Mütherich, J. Taralon and F. Wormald, *Le siècle de l'an mil* (Paris, 1973)

Grundy, L., *Books and Grace: Ælfric's Theology*, King's College London Medieval Studies 6 (London, 1991)

Günzel, B. *See* Ælfwine

Gutmann, J., ed., *The Image and the Word* (Missoula, MT, 1977)

Häring, N. M., 'St Augustine's Use of the Word *Character*', *Mediaeval Studies* 14 (1952), 79–97

Hanslik, R. *See* Benedictine Rule

Hanssens, J. M. *See* Amalarius

Harris, R. M., 'The Marginal Drawings of the Bury St Edmunds Psalter (Rome, Vatican Library, MS Reg. lat. 12)' (unpubl. PhD dissertation, Princeton Univ., 1960)

Harrison, C., *Beauty and Revelation in the Thought of Saint Augustine* (Oxford, 1992)

Hart, C. R., *The Early Charters of Eastern England* (Leicester, 1966)

Haymo of Auxerre. *Expositio in Apocalypsin B. Ioannis*: PL 117, 937–1220 *Homiliae*: PL 118, 11–816

*In Epistolam II ad Thessalonicenses*: PL 117, 777–84

Heimann, A., 'Three Illustrations from the Bury St Edmunds Psalter and their Prototypes', *JWCI* 29 (1966), 39–59

Henderson, G., *Bede and the Visual Arts*, Jarrow Lecture (1980)

*Losses and Lacunae in Early Insular Art*, University of York, Medieval Monograph Series 3 (1982)

'The Idiosyncrasy of Late Anglo-Saxon Religious Imagery', in *England in the Eleventh Century. Proceedings of the 1990 Harlaxton Symposium*, ed. C. Hicks, Harlaxton Medieval Studies 2 (Stamford, 1992), 239–49

Hesbert, R.-J. *See* Antiphons

Heslop, T. A., 'The Production of *de luxe* Manuscripts and the Patronage of King Cnut and Queen Emma', *ASE* 19 (1990), 151–95

'A Dated "Late Anglo-Saxon" Illuminated Psalter', *AntJ* 72 (1992), 171–4

Hexateuch. *The Old English Illustrated Hexateuch (British Museum Cotton Claudius B. iv)*, ed. C. R. Dodwell and P. Clemoes, EEMF 18 (Copenhagen, 1974) *For an edition of the text see under* Ælfric

Higgitt, J., 'Glastonbury, Dunstan, Monasticism and Manuscripts', *Art History* 2 (1979), 275–90

Hilary. *Tractatus super Psalmos*, ed. A. Zingerle, CSEL 22 (Vienna, 1891)

Hill, E. *See* Augustine of Hippo

Hill, J., 'Ælfric's Use of Etymologies', *ASE* 17 (1988), 35–44

Hincmar. *De una et non trina Deitate*: PL 125, 473–618

Hippolytus. *De refutatione omnium haeresium*: PG, 16, 3017–454

   *Sermo in sancta Theophania*: PG 10, 851–62

Hoffmann, W. *See* Stuttgart Psalter

Holder, A. G. *See* Bede

Homburger, O., *Die Anfänge der Malschule von Winchester im X. Jahrhundert* (Leipzig, 1912)

   'L'art carolingien de Metz et l'"'école de Winchester"'', in *Essais en l'honneur de Jean Porcher: Etudes sur les manuscrits à peintures*, ed. O. Pächt (Paris, 1963), pp. 35–46

Hrabanus Maurus. *Commentaria in Ezechielem*: PL 110, 497–1086

   *De laudibus sanctae crucis*: PL 107, 133–294

Hubert, J., J. Porcher and W. F. Volbach, *Europe in the Dark Ages*, trans. S. Gilbert and J. Emmons (London, 1969)

   *Carolingian Art*, trans. J. Emmons, S. Gilbert and R. Allen (London, 1970)

Hudson, J. E. *See* Bede

Hughes, A. *See* Wulfstan II of Worcester

Hunt, R. W. *See* Dunstan

Hurlbut, S. A., *The Picture of the Heavenly Jerusalem in the Writings of Johannes of Fécamp, 'De contemplativa vita' and in the Elizabethan Hymns* (Washington, DC, 1943)

Hurst, D. *See* Bede *and* Gregory the Great

Irenaeus. *Contra haereses*: PG 7, 433–1224

   *The Demonstration of the Apostolic Preaching*, trans. J. A. Robinson, (London, 1920)

Isidore. *Isidori Hispalensis episcopi Etymologiarum sive originum libri xx*, ed. W. M. Lindsay, 2 vols. (Oxford, 1911)

   *Quaestiones in Vetus Testamentum: in Genesin*: PL 83, 207–88

   *Sententiae*: PL 83, 1153–200

Jeauneau, E. *See* John Scotus

Jerome. *Breviarium in Psalmos*: PL 26, 821–1270

   *Epistolae*: PL 22, 325–1224

   *In Abacuc prophetam*, ed. M. Adriaen, CCSL 76A (Turnhout, 1970), 579–654

   *In Esaiam*, ed. M. Adriaen, CCSL 73–73A (Turnhout, 1963)

   *In Hieremiam*, ed. S. Reiter, CCSL 74 (Turnhout, 1960)

John of Damascus. *De imaginibus*: PG 94, 1231–420, trans. D. Anderson, *St John of Damascus, On the Divine Images* (Crestwood, NY, 1980)

John of Fécamp. *Ad imperatricem viduam*: J. Leclercq and J.-P. Bonnes, *Un maître de la vie spirituelle au XIe siècle: Jean de Fécamp*, Etudes de théologie et d'histoire de la spiritualité 9 (Paris, 1946), 211–17

    *Ad sanctimonialem*: *ibid.*, pp. 205–10

    *Confessio fidei*: PL 101, 1027–98

    *Confessio theologica*: Leclercq and Bonnes, *ibid.*, pp. 110–83

    *Libellus de scripturis et verbis patrum*: A. Wilmart, 'Deux préfaces spirituelles de Jean de Fécamp', *Revue d'ascétique et de mystique* 18 (1937), 36–41

    *Prayer to God the Father* [probably not by John of Fécamp]. Ptd under *Sancti Anselmi orationes*, no. ii, in PL 158, 858–65 and Augustine, *Meditationum liber unus*, chs. v–viii, in PL 40, 904–8

    *Summe sacerdos*: A. Wilmart, *Auteurs spirituels et textes dévots* (Paris, 1932), pp. 101–25

John Scotus. PL 122

    *Commentarius in Evangelium Iohannis*: *Jean Scot, Commentaire sur l'évangile de Jean*, ed. E. Jeauneau, *Sources chrétiennes* 180 (Paris, 1972)

    *De hominis opificio*: M. Cappuyns, 'Le "De imagine" de Grégoire de Nysse traduit par Jean Scot Erigène', *Recherches de théologie ancienne et médiévale* 32 (1965), 205–62

    *Expositiones in Ierarchiam coelestem*, ed. J. Barbet, CCCMed 31 (Turnhout, 1975)

    *Omelia Iohannis Scoti*: *Jean Scot, Homélie sur le Prologue de Jean*, ed. E. Jeauneau, *Sources chrétiennes* 151 (Paris, 1969)

    *Periphyseon*: *Iohannis Scotti Eriugenae Periphyseon (De divisione naturae)*, ed. and trans. J. P. Sheldon-Williams, Scriptores Latini Hiberniae 7, 9 and 11 (Dublin, 1968–81)

John, E., 'The World of Abbot Ælfric', in *Ideal and Reality in Frankish and Anglo-Saxon Society. Studies Presented to J. M. Wallace-Hadrill*, ed. P. Wormald, D. Bullough and R. Collins (Oxford, 1983), pp. 300–16

Johnston, P. M., in notes section (no title) of *Proceedings of the Society of Antiquaries* 24 (1911–12), 159–70

Jonas of Orleans. *De cultu imaginum*: PL 106, 305–88

Jones, C. W. *See* Bede

Jones, W. R., 'Art and Christian Piety: Iconoclasm in Medieval Europe', in *The Image and the Word*, ed. J. Gutmann (Missoula, MT, 1977), pp. 75–105

Kalb, A. *See* Augustine of Hippo

Kantorowicz, E. H., 'The Quinity of Winchester', in his *Selected Studies*, ed. M. Cherniavsky and R. E. Giesey (New York, 1965), pp. 100–20

Kartsonis, A. D., *Anastasis: The Making of an Image* (Princeton, NJ, 1986)

Katzenellenbogen, A., 'The Image of Christ in the Early Middle Ages', in *Life and*

*Thought in the Early Middle Ages*, ed. R. S. Hoyt (Minneapolis, MN, 1967), pp. 66–84

Kauffmann, C. M., *Romanesque Manuscripts 1066–1190*, A Survey of Manuscripts Illuminated in the British Isles 3 (London, 1975)

Keefer, S. L. and D. R. Burrows, 'Hebrew and the *Hebraicum* in Late Anglo-Saxon England', *ASE* 19 (1990), 67–80

Keenan, H. T., ed., *Typology and English Medieval Literature*, Georgia State Literary Studies 7 (New York, 1992)

Kelly, J. N. D., *Early Christian Creeds*, 3rd ed. (London, 1972)
*Early Christian Doctrines*, 5th ed. (London, 1985)

Ker, N. R., *Catalogue of Manuscripts containing Anglo-Saxon* (Oxford, 1957)

Kessler, H. L., *The Illustrated Bibles from Tours*, Studies in Manuscript Illumination 7 (Princeton, NJ, 1977)
'Pictorial Narrative and Church Mission in Sixth-Century Gaul', in *Pictorial Narrative in Antiquity and the Middle Ages*, ed. H. L. Kessler and M. S. Simpson, Studies in the History of Art 16 (1985), 75–91
'Reading Ancient and Medieval Art', *Word and Image* 5.1 (1989), 1
*See also* Weitzmann

Kessler, H. L. and M. S. Simpson, ed., *Pictorial Narrative in Antiquity and the Middle Ages*, Studies in the History of Art 16 (1985)

Keynes, S., 'King Athelstan's Books', in *Learning and Literature in Anglo-Saxon England. Studies Presented to Peter Clemoes on the Occasion of his Sixty-Fifth Birthday*, ed. M. Lapidge and H. Gneuss (Cambridge, 1985), pp. 143–201

Kidd, J. A., 'The *Quinity of Winchester* Reconsidered', *Studies in Iconography* 7–8 (1981–2), 21–33

Kitzinger, E., 'The Cult of Images in the Age before Iconoclasm', in *The Art of Byzantium and the Medieval West: Selected Studies by E. Kitzinger*, ed. W. E. Kleinbauer (Bloomington, IN, 1976), pp. 91–156 and *Dumbarton Oaks Papers* 8 (1954), 83–150
'Christian Imagery: Growth and Impact', in *Age of Spirituality*, ed. K. Weitzmann (New York, 1980), pp. 141–63

Klein, P. K. *See* Trier Apocalypse

Kleinbauer, W. E., ed., *Modern Perspectives in Western Art History* (New York, 1971)

Knowles, D., *The Monastic Order in England. A History of its Development from the Times of St Dunstan to the Fourth Lateran Council, 943–1216*, 2nd ed. (Cambridge, 1963)
*The Evolution of Medieval Thought* (London, 1962)

Koehler, W. R. W., *Die karolingischen Miniaturen im Auftrage des deutschen Vereins für Kunstwissenschaft* I–III (Berlin, 1930–60)
*See also* Drogo Sacramentary

Koehler, W. R. W. and F. Mütherich, *Die karolingischen Miniaturen im Auftrage des deutschen Vereins für Kunstwissenschaft* IV–V (Berlin, 1971–82)

Krapp, G. P. and E. van K. Dobbie. *See* The Anglo-Saxon Poetic Records

Kuypers, A. B. *See* Book of Cerne

Ladner, G. B., 'The Concept of the Image in the Greek Fathers and the Byzantine Iconoclastic Controversy', *Dumbarton Oaks Papers* 7 (1953), 3–34

'Ad imaginem Dei: the Image of Man in Mediaeval Art', in *Modern Perspectives in Western Art History*, ed. W. E. Kleinbauer (New York, 1971), pp. 432–61

Laistner, M. L. W., *Thought and Letters in Western Europe, AD 500 to 900*, rev. ed. (London, 1957)

*See also* Bede

Lambot, D. C. *See* Godescalc

Lapidge, M., 'A Tenth-Century Metrical Calendar from Ramsey', *RB* 94 (1984), 326–69

'Æthelwold as Scholar and Teacher', in *Bishop Æthelwold. His Career and Influence*, ed. B. Yorke (Woodbridge, 1988), pp. 89–117

Lapidge, M., ed., *Anglo-Saxon Litanies of the Saints*, HBS 106 (London, 1991)

*See also* Bischoff, Byrhtferth *and* Wulfstan of Winchester

Lapidge, M. and H. Gneuss, ed., *Learning and Literature in Anglo-Saxon England. Studies Presented to Peter Clemoes on the Occasion of his Sixty-Fifth Birthday* (Cambridge, 1985)

*Laterculus Malalianus*. J. Stevenson, ed., *The 'Laterculus Malalianus' and the School of Archbishop Theodore*, CSASE 14 (Cambridge, 1995)

Lasko, P., *Ars sacra 800–1200* (Harmondsworth, 1972)

Laufner, R. *See* Trier Apocalypse

Leclercq, J., 'Ecrits spirituels de l'école de Jean de Fécamp', *Studia Anselmiana* 20 [*Analecta Monastica* 1] (1948), 91–114

'Etudes sur le vocabulaire monastique du moyen âge', *Studia Anselmiana* 48 (1961)

'Etudes sur le vocabulaire de la contemplation au moyen âge', *Studia Anselmiana* 51 (1963)

*The Love of Learning and the Desire for God, a Study of Monastic Culture*, 2nd ed., trans. C. Misrahi (New York, 1974)

'*Otium monasticum* as a Context for Artistic Creativity', in *Monasticism and the Arts*, ed. T. G. Verdon (Syracuse, NY, 1984), pp. 63–80

*See also* Benedict of Aniane *and* Bernard of Clairvaux

Leclercq, J. and J.-P. Bonnes, *Un maître de la vie spirituelle au XIe siècle: Jean de Fécamp*, Etudes de théologie et d'histoire de la spiritualité 9 (Paris, 1946)

Lehmann-Brockhaus, O., *Lateinische Schriftquellen zur Kunst in England, Wales und Schottland vom Jahre 901 bis zum Jahre 1307*, 5 vols. (Munich, 1955–60)

Leo I, Pope. *Epistolae*: PL 54, 593–1218

# Bibliography

*Tractatus septem et nonaginta*, ed. A. Chavasse, 2 vols., CCSL 138–138A (Turnhout, 1973)

Leofric Collectar. *The Leofric Collectar (Harl. MS. 2961)*, ed. E. S. Dewick and W. H. Frere, 2 vols., HBS 45 and 56 (London, 1914 and 1921)

Leofric Missal. *The Leofric Missal as Used in the Cathedral of Exeter during the Episcopate of its First Bishop AD 1050–1072*, ed. F. E. Warren (Oxford, 1883)

Lerer, S., *Literacy and Power in Anglo-Saxon Literature* (Lincoln, NE, 1991)

*Liber vitae. See* New Minster

*Libri Carolini sive Caroli Magni Capitulare de imaginibus*, ed. H. Bastgen, MGH, Leges in quarto C, Concilia II, Suppl. (Hanover, 1924)

Lindsay, W. M. *See* Isidore

Loerke, W., ' "Real Presence" in Early Christian Art', in *Monasticism and the Arts*, ed. T. G. Verdon (Syracuse, NY, 1984), pp. 29–51

Luibheid, C. *See* ps.-Dionysius

McGinn, B., *The Presence of God: a History of Western Christian Mysticism* I, *The Foundations of Mysticism, Origins to the Fifth Century* (London, 1991)
    II, *The Growth of Mysticism, From Gregory the Great to the Twelfth Century* (London, 1994)

Making of England. *The Making of England. Anglo-Saxon Art and Culture AD 600–900*, ed. L. Webster and J. Backhouse (London, 1991)

Mansi, J. D., ed., *Sacrorum conciliorum nova et amplissima collectio* V and XII (Florence, 1761 and 1766)

Marenbon, J., *From the Circle of Alcuin to the School of Auxerre*, Cambridge Studies in Medieval Life and Thought 15 (Cambridge, 1981)

Markus, R. A., 'St Augustine on Signs', *Phronesis* 2 (1957), 60–83

Martin, E. J., *A History of the Iconoclastic Controversy* (London, 1930)

Martin, J. *See* Augustine of Hippo

Martin, L. T. *See* Bede

Mathews, T. F., *The Clash of Gods. A Reinterpretation of Early Christian Art* (Princeton, NJ, 1993)

Matter, E. A. *See* Paschasius Radbertus

Mayr-Harting, H., *Ottonian Book Illumination. An Historical Study*, 2 vols. (London, 1991)

Mellinkoff, R., 'The Round, Cap-Shaped Hats Depicted on Jews in BM Cotton Claudius B. iv', *ASE* 2 (1973), 155–65

Metz Coronation Sacramentary. *Sakramentar von Metz Fragment, MS lat. 1141, Bibl. Nat. Paris, Vollständige Faksimile-Ausgabe*, ed. F. Mütherich (Graz, 1972)

Metz, P., *The Golden Gospels of Echternach, Codex Aureus Epternacensis* (London, 1957)

Meyvaert, P., *Bede and Gregory the Great*, Jarrow Lecture (Jarrow, 1964)

'Bede and the Church Paintings at Wearmouth-Jarrow', *ASE* 8 (1979), 63–77

'A New Perspective on the Ruthwell Cross: Ecclesia and Vita Monastica', in *The Ruthwell Cross: Papers from the Colloquium Sponsored by the Index of Christian Art, Princeton University, 8 December 1989*, ed. B. Cassidy, Index of Christian Art Occasional Papers 1 (Princeton, NJ, 1992), 95–166

Minns, D., *Irenaeus* (London, 1994)

Missal. *See* Leofric Missal, New Minster *and* Robert of Jumièges

Mitchell, W. J. T., *The Language of Images* (Chicago and London, 1974)

*Iconology, Image, Text, Ideology* (Chicago and London, 1986)

Molin, J.-B., 'Les manuscrits de la "Deprecatio Gelasii", usage privé des psaumes et dévotion aux litanies', *EL* 90 (1976), 113–48

Moran, D., *The Philosophy of John Scottus Eriugena. A Study of Idealism in the Middle Ages* (Cambridge, 1989)

Morin, G. *See* Caesarius of Arles

Morris, R. *See* Blickling Homilies

Morrish, J. J., 'Dated and Datable Manuscripts Copied in England During the Ninth Century: A Preliminary List' *Mediaeval Studies* 50 (1988), 512–38

Mountain, W. J. *See* Athanasian Creed *and* Augustine of Hippo

Mütherich, F., *See* Drogo Sacramentary, Gospels of Otto III, Grodecki, Koehler *and* Metz Coronation Sacramentary

Mütherich, F. and J. E. Gaehde, *Carolingian Painting* (London, 1977)

Muir, B. J., ed., *A Pre-Conquest English Prayer-book (BL MSS Cotton Galba A. xiv and Nero A. ii (ff. 3–13))*, HBS 103 (London, 1988)

Mutzenbecher, A. *See* Augustine of Hippo

Mynors, R. A. B. *See* Bede

Nees, L., *The Gundohinus Gospels* (Cambridge, MA, 1986)

'Image and Text: Excerpts from Jerome's "De Trinitate" and the Maiestas Domini Miniature of the Gundohinus Gospels', *Viator* 18 (1987), 1–21

New Minster. *Liber Vitae: Register and Martyrology of New Minster and Hyde Abbey, Winchester*, ed. W. de G. Birch, Hampshire Record Society (London, 1892)

*The Missal of the New Minster Winchester (Le Havre, Bibliothèque municipale MS 330)*, ed. D. H. Turner, HBS 93 (London, 1962)

Nichols, A., *The Art of God Incarnate. Theology and Image in Christian Tradition* (London, 1980)

Nocent, H. *See* Ælfric

Norberg, D. *See* Gregory the Great

Oakeshott, W., *The Mosaics of Rome from the Third to the Fourteenth Centuries* (London, 1967)

O Carragáin, E., 'A Liturgical Interpretation of the Bewcastle Cross', in *Medieval Literature and Antiquities, Studies in Honour of Basil Cottle*, ed. M. Stokes and T. L. Burton (Cambridge, 1987), pp. 15–42

O'Connell, R. J., *Art and the Christian Intelligence in St Augustine* (Oxford, 1978)

Ogilvy, J. D. A., *Books Known to the English, 597–1066* (Cambridge, MA, 1967)

Ohlgren, T. H., *Insular and Anglo-Saxon Illuminated Manuscripts: An Iconographic Catalogue c. AD 625 to 1100* (New York, 1986)

    *Anglo-Saxon Textual Illustration. Photographs of Sixteen Manuscripts with Descriptions and Index*, Medieval Institute Publications, Western Michigan University (Kalamazoo, MI, 1992)

Okasha, E. and J. O'Reilly, 'An Anglo-Saxon Portable Altar: Inscription and Iconography', *JWCI* 47 (1984), 32–51

Old English Hexateuch. *See* Hexateuch

Openshaw, K. M., 'The Battle Between Christ and Satan in the Tiberius Psalter', *JWCI* 52 (1989), 14–33

    'The Symbolic Illustration of the Psalter: an Insular Tradition', *Arte medievale*, 2nd series, 6.1 (1992), 41–60

O'Reilly, J., 'St John as a Figure of the Contemplative Life: Text and Image in the Art of the Anglo-Saxon Benedictine Reform', in *St Dunstan: his Life, Times and Cult*, ed. N. Ramsay, M. Sparks and T. Tatton-Brown (Woodbridge, 1992), pp. 165–85

    *See also* Okasha

Otto III. *See* Gospels of Otto III

Pächt, O., 'The Illustrations of St Anselm's Prayers and Meditations', *JWCI* 19 (1956), 68–83

    *See also* Porcher

Panofsky, E. *Meaning in the Visual Arts* (Harmondsworth, 1970)

Parsons, D., ed., *Tenth-Century Studies. Essays in Commemoration of the Millennium of the Council of Winchester and the Regularis Concordia* (London, 1975)

Paschasius Radbertus. *De corpore et sanguine Domini*, ed. B. Paulus, CCCMed 16 (Turnhout, 1969), 1–131

    *De partu virginis and Epistula Beati Hieronymi ad Paulam et Eustochium, De assumptione Sanctae Mariae Virginis*, ed. E. A. Matter and A. Ripberger, CCCMed 56C (Turnhout, 1985)

    *Expositio in Psalmum xliv*, ed. B. Paulus, CCCMed 94 (Turnhout, 1991)

    *Sermones i–iii, De assumptione*: PL 96, 239–57

Paul the Deacon. *Homiliarius*: PL 95, 1159–584

Paulinus of Aquilea. *Libellus contra Elipandum*: PL 99, 151–66

Paulus, B. *See* Paschasius Radbertus

Pelikan, J., *The Christian Tradition. A History of the Development of Doctrine*, 5 vols. (Chicago, 1971–89)

    *Imago Dei: the Byzantine Apologia for Icons* (New Haven and London, 1990)

Pine-Coffin, R. S. *See* Augustine of Hippo

Plummer, C. *See* Bede

Pollitt, J. J., *The Ancient View of Greek Art. Criticism, History and Terminology* (New Haven, CT and London, 1974)

Pope, J. C. *See* Ælfric

Porcher, J. *Essais en l'honneur de Jean Porcher. Etudes sur les manuscrits à peintures*, ed. O. Pächt (Paris, 1963)
  *See also* Hubert

*Portiforium Wulstani. See* Wulfstan II of Worcester

Prescott, A., 'The Text of the Benedictional of St Æthelwold', in *Bishop Æthelwold. His Career and Influence*, ed. B. Yorke (Woodbridge, 1988), pp. 119–47

Primasius. *Commentaria super Apocalypsim*: PL 68, 793–936

Quirk, R. N., 'Winchester Cathedral in the Tenth Century', *ArchJ* 114 (1957), 28–68
  'Winchester New Minster and its Tenth-Century Tower', *JBAA* 3rd ser. 24 (1961), 16–54

Quodvultdeus. *Adversus quinque haereses*, ed. R. Braun, CCSL 60 (Turnhout, 1976), 261–301
  *Contra Iudaeos, paganos et Arrianos*, ed. R. Braun, CCSL 60 (Turnhout, 1976), 227–58
  *Sermo de symbolo*, ed. R. Braun, CCSL 60 (1976), 305–63

Ralph Glaber. *Rodulfi Glabri, Historiarum libri quinque*, ed. and trans. J. France (Oxford, 1989),

Ramsay N., M. Sparks and T. Tatton-Brown, ed., *St Dunstan: his Life, Times and Cult* (Woodbridge, 1992)

Ratramnus. *Contra Graecorum opposita*: PL 121, 225–346

Raw, B. C., 'The Drawing of an Angel in MS 28, St John's College, Oxford', *JWCI* 18 (1955), 318–19
  '*The Dream of the Rood* and its Connections with Early Christian Art', *MÆ* 39 (1970), 239–56
  'The Probable Derivation of Most of the Illustrations in Junius 11 from an Illustrated Old Saxon *Genesis*', *ASE* 5 (1976), 133–48
  *The Art and Background of Old English Poetry* (London, 1978)
  *Anglo-Saxon Crucifixion Iconography and the Art of the Monastic Revival*, CSASE 1 (Cambridge, 1990)
  'Biblical Literature: the New Testament', in *The Cambridge Companion to Old English Literature*, ed. M. Godden and M. Lapidge (Cambridge, 1991), pp. 227–42
  'What do we Mean by the Source of a Picture?' in *England in the Eleventh Century. Proceedings of the 1990 Harlaxton Symposium*, ed. C. Hicks, Harlaxton Medieval Studies 2 (Stamford, 1992), 285–300
  'Why does the River Jordan Stand Still? (*The Descent into Hell*, 103–6)', *Leeds Studies in English* ns 23 (1992), 29–47

'Verbal Icons in Late Old English', *The Bible and Early English Literature from the Beginnings to 1500: Proceedings of the Second G. L. Brook Symposium held in the University of Manchester, 1993*, ed. A. R. Rumble, S. C. Weinberg, J. J. Anderson and G. R. Owen-Crocker, *Bulletin of the John Rylands University Library of Manchester* 77.3 (1995), 121–39

*Regularis concordia Anglicae nationis monachorum sanctimonialiumque*, ed. T. Symons (London, 1953)

Reiter, S. *See* Jerome

Ripberger, A. *See* Paschasius Radbertus

Ritzke-Rutherford, J., *Light and Darkness in Anglo-Saxon Thought and Writing*, Sprache und Literatur, Regensburger Arbeiten zur Anglistik und Amerikanistik 17 (Frankfurt, 1979)

'Anglo-Saxon Antecedents of the Middle English Mystics', in *The Medieval Mystical Tradition in England. Papers Read at the Exeter Symposium, July 1980*, ed. M. Glasscoe (Exeter, 1980), pp. 216–33

Robert of Jumièges. *The Missal of Robert of Jumièges*, ed. H. A. Wilson, HBS 11 (London, 1896)

Robertson, D. W. *See* Augustine of Hippo

Robinson, J. A. *See* Irenaeus

Rochais, H. *See* Bernard of Clairvaux

Rosenthal, J., 'The Historiated Canon Tables of the Arenberg Gospels' (unpubl. PhD dissertation, Columbia Univ., 1974)

'Three Drawings in an Anglo-Saxon Pontifical: Anthropomorphic Trinity or Threefold Christ?', *Art Bulletin* 63 (1981), 547–62

'The Pontifical of St Dunstan', in *St Dunstan: his Life, Times and Cult*, ed. N. Ramsay, M. Sparks and T. Tatton-Brown (Woodbridge, 1992), pp. 143–63

Sacramentary of Robert of Jumièges. *See* Robert of Jumièges

Sahas, D. J., *Icon and Logos: Sources in Eighth-Century Iconoclasm* (Toronto, 1986)

Salmon, P., *Analecta liturgica: extraits des manuscrits liturgiques de la Bibliothèque Vaticane. Contribution à l'histoire de la prière chrétienne*, Studi e testi 273 (1974)

'Livrets de prières de l'époque carolingienne', *RB* 86 (1976), 218–34 and *RB* 90 (1980), 147–9

Schapiro, M., 'The Image of the Disappearing Christ: the Ascension in English Art around the Year 1000', *Gazette des Beaux-Arts*, 6th ser., 23 (1943), 135–52, repr. in his *Selected Papers Vol. 3* (1980), pp. 266–87

'On Some Problems in the Semiotic of Visual Art, Field and Vehicle in Image-sign', *Semiotica* 1.3 (1969), 223–42

*Selected Papers, Vol. 3: Late Antique, Early Christian and Mediaeval Art* (London, 1980)

Schiel, H. *See* Codex Egberti

Schiller, G., *Ikonographie der Christlichen Kunst*, 5 vols. (Gutersloh, 1966–91)
  *Iconography of Christian Art*, 2 vols., trans. J. Seligmann (London, 1971–2)
Schmaus, M. *See* Augustine of Hippo
Schmitt, F. S. *See* Anselm
Scragg, D. G. *See* Vercelli Homilies
Sendler, E., *The Icon, Image of the Invisible. Elements of Theology, Aesthetics and Technique*, trans. S. Bigham (Torrance, CA, 1988)
Sheldon-Williams, J. P. *See* John Scotus
Shepherd, M. H., 'Christology: a Central Problem of Early Christian Theology and Art', in *Age of Spirituality*, ed. K. Weitzmann (New York, 1980), pp. 101–20
Sisam, K., 'MSS Bodley 340 and 342: Ælfric's *Catholic Homilies*', in his *Studies in the History of Old English Literature* (Oxford, 1953), pp. 148–98
Skeat, W. W. *See* Ælfric
Smalley, B., *The Study of the Bible in the Middle Ages*, 2nd ed. (Notre Dame, Indiana, 1964)
Smaragdus. *Diadema monachorum*: PL 102, 593–690
  *Epistola de processione Spiritus Sancti*: PL 98, 923–9
Smetana, C. L., 'Ælfric and the Early Medieval Homiliary', *Traditio* 15 (1959), 163–204
  'Ælfric and the Homiliary of Haymo of Halberstadt', *Traditio* 17 (1961), 457–69
Smith, G. D., *The Teaching of the Catholic Church* (London, 1952)
Southern, R. W., *Saint Anselm and his Biographer. A Study of Monastic Life and Thought 1059–c.1130* (Cambridge, 1966)
Sparks, M. *See* Ramsay
Stevenson, J. *See Laterculus Malalianus*
Stubbs, W. *See* Dunstan
Stuttgart Psalter. *Der Stuttgarter Bilderpsalter, Bibl. fol. 23, Württembergische Landesbibliothek Stuttgart*, ed. W. Hoffman *et al.*, 2 vols. (Stuttgart, 1965–8)
Symons, T. See *Regularis concordia*
Szarmach, P. E., ed., *Sources of Anglo-Saxon Culture*, Studies in Medieval Culture 20 (Kalamazoo, MI, 1986)
  *Studies in Earlier Old English Prose* (New York, 1986)
  *See also* Vercelli Homilies
Taralon, J. *See* Grodecki
Tatton-Brown, T. *See* Ramsay
Taylor, H. M., *Anglo-Saxon Architecture* III (Cambridge, 1978)
Taylor, H. M. and J. Taylor, *Anglo-Saxon Architecture*, 2 vols. (Cambridge, 1965)
Temple, E., *Anglo-Saxon Manuscripts 900–1066*, A Survey of Manuscripts Illuminated in the British Isles 2 (London, 1976)

The Anglo-Saxon Poetic Records: A Collective Edition, ed. G. P. Krapp and E. van K. Dobbie, 6 vols. (New York, 1931–42)

Theodulf, De Spiritu Sancto: PL 105, 239–76

Thorpe, B. See Ælfric

Torrance, T. F., The Trinitarian Faith. The Evangelical Theology of the Ancient Catholic Church (Edinburgh, 1993)

Treschow, M., 'Echoes of the Periphyseon in the Third Book of Alfred's Soliloquies', N&Q ns 40 (1993), 281–6

Trier Apocalypse. Trierer Apokalypse. Vollständige Faksimile-Ausgabe im Originalformat des Codex 31 der Stadtbibliothek Trier, ed. R. Laufner and P. K. Klein, 2 vols. (Graz, 1975)

Tschan, F. J., Saint Bernward of Hildesheim, 3 vols., Publications in Mediaeval Studies, University of Notre Dame, 6, 12 and 13 (Notre Dame, IN, 1942–52)

Tudor-Craig, P. See Gem

Turner, D. H., 'The Prayer-Book of Archbishop Arnulph II of Milan', RB 70 (1960), 360–92

See also Golden Age and New Minster

Unterkircher, F., Zur Ikonographie und Liturgie des Drogo-Sakramentars (Graz, 1977)

Ure, J. M., See Benedictine Office

Utrecht Psalter. The Illustrations of the Utrecht Psalter, ed. E. T. de Wald (Princeton, NJ, 1933)

Utrecht-Psalter: Vollständige Faksimile-Ausgabe im Originalformat der Handschrift 32 aus dem Besitz der Bibliothek der Rijksuniversiteit te Utrecht, ed. K. van der Horst and J. H. A. Engelbregt, 2 vols. (Graz, 1984)

van den Hout, M. P. J. See Augustine of Hippo

van der Horst, K. See Utrecht Psalter

Vercelli Homilies. Die Vercelli-Homilien i–viii, ed. M. Förster, Bibliothek der angelsächsischen Prosa 12 (Hamburg, 1932)

Vercelli Homilies ix–xxiii, ed. P. E. Szarmach (Toronto, 1981)

The Vercelli Homilies and Related Texts, ed. D. G. Scragg, EETS os 300 (London, 1992)

Verdon, T. G., ed., Monasticism and the Arts (Syracuse, NY, 1984)

Verheijen, L. See Augustine of Hippo

Verhelst, D. See Adso of Montier-en-Der

Vespasian Psalter. The Vespasian Psalter (British Museum Cotton Vespasian A. i), ed. D. H. Wright, EEMF 14 (Copenhagen, 1967)

Volbach, W. F. See Hubert

Wærferth of Worcester. Bischof Wærferths von Worcester Ubersetzung der Dialoge Gregors des Grossen über das Leben und die Wundertaten Italienischer Väter und über die Unsterblichkeit der Seelen, ed. H. Hecht, Bibliothek der angelsächsischen Prosa 5 (Darmstadt, 1965)

Waitz, G. *See* Adémar of Chabannes

Warner, G. F., *Descriptive Catalogue of Illuminated Manuscripts in the Library of C. W. Dyson Perrins*, 2 vols. (Oxford, 1920)
   *See also* Benedictional

Warren, F. E., *See* Leofric Missal

Webb, J. F. *See* Bede

Weber, R. *See* Ambrosius Autpertus

Webster, L. *See* Golden Age *and* Making of England

Weitzmann, K., ed., *Age of Spirituality: a Symposium* (New York, 1980)

Weitzmann, K. and H. L. Kessler, *The Cotton Genesis, British Library Codex Cotton Otho B. vi*, The Illustrations in the Manuscripts of the Septuagint I, Genesis (Princeton, NJ, 1986)

Willems, R. *See* Augustine of Hippo

Wilmart, A., 'Les prières envoyées par Saint Anselme à la comtesse Mathilde en 1104', *RB* 41 (1929), 35–45
   'The Prayers of the Bury Psalter', *Downside Review* 48 (1930), 198–216
   *Auteurs spirituels et textes dévots du moyen âge latin: études d'histoire littéraire* (Paris, 1932)
   'Cinq textes de prière composés par Anselme de Lucques pour la Comtesse Mathilde', *Revue d'ascétique et de mystique* 19 (1938), 23–72
   *Precum libelli quattuor aevi Karolini* (Rome, 1940)
   *See also* Goscelin *and* John of Fécamp

Wilson, D. M., *Anglo-Saxon Ornamental Metalwork 700–1100 in the British Museum*, Catalogue of Antiquities of the Later Saxon Period 1 (London, 1964)

Wilson, H. A., *See* Benedictional *and* Robert of Jumièges

Winchester. *See* New Minster

Winterbottom, M. *See* Wulfstan of Winchester

Woollcombe, K. J., 'The Biblical Origins and Patristic Development of Typology', *Studies in Biblical Theology* 22 (1957), 39–75

Wormald, F., *English Drawings of the Tenth and Eleventh Centuries* (London, 1952)
   *The Miniatures in the Gospels of St Augustine, Cambridge, Corpus Christi College MS 286* (Cambridge, 1954), and in *Collected Writings* I, 13–35
   *The Benedictional of St. Ethelwold* (London, 1959), and in *Collected Writings* I, 85–100
   'An English Eleventh-Century Psalter with Pictures, British Library, Cotton MS Tiberius C. vi', *Walpole Society* 38 (1962), 1–13, and in *Collected Writings* I, 123–37
   'Late Anglo-Saxon Art: some Questions and Suggestions', in *Studies in Western Art*, ed. M. Meiss (Princeton, NJ, 1963), pp. 19–26, and in *Collected Writings* I, 105–10

# Bibliography

'The "Winchester School" before St Æthelwold', in *England before the Conquest. Studies in Primary Sources presented to Dorothy Whitelock*, ed. P. Clemoes and K. Hughes (Cambridge, 1971), pp. 305–13, and in *Collected Writings* I, 76–84

*Collected Writings I: Studies in Medieval Art from the Sixth to the Twelfth Centuries*, ed. J. J. G. Alexander, T. J. Brown and J. Gibbs (Oxford, 1984)

*See also* Grodecki

Wormald, P., D. Bullough and R. Collins, ed., *Ideal and Reality in Frankish and Anglo-Saxon Society. Studies presented to J. M. Wallace-Hadrill* (Oxford, 1983)

Wrenn, C. L., *A Study of Old English Literature* (London, 1967)

Wright, D. H. *See* Vespasian Psalter

Wulfstan of Winchester. *Wulfstan of Winchester, The Life of St Æthelwold*, ed. M. Lapidge and M. Winterbottom (Oxford, 1991)

Wulfstan of Worcester. *The Homilies of Wulfstan*, ed. D. Bethurum (Oxford, 1957)

Wulfstan II of Worcester. *The Portiforium of Saint Wulstan (Corpus Christi College, Cambridge, MS 391)*, ed. A. Hughes, 2 vols., HBS 89–90 (London, 1958–60)

Yorke, B. A. E., ed., *Bishop Æthelwold. His Career and Influence* (Woodbridge, 1988)

Zingerle, A. *See* Hilary

Zycha, J. *See* Augustine of Hippo

211

# Index

Aachen, Synod of, 8

Aaron's rod, 122–3, 127–8, 154

Abingdon, links with Corbie, 97 n. 99, 158 n. 79

Abraham, 78–80, 99, 101, 163

Adam, 101, 132

Adémar of Chabannes, 23–4

Adoptionism, 8–9, 42, 45, 61

Adso of Montier-en-Der, 22–3

Ælfric, abbot of Eynsham

    All Saints, 126–7; Antichrist, 21–3; Arius, 25; Ascension, 5; Athanasian Creed, influence of, 32–4, 45; Augustine, influence of, 2, 32, 35–9; bronze serpent, 70; Christ: acknowledged by creation, 111; creation and re-creation through, 46–8; as image of Father, 96; opening heaven, 50–1; pre-existent, 105; presence of, 5; risen body of, 45, 50; rod of, 122; two natures of, 45–52, 64–6, 158; visible form of God, 4, 66–8; church Councils, 7–8; creation as reflection of the divine, 82; 'De dominica oratione', 32; 'De fide catholica', 31–9; ps-Dionysius, knowledge of, 96; divinization, 43–4; Epiphany, 110; faith, 22, 28; and understanding, 31; Feast of Trinity, 10–11; God: as artist, 96; creating by measure, number, weight, 83; distinct from creation, 81; filling earth and heaven, 138; holding world in his hands, 167; throned on globe, 138–9, 182; unity of, 4, 40, 139–40, 142, 167; good works, 22, 34; idolatry, 56–7; 'In letania maiore', 32; Jerusalem/Sion, 86; Jews, 25–6; John the Evangelist, 64–6; John Scotus, knowledge of, 96; Judas, 160–1; Last Days, 19–22; letters to Archbishop Wulfstan, 7–8; and Bishop Wulfsige, 7–8, n. 4; and monks of Eynsham, 11; Mary, 48–9, 165; Moses, 103–4; Old and New Testaments, 25, 104–5; Paschasius Radbertus, knowledge of, 158, 165; Peter, 28, 56, 181; Psalms, 170; reputation of, 2–3; Rogation sermons, 30, 32; Sabellius, 38; Stephen, 146; translations of *Pater noster* and Creeds, 30; Trinity: at Baptism, 41–2; creation by, 46, 56, 64, 107, 140; images of: Abraham's visitors, 80; fire/ sun, 34–5; human soul, 35–8; three loaves, 32, 39; inner relations of, 34–5, 38, 40–1; unity of action, 81; typology, use of, 96; wise and foolish virgins, 19

Ælfwine, abbot of New Minster

    represented at feet of St Peter, 176, 181, 183, 185–6; mentioned in inscription to Crucifixion picture, 178, 185; sealed with cross, 185–6